Violence in the Films
of Stephen King

Lexington Books Horror Studies

Series Editor

Carl Sederholm, Brigham Young University

Lexington Books Horror Studies is looking for original and interdisciplinary monographs or edited volumes that expand our understanding of horror as an important cultural phenomenon. We are particularly interested in critical approaches to horror that explore why horror is such a common part of culture, why it resonates with audiences so much, and what its popularity reveals about human cultures generally. To that end, the series will cover a wide range of periods, movements, and cultures that are pertinent to horror studies. We will gladly consider work on individual key figures (e.g. directors, authors, show runners, etc.), but the larger aim is to publish work that engages with the place of horror within cultures. Given this broad scope, we are interested in work that addresses a wide range of media, including film, literature, television, comics, pulp magazines, video games, or music. We are also interested in work that engages with the history of horror, including the history of horror-related scholarship.

Titles in the Series

Violence in the Films of Stephen King

Edited by

Tony Magistrale and Michael J. Blouin

LEXINGTON BOOKS
Lanham • Boulder • New York • London

Published by Lexington Books
An imprint of The Rowman & Littlefield Publishing Group, Inc.
4501 Forbes Boulevard, Suite 200, Lanham, Maryland 20706
www.rowman.com

6 Tinworth Street, London SE11 5AL, United Kingdom

British Library Cataloguing in Publication Information Available

Library of Congress Cataloging-in-Publication Data

Names: Magistrale, Tony, 1952– editor. | Blouin, Michael J., 1984– editor.
Title: Violence in the films of Stephen King / edited by Tony Magistrale, Michael J. Blouin.
Description: Lanham : Lexington Books, 2021. | Series: Lexington Books horror studies | Includes bibliographical references and index. | Summary: "Contributors analyze the theme of violence in the film adaptations of Stephen King's work, ranging from his earliest movies to the most recent, through a variety of lenses"— Provided by publisher.
Identifiers: LCCN 2021017870 (print) | LCCN 2021017871 (ebook) | ISBN 9781793635792 (cloth) | ISBN 9781793635808 (epub) | ISBN 9781793635815 (pbk)
Subjects: LCSH: King, Stephen, 1947– Film adaptations. | American fiction—20th century—Film adaptations. | American fiction—21st century—Film adaptations. | Violence in motion pictures. | Horror films—History and criticism.
Classification: LCC PS3561.I483 Z912 2021 (print) | LCC PS3561.I483 (ebook) | DDC 791.43/6164—dc23
LC record available at https://lccn.loc.gov/2021017870
LC ebook record available at https://lccn.loc.gov/2021017871

♾™ The paper used in this publication meets the minimum requirements of American National Standard for Information Sciences—Permanence of Paper for Printed Library Materials, ANSI/NISO Z39.48-1992.

Contents

Introduction

Tony Magistrale and Michael J. Blouin

Violence is both everywhere and nowhere in the studies of Stephen King's fictional universe. Recent works uncover violence in relatively unexpected places: Douglas Cowan locates it in the religious subtext of King's works; John Sears and Heidi Strengell locate it in a textual or generic breakdown; Michael Blouin locates it in King's political vision.[1] Yet violence remains a *secondary* feature in many of these studies—that is, it proves to be just one aspect among many others. Religion, deconstruction, and politics all involve violence, certainly, but almost always as a symptom rather than the illness itself. This volume investigates the role of violence in the films of Stephen King on its own terms. As the maestro behind some of America's most blood-stained frames, King invites us to investigate our complicated savagery as both actors and spectators: our impulse to do harm to others (and the perverse pleasure many of us find in watching it); our national legacy of genocide and war; our inability to imagine a world without needless bloodshed.

One of the shared conclusions raised by several of the contributors to this collection—Findley, Simpson, Muller—is that the King film canon has grown more violent since at least the start of the new Millennium. Their individual chapters argue different explanations for this occurrence, ranging from villains making use of advanced computer technology to foment greater levels of violence to advanced camera technology now available to cinematographers and directors for filming violence from unique and more intimate angles. In addition to evolving levels of violence present in King adaptations, however, it is also clear that the gendered perspective on the treatment of this subject has likewise shifted dramatically. Early King films, such as *Salem's Lot, The Shining, The Stand, Cujo, Bag of Bones*, are relatively traditional in their presentation of violent behavior: out of control men threatening and just as often exacting violence against women; women, in turn, portrayed as helpless victims. As Frannie Goldsmith, the pregnant Eve of the new Eden in *The Stand* recognizes, much to her dismay, without the protective umbrella of civilization, "this was going to be a stinking macho world again, at least for a while" (528).

Since *Misery* (1990) and through the release of movies made from King's "feminist decade" of the 1990s through to the present day, however, a true shift has taken place in this orientation. It appears to us that the women who have emerged from King's canon over the last twenty-five years have responded strongly to Lant and Thompson's assertion back in 1998 that "King's women . . . have really not come a long way from the politically and discursively powerless times of their disenfranchised mothers and grand-mothers" (6). While it is probably accurate that they may still be politically disenfranchised (whatever that means), they are definitively not powerless.

Cinematic heroines, such as Dolores Claiborne (1995), Jessie Burlingame (*Gerald Game* [2017]), Tess Thorne (*Big Driver*), Darcy Anderson (*A Good Marriage*), and Emily in *The Gingerbread Girl* (currently in film production), for example, have emerged from beneath the penumbra of victimhood, will-ing and more than capable in the course of their respective films to employ violence against men as a means for self-survival. This is certainly indicative of the empowerment of women brought about through decades of American feminism, and King's own narrative response to the pervasive reality of domestic violence (because all of the aforementioned violent females are responding to particular domestic situations). While some of these women may still occupy domestically centered roles as mothers and wives who are economically dependent on male spouses, none of them tolerate the sexual and psychological abuse that once attended male privilege. Rape and other forms of sexual maladjustment found in the King universe have forced women to break with traditional feminine behavior; to survive these vicious circumstances, they must act like men. And curiously, their justifiable employment of violence against sexually abusive men serves as a liberating experience that points the way to further degrees of self-empowerment and supportive connections with other women. It is as if possessing the courage to usurp violence from a masculine-gendered domain results not only in self-rescue and revenge, but enlightenment as well.

Yet even as King's cinematic universe engages with these concerns, a number of essays in this book—including contributions from Blouin, Findley, Grady, Crockett, and Indrisano—critique a number of these films for their exploitative qualities. It remains difficult, these authors contend, to draw a clear line between *necessary violence*, which is to say, violence with nar-rative as well as ethical significance, and *sensationalist violence* (violence evoked to titillate, repulse, or even comfort). How are viewers to delineate these two categories? For example, one might view the excruciating violence of Rob Reiner's *Misery* as necessary, since the plot requires Annie Wilkes (Kathy Bates) to be brutal in order to heighten the feelings of paralysis in Paul Sheldon (James Caan). On the other hand, one might describe the scene in

which Annie hobbles Paul with a wooden block and a mallet as sensationalist, since this ghastly moment (arguably) does little to advance the storyline
and it raises possible concerns about how much violence is too much. (The
familiar litany of complaints includes desensitized audiences as well as the
glorification of savagery.) Of course, these concerns become even further
magnified when filmmakers depict certain kinds of acts on screen. It is one
thing to paralyze a middle-aged white, male writer, the popular logic goes;
it is quite another thing to linger on images of already disenfranchised and
oft-abused groups such as women, people of color, homosexuals, or children.
Just why is it that certain Stephen King films relish in grotesque violence
against the most vulnerable populations? Perhaps these works are simply bor-
rowing from a long tradition of exploitative cinema in which brutal imagery
caters to the supposedly sadistic appetites of a specific clientele. Or perhaps
they are speaking, at a deeper level, to a permeable boundary between the
status quo and the unspeakable, that which resists symbolization (a pastime
that stretches back to Gothic mainstays like "Monk" Lewis and, further back,
to Ovid and the Roman Colosseum)? Either way, King's filmic universe
routinely risks drifting into violence-for-violence-sake, and so it begs us to
consider possible demarcations between the necessary and sensationalist vari-
ants of this sanguinary cinema.

Perhaps, then, it is the necessary violence that we must investigate in
greater detail. Contributors, including Olsen, Reuber, Magistrale, and
McAleer, attempt to make meaning out of the violent logic of certain King
films by highlighting the redemptive qualities of certain kinds of violence or
imagining a better, more peaceful future. When do gruesome displays help
to revise our definition of "justice"? When do specific modes of aggression
trigger their antithesis—that is to say, not some naïve utopianism, but a
healthy antagonism that need not end in casualties? Summoning the specters
of King's *The Stand*—recently remade for television—we could work to
imagine a society built upon something other than murderous power struggles
(as difficult as that proposal may prove to be). As Muller and Clemence illustrate in this volume, violence is stitched into the most intimate fabrics of our
lives, and it can be terribly difficult to spot, let alone address in a sustained
fashion. After all, violence manifests in seemingly innocuous guises: a simple
economic transaction; participation on an online platform; a passive glance at
a stranger. Violence structures our lives to a degree that efforts to rectify this
condition will inevitably prove arduous. This bleak reality, however, reminds
us of just why the films of Stephen King are so invaluable as a site for further
study. As reflections of our darkest demons and brightest angels, these works
afford us an opportunity to discuss a less violent tomorrow. Let us begin our
work today.

The first four chapters contained in this book deal specifically with aspects of violence as they are experienced by women in Stephen King's film canon. King's cinematic women are worthy of a book itself, as his fifty-plus movies provide us with a wide variety of female characters. Sarah E. Turner's opening chapter commences this examination by addressing those violent women who often appear in his films with special attention devoted to the first "violent" King woman, Carrie White. Reading *Carrie* (1976) as a prototypical feminist film, Turner argues that De Palma's movie pulls together three images of fiercely disruptive females in the creation of the main protagonist's filmic construction: the Witch, Lady Macbeth, and the Roe v. Wade Supreme Court decision legalizing abortion from the time era commensurate with the creation of Carrie's character in the mid-seventies.

The movies adapted from Stephen King's fiction are often indebted to classic horror icons—Dracula, Frankenstein, Mr. Hyde. Tony Magistrale's chapter on *Stephen King's A Good Marriage* (2014) discusses the Jekyll and Mr. Hyde doppelganger trope when it appears to disrupt a middle-class suburban marriage. Based on the real-life story of the infamous BTK killer, *A Good Marriage* presents the dilemma a wife must confront when she accidentally discovers that her husband is a violent sexual predator. Magistrale's analysis also explores the relationship that is subsequently forged between Darcy Anderson, the wife in *Good Marriage*, and other feminist heroines elsewhere in the King film canon, and thus continues the discussion raised by Sarah Turner's introduction of the earliest version of a violent King woman.

Phoenix Crockett and Stephen Indrisano consider the exploitative violence in the miniseries adaptation *Bag of Bones* (2011). In particular, their chapter looks at the sexist and racist underpinnings of the violence that the series portrays (and, of at least equal import, the scenes of violence that it omits). Why is *Bag of Bones* willing to show violence against women in such vivid detail, Crockett and Indrisano ask, and why do some of its scenes of racialized violence adopt such a supposedly "titillating" tenor? In short, they highlight a very thin line between meaningful or necessary violence and the kinds of exploitative violence too often recycled in King's filmic adaptations.

For several years Stephen King worked on a fictional account of the Patty Hearst kidnapping titled *The House on Value Street*. Not able to complete the novel satisfactorily, he went on to write *The Stand* (1978) and employed Donald DeFreeze, one of the leaders of the Symbionese Liberation Army (SLA), as the prototype for the character Randall Flagg in the novel. His interest in the Patty Hearst story also led King to name the dog Cujo after Willie Lawton Wolfe, another founder of the SLA, whose nickname was "Kahjoh," which the media misspelled as "Cujo." In her chapter on *Cujo* the movie (1983), Sarah Nilsen argues that King's interest in the particular violence associated with the Patty Hearst saga continued to haunt the author to the point that the novel/ film synthesized a triangulation among the vicious masculinities coalescing in King's imagination: the males of the SLA; Steve Kemp, Donna Trenton's adulterous lover; Frank Dodd, the serial rapist-killer that haunts the fringes of *Cujo*; and the rabid St. Bernard duly named Cujo. Trapped in the confines of her incapacitated Pinto and forced to submit to a relentless assault, Donna finds herself in a situation that comes to resemble markedly the closeted ordeal and physical assault Patty Hearst underwent as a captive of the SLA after her kidnapping.

Just as women characters appear often as both victims of and resilient heroines responding to masculine violence as it appears in the King film universe, adolescent children likewise find themselves drawn unwittingly into violent situations. In her study of the film adaptation of *Doctor Sleep* (2019), Mary Findley tracks a disturbing trend in King's fictional universe from the loss of childhood innocence to a normalization of violence against children. Although King condemns certain violent aspects of American society (like overzealous gun use), his willingness to depict the violent abuse of children has escalated steadily over the years. Findley argues that It is time for us to interrogate this "kiddie torture porn" and to evaluate the culpability of the films of Stephen King in its general prevalence.

Extending the central argument that he and Tony Magistrale presented in *Stephen King and American History* (2020), Blouin reads the two-part adaptations of *IT* from director Andy Muschietti (2017 and 2019, respectively) as extended meditations upon the violent impetus of American History. In renditions that deal with children as well as adults, these films depict the History of Derry as an entropic cycle in which actors are compelled, by invisible forces, to "make their mark"—that is, at least in this context, to leave scars on the face of the world. Characters violently etch their signature into harmless surfaces (casts; bodies; overpasses). Yet, even as Muschietti's films critique this bloody trajectory, they seem unable to imagine non-violent alternatives that do not simply retreat into platitudes. Indeed, Blouin argues this final paralysis echoes a much larger preoccupation of King's fictional universe.

The King Hollywood pantheon is enormous and therefore embraces a wide definition of success, regardless of how we define the term—ranging from regrettable adaptations of the multiple iterations of *Children of the Corn* and the cult classic *Maximum Overdrive* (1986) to the acclaimed and brilliant work found in Kubrick's *The Shining* (1980) and Darabont's *The Shawshank Redemption* (1994). Danel Olsen's take on *The Shining*—arguably the best of the horror films included in this volume, and certainly the one possessing the longest academic resumé and largest world-wide fan base—begins by comparing it to the later Stephen King film adaptation *1408* (2007) in an attempt to explain why, despite their similarities in plots and horror tropes, *The Shining* has emerged as a deathless tour de force while *1408* has not. A large part of his argument centers around the role the ghosts play in Kubrick's film. Unlike the various specters that populate *1408* and share mostly a relentless fury, Kubrick's revenants are, according to Olsen, "untraditional," by which he means that they are "more like real people—you can imagine how callous and casually dominating they were in real life by meeting them in death."

Dealing with this volume's theme of violence head-on, Maura Grady sees contrasting levels of it at work in King's fictional versions of *Rita Hayworth and Shawshank Redemption* and *The Green Mile* and Frank Darabont's cinematic renditions of these two books. In explaining why Darabont felt compelled to tone down the violence presented in these two novels, Grady explores issues such as the awareness of differing audiences, film censorship, and the contrasts between visualized and imaginative presentations of violence. Related to this comparison, Grady's chapter also considers the differences between the film versions of *Shawshank* and *The Green Mile*.

The chapters authored respectively by Brian Kent and Philip Simpson undertake discussions of the most recently released King televised miniseries. Since *Salem's Lot* (1979) first appeared on television, King's novels have regularly been introduced as adaptations designed for both the large and small screen. Brian Kent ranges among the various themes located in the Bill Hodges' trilogy (based on King's novels *Mr. Mercedes, Finders Keepers*, and *End of Watch*) in three season's worth of adaptations that debuted on Netflix from 2014–16; his chapter is especially attentive to the role of Brady Hartsfield, dubbed "the Mercedes Killer," and one of King's most diabolical villains. Brady and Hodges are the central figures that link the series' televised terror, and Brady as a home-grown terrorist is reflective of King's expanding employment of violence in his most recent novels/ film iterations. Adept at using his computer expertise to terrorize retired detective Hodges, Brady's magnum opus is to propagate a scene of mass carnage so that he, like the Columbine school shooters, will be immortalized in its fiery consequence. Kent is interested in explaining why Brady focuses his attention on Hodges as well as probing the effect Brady produces on television audiences witnessing these acts of domestic terror.

Phil Simpson examines King's reputation as a purveyor of fictional violence, particularly in the television adaptation of one of his most recent works, *The Outsider* (2018). According to Simpson, this adaptation reveals how "the contagion of violence" spreads through familiar as well as unfamiliar channels. *The Outsider* specifically recognizes the locus of violence in the recent proliferation of political Others. Even more interesting for Simpson, however, are the multiple ways in which the media (including, perhaps, King's brand itself) perpetuates the very violence that it depicts—the inherent antagonism of "fake news"; the intrinsically inflammatory nature of "going viral."

As Simpson supplies a contemporary political context for interpreting violence in *The Outsider*, Matt Muller's essay examines the vampiric presence of the camera in two King adaptations, *The Outsider* and *Doctor Sleep*, from its invasive or surveillance point of view. Muller contends that both films feature highly sexualized violence often technically rendered through a drone's top-down camera shots that remain typically associated with military surveillance and termination. This unique cinematic perspective deepens the characters and audience's shared sense of paranoid horror while revealing the violence inherent in contemporary forms of surveillance.

Muller's emphasis on the covert violence of capitalism is also considered by Jason Clemence in his argument that the film adaptation of *1922* (2017) appears to reflect, upon first blush, the much-ballyhooed tension between urban and rural America. To understand this apparent tension, the film mines heavily from specific veins within the horror genre, including prominently "backwoods" and "suburban horror." And yet, despite the painful schism that ostensibly separates city life from so-called flyover country, Clemence contends that a cross-current runs beneath both spheres of *1922*: the bloody maintenance of capitalist patriarchy, which Clemence compellingly calls the "larger machinery of American violence."

Alexandra Reuber explores the history of violence in the films of Stephen King with a study of Frank Darabont's *The Mist* (2007), wherein she traces parallels between the COVID-19 pandemic and the community crisis that occurs in King's plotline. Using the General Aggression Model (GAM), Reuber investigates the various ways in which the characters of *The Mist* devolve into violence against one another. She ultimately argues that *The Mist* has a good deal to teach us about American responses to the pandemic, particularly when it comes to making difficult sacrifices for the general good.

Patrick McAleer's final chapter in this volume is a philosophical exegesis on the role of vigilante justice in Stephen King's universe, specifically in the film adaptation of *Big Driver* (2014). The film forces viewers to question when revenge and retribution are considered "legitimate" (and who gets to decide on this designation). Although perhaps cathartic, how is King's spectator supposed to determine when, if ever, vengeful murder is "reasonable"? McAleer wonders if the sense of "justice" in *Big Driver* may be overly simplistic, and if its utopian undercurrent encourages us to bypass serious scrutiny of the film's violence; at the same time, he posits, King's films do pause to deliberate upon "just" violence, and this act of pausing, at the very least, invites us to reflect upon the violent underbelly of American culture.

NOTES

1. See Douglas Cowan's *America's Dark Theologian: The Religious Imagination of Stephen King* (New York: NYU Press, 2018), John Sears's *Stephen King's Gothic* (Cardiff, UK: University of Wales Press, 2011), Heidi Strengell's *Dissecting Stephen King: From the Gothic to Literary Naturalism* (Madison, WI: Popular Press, 2006), and Michael Blouin's *Stephen King and American Politics* (Cardiff, UK: University of Wales Press, 2021).

WORKS CITED

King, Stephen. *The Stand* [Complete and Uncut Edition.] NY: Doubleday, 1978. 1990. Print.
Lant, Kathleen Margaret, and Theresa Thompson. "Imagining the Worst: Stephen King and the Representation of Women." *Imagining the Worst: Stephen King and the Representation of Women.* Eds. Kathleen Margaret Lant and Theresa Thompson. Westport, CT: Greenwood Press, 1998. 3–8. Print.

Chapter 1

Stephen King's *Carrie*

Victim No More?

Sarah E. Turner

"Yet who would have thought the old man to have had so much blood in him?" (*Macbeth* 5. 1. 30-4)

From the eponymously titled *Carrie* (1974) and Wendy who is victimized in *The Shining* (1977), to the women who fall victim to the serial killer Frank Dodd in *The Dead Zone* (1979), Linda Dufresne, the murdered wife in *The Shawshank Redemption* (1994), and the young sisters raped and killed by Wild Bill in *The Green Mile* (1996), King's early work and its filmic representations are littered with the bodies of women. However, in his 1987 *Misery*, readers are introduced to Annie Wilkes, the sadistic über fan of Paul Sheldon, who, before being killed by Sheldon, inflicts mental and physical abuse on the imprisoned Sheldon. And in *Dolores Claiborne* (1995), the once victim Dolores turns vigilante and kills her husband who has abused their daughter. More recently, in *A Good Marriage* (2010), Darcy Anderson kills her husband who has been a serial killer for most of their twenty-five-year marriage. King, who in a now famous 1983 *Playboy* interview responds to the interviewer's accusation of "hav[ing] a problem with women in your books" with "it's probably the most justifiable of all those [criticisms] leveled at me . . . I recognize the problems but can't yet rectify them" (Norden), clearly struggles with his female characters and yet his books and movies continue to intrigue and entertain.

But America's Storyteller is also, or more importantly, a cultural critic, engaging with issues and politics and questions at the heart of a troubled America. This chapter, then, will explore the issue of King's violent women, focusing on one in particular: the earliest "violent" woman, Carrie White, and the cultural moments from which she emerged not to establish King as a feminist or a misogynist as others have attempted to argue in earlier studies, but instead to connect this "violent" woman to an emerging female consciousness that culminated in the creation of the #MeToo movement that began in 2006.[1]

In 1973, the Supreme Court in a 7 to 2 ruling decided in favor of Roe in the now landmark abortion ruling of Roe v. Wade, giving women power over their own bodies regarding abortion. In that same year, journalist and writer Barbara Ehrenreich published *Witches, Midwives, and Nurses: A History of Women Healers*, at about the same time that King's wife found his original manuscript of *Carrie* in the garbage. What interests me is the confluence of these three seemingly disparate events and how they contributed to the commercial success of De Palma's filmic representation of King's novel and thus seemed to jump start King's career.

Historians and writers such as Ehrenreich tell us that up until the late 19th century abortion was legal in this country up to the fourth month of pregnancy. A combination of events in the mid- to late-19th century led to the regulation and criminalization of abortion: the American Medical Association, founded in 1847, fought to criminalize abortion as a means to establish their medical monopoly and undermine those whom they saw as competitors, namely midwives and homeopaths. And, in a move sounding terrifyingly familiar to the 2020 moment, nativists (MAGA in today's terms) concerned about the declining birth rates amongst white American-born Protestant women and the increasing numbers of immigrants also supported the efforts to regulate abortion.

In the introduction to *Witches, Midwives, and Nurses*, Ehrenreich describes the male-dominated field of medicine both historically and contemporaneously to the early 1970s:

> Women have always been healers. They were the unlicensed doctors and anatomists of western history. They were abortionists, nurses and counsellors. They were pharmacists, cultivating healing herbs and exchanging the secrets of their uses. They were midwives, travelling from home to home and village to village. For centuries women were doctors without degrees, barred from books and lectures, learning from each other, and passing on experience from neighbor to neighbor and mother to daughter. They were called "wise women" by the people, witches or charlatans by the authorities. (2)

Midwives and women healers become witches and charlatans in the male medical rhetoric, a threat to the health care profession, framed as male, and thus excluded from major medical decisions, policies, and practices. Abortion then, a woman's right to choose, was initially criminalized to ensure the male medical monopoly and to disenfranchise women who sought to practice medicine. That midwives and female healers became defined and persecuted as witches further underscores the desire to control the female body, and for many, this includes the right to choose. Ehrenreich continues,

Witches lived and were burned long before the development of modern medical technology. The great majority of them were lay healers serving the peasant population, and their suppression marks one of the opening struggles in the history of man's suppression of women as healers. The other side of the suppression of witches as healers was the creation of a new male medical profession, under the protection and patronage of the ruling classes. (6)

The fate of so many women condemned as witches was burning, in addition to drowning, hanging, and stoning; Joan of Arc herself was condemned as a sorceress (and a fraud, heretic, and cross-dresser) and was burned at the stake in 1431. Thus, King's decision to have Carrie destroy the high school and the town of Chamberlain by burning it to the ground provides a fascinating engagement with, and inversion of, the fate of witches as Carrie herself is ostracized and perceived as threatening and labeled a witch by her own mother. De Palma's Margaret White refers to her daughter as a witch at the moment Carrie leaves for the prom while King's Margaret first calls Carrie a witch at age three after she causes the rocks to fall from the sky and damage their roof: "it's you it's you devils spawn witch imp of the devil it's you doing it" (70) and again when Carrie announces she does not want to live her Momma's life and is going to the prom—"Witch. It says in the Lord's Book: Thou shalt not suffer a witch to live" (74). Margaret White conflates witches with the Devil and sees Carrie's telekinetic abilities as the "Devil's Power working in Carrie" (110), a conflation exploited by De Palma in his film. While both men position Carrie as a witch and therefore a threat, King and De Palma exploit competing versions/visions of witch—King's Carrie as the traditional healer and abortion practitioner who is still perceived as a threat to the status quo versus De Palma's with both Margaret—who he refers to as a crone, albeit a sexy crone—and Carrie as the monster/threat to be eradicated.

Brian De Palma has famously acknowledged his debt to Gustave Moreau's 1851's portrait of Lady Macbeth as the inspiration for the seminal shot of Carrie—drenched in pig's blood and backlit by flames—as well as her posture and gait in the later parts of the film.

And clearly at some level King had her in mind as well—as readers are told that Carrie was "unaware that she was scrubbing her bloodied hands against her dress like Lady Macbeth" after the destruction of the high school and town (140). And yet, the two men have competing visions of both Lady Macbeth and Carrie; for De Palma, the women are destructive, unnatural, a threat to the heteronormative patriarchal culture of their time. For King, Carrie is, at the very least, disruptive and a threat to the existing patriarchal culture of suburban America but is not necessarily unnatural. Both Lady Macbeth and Carrie stand in defiance of the patriarchy and clearly defined and prescribed gender roles. Lady Macbeth, in her violation of the Elizabethan great chain

Left: Carrie (1976) juxtaposed with Right: Gustave Moreau's Study for Lady Macbeth, c. 1851. Left: *Carrie*, Dir. Brian De Palma. Red Banks Films, 1976. DVD. Screenshot captured by author. Right: Gustave Moreau, c. 1851. Musée National Gustave-Moreau. Painting.

of being, also acts to violate the king's divinity and the rules of domestic hospitality by goading Macbeth into action. Shakespeare, like King with Carrie, may be critical of Lady Macbeth's actions, but he creates a powerful woman whose actions insofar as they stand in defiance of traditional woman's role bridled by patriarchal law and custom may be read as the precursor to Carrie as "witch/abortionist." Both King and De Palma see Carrie as a threat, but King's Carrie embodies the empowering but "threatening" potential of Roe v. Wade, while De Palma's Carrie is an outlier, a threat to traditional femininity as defined and oppressed by the patriarchy. These two views set up the tension at the heart of this reading of Carrie that seeks to reclaim her—to move her from ostracized victim to subversive challenger.

Even the title of Victoria Madden's 2017 insightful study of *Carrie*—"We Found the Witch, May We Burn Her?"—works to locate Carrie in the realm of witches and outsiders who present a threat to the status quo, in this case, American suburbia and conformity. Madden works to define King's *Carrie* as a quintessentially American Gothic tale, in part because of its suburban locale and in part because she, Madden, draws upon both Freud's sense of the uncanny and Kristeva's sense of the abject to explore how Carrie literally expresses "sociocultural concerns in an age of uncertainty" (7). The abject and its emphasis on the body—on waste and fluids and expulsion—is not gothic in the sense that Madden argues, but instead may be read as a per- sonification or manifestation of the future as envisioned by those opposed to the women's right to choose. What this means, I would argue, is that the sociocultural concerns expressed and explored in *Carrie* are not those of the homogeneous suburban need to/fear of containing the 'other'; instead, what *Carrie* is exploring is the impact of the 1973 Supreme Court Decision in Roe v. Wade. King reveals that "I never got to like Carrie White and I never trusted Sue Snell's motives in sending her boyfriend to the prom with her, but I did have something there" (*On Writing*). The "something there" is King's exploration of the Roe v. Wade decision as it is inscribed on the bod- ies of these two young women. Inscribed on the body of King's Carrie is a cautionary tale of a woman empowered by choice, who, ultimately, must die in order to preserve the status quo; Sue, however, is not simply constructed as Carrie's foil as King's own admission implies. Ultimately, Sue rejects the image of conformity Chamberlain imposes on her and may be read instead as feminist manifestation of the uncanny: a woman who ultimately rejects imposed gender roles and expectations.

Madden states that when she "unleash[es] her powers on her peers, Carrie effectively denounces the rites of passage she must observe in order to become an accepted member of the community, thus hindering her own self-actualization" (17). Madden sees rites such as the prom, being crowned prom queen, and by extension, courtship, love, marriage, and children as the status quo of suburban America; these normative acts guarantee acceptance by the community, and by Carrie's rejection of them, Madden argues, Carrie "embraces her own abjection" and becomes "the monster" (17). However, I read Carrie's abjection through the lens of Roe v. Wade; the preponderance of blood that saturates the film—menstrual in the opening scenes, pig's at the prom—suggests the horror and perceived threat of the right to choose an abortion held by many conservative Americans at the time of the Supreme Court's decision. Carrie as monster is a warning—the liberating ramifications of the Roe v. Wade decision stand as a direct threat to the perpetuation of the conservative community made manifest by the American suburbs.

King himself acknowledges that "*Carrie* is largely about how women find their own channels of power, and what men fear about women and women's sexuality . . . which is only to say that, writing the book in 1973 and only out of college three years, I was fully aware of what Women's Liberation implied for me and others of my sex. The book is, in its more adult impli- cations, an uneasy masculine shrinking from a future of female equality" (*Danse Macabre* 171–2). Female equality including the right to choose an abortion. There is in King's construction of Carrie an obvious ambivalence

as if he himself oscillates between liking and fearing her; in 1981 he calls
her a "sadly misused teenager" (172) and then recognizes that she "starts out
as a nebbish victim and then *becomes a bitch goddess*, destroying an entire
town in an explosion of hormonal rage (Norden 1983). At the time of the
1973 Roe v. Wade decision, Maine was one of thirty states wherein abortion was still illegal; therefore, I would argue the following claim by King
may reflect to some extent his reaction (at the time) to the Supreme Court:
"You see, I view the world with what is essentially an old-fashioned frontier
vision. I believe that people can master their own destiny and confront and
overcome tremendous odds. . . . I also believe that the traditional values of
family, fidelity and personal honor have not all drowned and dissolved in
the trendy California hot tub of the 'me' generation" (Norden). His emphasis
in the earlier quotation on Carrie's hormonal rage and the graphic, textual
exploitation of the onset of her menses suggests to me that abortion and the
right to choose were/are a subtext of his novel. His Chamberlain, Maine is
"old-fashioned"—the neighbors all know each other; high school students
dream of being crowned prom queen and king; football players rule the
social hierarchy; horny teens have awkward, heterosexual sex in the back
of their cars. This cultural bifurcation might be reflected in how often King
takes us back to the 1950s and early 1960s in his fictional settings: *Stand by
Me*, *11/26/64*, *IT*. He likes to explore those "cusp" moments when America
is on the verge of great cultural shifts; the precursor to these later texts that
focus on the cusp is *Carrie* and his exploration of the impact of Roe v. Wade
on "traditional family values."

Indeed, Sue Snell's decision to instruct Tommy to take Carrie to the prom
instead of her, despite the fact that she has the "perfect" dress, reminds
readers/the audience of the rite of passage and centrality of the prom in the
text—the coming of age for the seniors—graduation from adolescence to
suburban life as defined by marriage and children. However, in the novel,
when contemplating the prom and her relationship with Tommy, Sue sees her
future unfolding and is horrified:

> The word she was avoiding was expressed in *To Conform*, in the infinitive, and
> it conjured up miserable images of hair in rollers, long afternoons in front of the
> ironing board in front of the soap operas while hubby was off busting heavies in
> an anonymous Office; of joining the PTA and then the country club . . . of pills
> in circular yellow cases without number to insure against having to move out of
> the misses' sizes before it became absolutely necessary and against the intrusion
> of repulsive little strangers who shat in their pants and screamed for help at two
> in the morning . . . of fighting with desperate decorum to keep the niggers out of
> Kleen Korners . . . armed with signs and petitions and sweet, slightly desperate
> smiles. (53, original italics)

Overlooking (for now) the overt racism expressed by this vision of her horrifying future, readers see a *Leave It to Beaver* June Cleaver life in store for Sue, who has finally given up her virginity to Tommy whom she imagines as a suitable husband in the future. However, it is difficult to imagine June Cleaver ever referring to her offspring as "repulsive little strangers," which again is a tangible reminder of the ambiguity throughout *Carrie.* King seems not ambivalent but undecided about Roe v. Wade as he explores the impact of the decision throughout the novel, choosing to set the novel in 1979, some six years after the Supreme Court's decision where the potential implications of that decision would be more obvious and demonstrable than in the months immediately following it. And yet, at the end of the novel, it is Carrie who 'saves' Sue from this future albeit in an apocalyptic fashion—literally leveling the town and incinerating close to seventy of their classmates. *I forget this part la*

In the weeks leading up to the prom, Sue and Tommy have had sex in the novel seven times; Sue reveals that "the first time had hurt like hell . . . [like] being reamed out with a hoe handle" (36). And Tommy had put the "rubber on wrong" (36) too. The violent image of the hoe handle and the complete lack of pleasure (for Sue) associated with sex seems puritanical; is this another example of King's "traditional family values"? Indeed, King's treatment of sex is seldom positive—it's never really about pleasure so much as it is a statement about morality or survival. Sue has earlier reflected on the fact that her period, always reliably regular, is over a week late, leading the reader as well as Sue to imagine she is pregnant. Is King conflating sex and pregnancy, thus arguing for abstinence until the prescribed moment of normative heterosexual marriage? Sue, after witnessing Carrie's death at the end of Part II, "became aware that something had begun to happen . . . Her rapid breathing slowed, slowed, caught suddenly as if on a thorn—And suddenly vented itself into one howling, cheated scream. As she felt the slow course of dark menstrual blood down her thighs" (171–172). In the minutes before this moment, Sue said it literally felt as though Carrie had entered her mind as she lay dying on the pavement. Carrie somehow "knows" Sue is pregnant, and her final act is to cause a miscarriage, to "abort" Sue's fetus. King's ambiguity is present in this moment as Sue screams when she feels the bleeding start; readers are left wondering if, despite her fears regarding her future conformity, she "wanted" that pregnancy. Do readers see Carrie at this point revengeful or magnanimous? Does she "see" Sue's future and desire to save her from the conformity expected by those around her? The "howling, cheated scream" marks this moment as ambiguous; although Sue has balked at the future she had imagined for herself, would she have chosen abortion if given the option?

Carrie's mother clearly conflates sex and sin, revealing to Carrie in their final confrontation, that she had premarital sex and a miscarriage:

"I should have killed myself when he put it in me," she said clearly. "After the first time, before we were married, he promised. Never again. He said we just . . . slipped. I believe him. I fell down and I lost the baby and that was God's judgement. I felt that the sin had been expiated. By blood. But sin never dies. Sin . . . never . . . dies." Her eyes glittered . . . "At first it was all right. We lived sinlessly. We slept in the same bed, belly to belly sometimes, and I could feel the presence of the Serpent, but we. never. did. until." (154)

Margaret White is a religious fanatic. The house is full of religious iconography, and in the novel, Carrie is frequently imprisoned in the closet where she is forced to pray and contemplate her supposedly sinful thoughts. In the film, the only time her mother successfully forces her into the closet is after their discussion during which Margaret expounds upon the link she sees between menstruation and sex: "After the blood, come the boys." The film also shows us an image of St. Sebastian martyred with arrows that hangs in the closet. The image points the way not only to penetration but also to orgasm in the face of the martyr, repeated again as it is in the death throes of Mrs. White. Her death in the novel occurs when Carrie literally slows and then stops her heart; however, in De Palma's vision, Margaret's death draws upon images of Christian martyrs and violent moments of martyrdom. Pauline Kael, writing for *The New Yorker* upon the film's release, first articulates this connection between Carrie's mother and Christian martyrs: "This fundamentalist mother is powerful and sexy, yet she sees herself as a virgin damaged by sex. When the wounded daughter retaliates against her mother's assault, and the kitchen utensils fly into Mama, pinning her like St. Sebastian, Piper Laurie's face is relaxed and at peace—she's a radiant martyr in a chromo." Margaret White is sacrificed, martyred, for her religious beliefs, and De Palma makes the most of the moment as the audience sees multiple markers of domesticity, of *kinder, küche,* and *kirche*—kitchen implements—flying at her and pinning her to the wall. This visual marks a significant change from the novel where Carrie slowly slows down her mother's heart-beat—until she simply stops her heart altogether; the Christian overtones, martyrdom, and sex appeal are not as obvious in the textual moment of her death. DePalma fetishizes Margaret's death; the camera angles, the various tools that "penetrate" her, her panting breath, and her body's death shudders reflect the masochistic lens of his camera and work to further conflate the link between sex and violence that runs throughout the film.

Depicting Margaret White as sexy is one example of the ways in which De Palma's *Carrie* and Lawrence D. Cohen's screenplay diverts significantly from the novel. In a 1977 interview, De Palma admitted that he "liked the idea of making Margaret White very beautiful and sexual, instead of the usual dried-up old crone at the top of the hill" (Childs and Jones). The result of those artistic choices was that Brian De Palma's 1976 *Carrie*, starring Sissy Spacek and John Travolta, was a critical and commercial success generating $33,800,000 at the box office and garnering a National Society of Film Critics Award for Best Female Actress for Spacek as well as Academy Award nominations for both Spacek and Piper Laurie.[2]

De Palma's version of *Carrie* is ninety-eight minutes in length, focusing specifically and only on the present-day life of the characters. Gone are the details about Carrie's childhood, and most importantly, her childhood experiences with her telekinesis that King provides in the novel. De Palma's decision to foreground the shower scene and to conflate Carrie's menstruation with the onset of her supernatural powers (which he downplays, and he also ignores Carrie's ability to penetrate people's thoughts and minds) creates a main character "out of control" of both her body and her bodily functions. Indeed, at one level, the whole film is about female bodies out of control: the mother, Chris. The "horror" of the film, De Palma seems to suggest, is the public moment of menstruation; not only does Carrie's entire PE class share in that moment, but also her PE teacher and the male school principal—the latter clearly uncomfortable with the topic and the bloody evidence on Miss Collins' white shorts where Carrie had grabbed her in her panic.[3] At one level, the class response to Carrie's panic when she begins to menstruate reflects how women are taught to hate their own bodies and particularly their periods—"plug it up" is more than just derisive mockery; it is the language of self-abjection. Societal taboos dictate that menstruation is "dirty"—something to hide—not something to publicize let alone celebrate. Indeed, Carrie's own mother conflates the blood with sin—and by extension sex. As critic Brian Eggert tells us,

Carrie's mother fears what her religion tells her is a connection between womanhood and sin, her classmates despise that she allowed her womanliness to show itself so externally in the locker room, and the audience fears the way her femininity materializes into jolts of telekinesis. These fears are representative of a history of misunderstanding and generalized fears toward women. And yet, *Carrie* was written by a male who recognizes his own fear of women and uses that against his main character and his reader. Moreover, the film was made by a director who was later accused of chauvinism and exploiting female sexuality in his films. (Eggert)

De Palma's Margaret White, after angrily watching Carrie leave for the prom, prophesizes that "Thou shalt not allow a witch to live." But, in King's original version, we read that "Momma smiled. Her bloody mouth made the smile grotesque, twisted. 'As Jezebel fell from the tower, let it be with you,' she said. 'And the dogs came and licked up the blood. It's in the Bible.

It's—'" (90). King keeps the focus on blood, in this case, the bloody mouth where Margaret has scratched herself, and the blood lapped up by dogs after Jezebel is thrown from a window by eunuchs.[4] Carrie is a witch, an outsider, in De Palma's world, monstrous because of her seemingly uncontrollable body and emotions. Indeed, film scholar Shelley Stamp Lindsey reads the horror at the heart of De Palma's *Carrie* as being located precisely in Carrie's "monstrous puberty." She writes, "By mapping the supernatural onto female adolescence and engaging the language of the fantastic, *Carrie* presents a masculine fantasy in which the feminine is constituted as horrific. In charting Carrie's path to mature womanhood, the film presents female sexuality as monstrous and constructs femininity as a subject position impossible to occupy" (34). De Palma's "masculine fantasy" denies any overt female sexuality in the film with the exception of the fellatio performed by Chris on Billy when she tries to convince him to participate in the attack on Carrie. But King's female characters are sexually active; Sue and Tommy have had sex seven times, readers are told; Chris and Billy frequently engage in violent, almost sadistic sex in the room above the bar; and Sue recalls her friends Helen Shyres and Jeanne Gault describing the first time they had done "It . . . that it only hurt for a minute—like getting a shot of penicillin—then it was roses" (36). DePalma's Sue is chaste; there is no suggestion that she and Tommy have ever done "it"—and, if and when these other girls menstruate, it is in the shadows, something to hide, an embarrassment.

Shelley Stamp Lindsey's reading of *Carrie* as monstrous is in response to other theorists who read De Palma's *Carrie* as a victim of a repressive society and the oppression she experiences at the hands of both the idealized suburban setting and her mother's religious fanaticism. However, I would extend her reading to include what really comprises the threat of female sexuality, which is, of course, a woman's right to choose. De Palma refuses to enter into this discussion; his *Carrie* is a classic horror film while the novel is an example of King's cultural commentary. Indeed, the original movie posters for the film read "A Taste for Terror . . . Take Carrie to the Prom." Stamp Lindsey argues that "monstrosity is explicitly associated with menstruation and female sexuality . . . [but] menstruation and female sexuality here are inseparable from the 'curse' of supernatural power, more properly the domain of horror films" (36). Reading Carrie's powers as a "curse" serves to disenfranchise Carrie herself; instead of taking charge of her life, she is "cursed" and thus must be saved—in De Palma's version, entombed with her mother in the bowels of the earth after their home is swallowed up in an apocalyptic vision. De Palma's horror story concludes with chaste Sue in her childhood bedroom suffering from nightmares and trauma as a result of the horrors of the prom while King's Sue experiences a spontaneous miscarriage (an abortion) at the moment of Carrie's death.

Gallup polling in 1975, the year before the release of De Palma's movie, found that "Two years after the court's decision, 54 percent of U.S. adults said they supported abortion under certain circumstances and another 21 percent said abortion always should be legal, while 22 percent of Americans said it should be illegal" (Santhanam). In King's vacillation between referring to Carrie as a victimized teen and a bitch, I would argue, it is possible to find evidence of his role as cultural critic and his ruminations on the decision. While never overtly displaying support or disdain for the Court's decision, King presents a snapshot of the hypothetical impact of the Roe ruling—as made evident by the preponderance of blood, the focus on menstruation, which also announces a woman's fertility, and the ending wherein Carrie causes Sue's spontaneous miscarriage. Carrie, a witch in the traditional sense of the word meaning a healer, nurse, abortionist, is confronted by both a conservative suburban setting and a religious zealot—both Chamberlain and Margaret White see Carrie as a threat—a monster or outsider—who must be destroyed before she destroys their traditional and patriarchal Christian family values. Moreover, the novel ends with the threat of genetic testing and the possibility of eugenics or state-sanctioned abortions to weed out future Carries—an aspect of King's cultural commentary completely overlooked by De Palma. *→ never noticed this...*

De Palma's obvious homage to Hitchcock's *Psycho* (1960) deliberately and thoroughly overlooks the political commentary evident in the novel; his focus is on the eroticism of the shower scene and the gratuitous full frontal nudity shots of the girls in the locker room. De Palma indicts himself in this interview: "The shower scene I always wanted to shoot in slow-motion. I wanted to get involved in this lyrical eroticism before the blood comes, and it's all wonderful, beautiful . . . the steam, Carrie's touching herself . . . and then WHAM!" (Childs and Jones). Masturbation and menstruation marginalize Carrie in De Palma's film; her sexuality makes her monstrous—something that must be first humiliated and then destroyed. Indeed, *The New Yorker*'s movie critic describes the movie as "scary and funny—a terrifyingly lyrical thriller" (Kael). King's Carrie is more destructive in that she razes the bulk *ah* of Chamberlain to the ground—attacking not simply the cruel teenagers who mortify her but also the town that ostracizes her. Her anger is not the result of, or extension of, repressed female sexuality alone as others have argued; instead, it is a reaction against the strictures of conservative American suburbia that would deny women the right to choose.

A close reading of the rhetorical choices utilized by Kael in her 1976 review reveals fascinating references to menstruation and pregnancy albeit through a problematic, misogynistic lens: she calls the film "a menstrual joke—a *film noir* in red" and refers to Carrie as seemingly "unborn—a fetus" (Kael). Menstruation becomes a joke while Carrie is infantilized. Yet both film and

novel rely heavily on the presence of blood, be it menstrual, pig, Margaret
White's, who cuts herself while sharpening the knife, Carrie's birth during
which her mother cut the umbilical cord with a kitchen knife. De Palma's
preponderance of blood is "blood for blood's sake"—shock value—which
clearly locates the film in the horror genre. The movie frequently conflates
blood, sex and violence: Chris performs oral sex on Billy in order to convince
him to kill the pig and participate in Carrie's mortification; Margaret sees
Carrie's menstrual blood as a sin, beating her and locking her in the prayer
closet; the audience sees Billy slap Chris's face on several occasions (which
in itself is problematic and perhaps connects to De Palma's misogyny);
Carrie's moment of triumph—Queen of the prom—is undercut by the buckets
of blood; Carrie's first menses precipitates an attack by the other girls in the
locker room; Miss Desjardins (PE teacher), braless, and therefore sexualized, yet marked by the bloody handprint on her white shorts. In a sense, all
the girls are "marked" by Carrie: Chris via her overreaction vendetta, Miss
Desjardins' shorts, Sue, who becomes Carrie by end of the text—friendless
and haunted by the legacy.

Ultimately, the reader of King's text is left with a sense of ambiguity:
King presents both sides of the abortion debate, albeit hyperbolically, but
he does not dictate how to read them. He creates tension between mother
and daughter that represents the duality of the debate around abortion and a
woman's right to choose. Margaret White is the hyperbolic manifestation of
the religious right—an extreme King seems to reject even as he creates her;
Carrie is the potentially monstrous implications of the Roe v. Wade decision: destructive, vindictive, unnatural, deadly. However, De Palma's movie
engenders no sense of ambiguity; Carrie is monstrous and must be destroyed,
as he acknowledges here:

> I don't know where I got the idea for the ending of *Carrie*. In the original script,
> the big climax was Carrie giving her mother a heart attack. I remember saying
> to the producer, "This is the big scene?! Carrie looks at her mother and she
> clutches her chest?! I don't think so!" You know, it's actually Sissy's hand that
> reaches out from the grave. They put her in a box under the ground. I planned
> on using someone else. I mean, who would know if it was her hand? But she
> wanted to do it. (Nashawaty)

Ending the film with Carrie's hand reaching out from the grave to grab
Sue's arm, even though the moment is embedded within Sue's nightmare,
signals De Palma's interpretation of Carrie as a monster, a hysterical woman
who must be destroyed.[5] While both men look to Lady Macbeth as Carrie's
antecedent, De Palma's metatextual references concentrate on the blood—
"out damned spot! Out, I say" (5.1.31) and by connection the need to

eradicate Carrie—while King acknowledges the potential, yet subversive, power that Carrie must wield.

NOTES

1. While the scope of this chapter is focused on *Carrie* and the figure of Carrie White, a longer project would also explore the women in many other King texts and their movie adaptations such as Annie Wilkes in *Misery*, and Darcy Anderson in *A Good Marriage*. Amy Canfield's insightful 2007 study "Stephen King's *Dolores Claiborne* and *Rose Madder*: A Literary Backlash against Domestic Violence" connects both these texts to a growing awareness of domestic violence. As an extension of Canfield's study, there is, I would argue, a clear connection between *Dolores Claiborne*, the Lorena Bobbit case, and the Violence Against Women Act passed by Congress in 1994. While King's novel *Dolores Claiborne* was published in 1992, a year before Bobbitt's actions and two years before her trial, director Taylor Hackford's *Dolores Claiborne* was released in 1995. Moreover, the 2013 remake of *Carrie* by Kimberly Peirce may be read as a response to the #MeToo movement as well as conservative challenges to Roe v. Wade taking place at the same time.

2. This is a stark contrast to the book as, initially, *Carrie* the book, King's first published novel, sold only 13,000 copies in hardcover and was purchased for $2,500 by Doubleday. The book now has sold over four million copies, and the movie was remade in 2013; this in addition to an ill-fated musical (1988) and an earlier remake flopped (*The Rage: Carrie 2*, 1999).

3. In the novel, the gym teacher's name is Miss Desjardins; De Palma does not offer an explanation for the name change.

4. Jezebel, the Bible tells us, worshipped the pagan god of fertility, and her insistence on the worship of Baal instead of Yahweh led to violence, murder, and destruction in the Old Testament (I Kings 21:5–16).

5. Brian Eggert argues that, "and while an argument could be made against Carrie for its voyeuristic tendencies, De Palma and Cohen have intentionally muted Carrie's prevalent psychic abilities, overly emphasized in King's book, to create a direct correlation between her emotional state and supernatural outbursts, transforming the character into a distinctly human protagonist whose fragile psyche gives way to her telekinetic retaliation. Where King's book featured a mysterious, seemingly unholy version of Carrie White who could create meteor showers and scan people's minds telepathically, the film considers Carrie and her abilities defined by her delicate state, tremendous emotions, and abhorrent persecution as a woman."

WORKS CITED

Canfield, Amy. "Stephen King's *Dolores Claiborne* and *Rose Madder*: A Literary Backlash against Domestic Violence." *The Journal of American Culture,* Dec. 2007, 30, 4.

Childs, Mike, and Alan Jones. Brian De Palma Interview. *Cinefantastique.* Volume 6, Number 1 Summer 1977.

De Palma, Brian, Director. *Carrie*. Red Bank Films, Nov. 3rd, 1976.

Eggert, Brian. *"Carrie."* The Definitives: Appreciations and Critical Essays on Great Cinema. *Deep Focus Review,* October 13, 2013.

Ehrenreich, Barbara, and Deirdre English. *Witches, Midwives, and Nurses: A History of Women Healers*. The Feminist Press, 1973.

Kael, Pauline. "The Curse: Brian De Palma's *Carrie*," *The New Yorker,* November 15, 1976.

King, Stephen. *Carrie*. Doubleday, 1974.

King, Stephen. *Danse Macabre: The Modern American Horror Movie*. Berkley Books, 1983.

King, Stephen. *On Writing: A Memoir of the Craft*. Charles Scribner's Sons, 2000.

Lindsey, Shelley Stamp. "Horror, Femininity, and Carrie's Monstrous Puberty." *Journal of Film and Video,* 43: (Winter 1991): 33–44.

Madden, Victoria. "We Found the Witch, May We Burn Her?: Suburban Gothic, Witch-Hunting, and Anxiety-Induced Conformity in Stephen King's *Carrie*." *The Journal of American Culture*, 40:1. 2017.

Nashawaty, Chris. "The Lives of Brian: Interview with Brian De Palma." *Entertainment Weekly* #898, September 22, 2006.

Norden, Eric. "Stephen King: Playboy Interview." *Playboy Magazine* (1983).

Santhanam, Laura. "How has public opinion about abortion changed since Roe v. Wade?" PBS NewsHour Special Report. Health July 20, 2018. https://www.pbs.org/newshour/health/how-has-public-opinion-about-abortion-changed-since-roe-v-wade.

Chapter 2

An American Hyde

Stephen King's A Good Marriage

Tony Magistrale

In his essay "Invisible Monsters: Vision, Horror and Contemporary Culture," Jeffrey Andrew Weinstock argues that in the history of western teratology, studies into cultural monstrosity have shifted from definitions that once focused on mere physical or outward appearance to include the interior realm of psychological aberration. In other words, postmodern monsters may look human, but are seething on the inside: "Through his antisocial actions, the psychopath and the murderous terrorist make visible the internal lack of humanity obscured by their human facades—they are monsters on the inside" (363). Mark Edmundson enlarges Weinstock's scale to assert that America has become a Gothic culture populated by monsters who are themselves possessed: "We all lead a double life; and our other, our *it*, could choose any moment to reassert itself" (59). Films adapted from Stephen King's novels often grapple with various definitions of monstrosity, ranging from omnivorous preternatural clowns to an inexplicable rampaging technology, with perhaps a couple of common denominators typically tying these various manifestations together: namely, a demonic supernatural core and a love of perpetrating random violence. Since the advent of the new millennium, however, the King cinematic monster has become more fixated in directing his violence at particular individuals. Even more significant, I think, is that recent incarnations of King monstrosity have centered on the emergence of the serial killer, a very human characterization who, as Weinstock points out, possesses neither supernatural energies nor the obvious physical abnormalities that in another era would have marked the antagonist as monstrous.

Several characters throughout the King canon meet the criteria for serial murderers. The wandering sociopath named Springheel Jack in the short story "Strawberry Spring" from King's first short story collection *Night Shift* is an early example. So is Frank Dodd, who makes appearances in both *The Dead Zone* and *Cujo* as the Castle Rock killer. Annie Wilkes, the infamous Dragon Lady in *Misery*, belongs to this category as well, as her efforts to relieve the suffering of the "poor things" (177) she eliminates in the maternity wards of various Boulder hospitals end up costing her both her job and reputation. These three characters notwithstanding, I cannot think of any King narrative prior to *A Good Marriage* (2010 novella; 2014 film) that focuses exclusively on the violent history of such a monster—putting a serial killer at the epicenter of a narrative. This is rather remarkable given King's enduring fascination and quasi-identification with this type of criminal. In his 1983 interview with *Playboy* magazine, the writer revealed that as an adolescent he "compiled an entire scrapbook on Charlie Starkweather, the Fifties mass murderer . . . I used to clip and paste every news I item could find on him, and then I'd sit trying to unravel the inner horror behind that ordinary face. I had a hard time hiding that from my mother." Later, in this same interview, when King was asked to speculate on what he might have done with his life had he not become a successful novelist, his startling response, most likely only half-joking, was that he "might very well have ended up there in the Texas tower with Charlie Whitman, working out my demons with a high-powered telescopic rifle. I *know* that guy Whitman. My writing has kept me out of that tower" (Underwood and Miller 41, 44). It is therefore noteworthy that a full-length exposé devoted to a serial slayer has taken so long to find its way into the King canon, especially in light of the fact that this writer has spent such an inordinate amount of time, if you will, studying the genre.

Further, it is one thing to inform the viewer of Annie Wilkes's infanticide killing spree through sanitized newspaper clippings recorded for an unspecified reason in a madwoman's scrapbook. Or to include Frank Dodd as a strictly peripheral character whose main role in *The Dead Zone* is to serve as John Smith's dark alter ego. Or to include references to the machinations of a serial murderer in "The Gingerbread Girl" and *Big Driver* when each of these narratives are really about "the strong women" Rebecca Frost has identified "who have endured tragedy and emerge victorious from their latest fight" (124). Something more intensely intimate occurs when an entire novel/film revolves around the grisly details of a serial murderer's work and its aftermath. Such is the case with Bob Anderson, the unassuming accountant, rare coin collector, and obsessively attentive father and husband in *A Good Marriage*, who has no qualms about returning to his mundane life even after biting off the penis of a twelve-year-old boy and murdering his mother. And in Brady Hartsfield, the highly disturbed techno-terrorist in the novels from the Bill Hodges trilogy, we have additional evidence of a King serial killer: a central character who directs his diabolical energies at Bill Hodges and his small *ka-tet* of friends and associates specifically, while also yearning to create mass casualties in the construction of an explosive device built to be detonated at a concert venue. Anderson can perhaps be viewed as an early prototype for the more disturbing portrait of Brady Hartsfield. However, the difference between these two is that Brady can barely function in everyday society, and barely contains his psychopathic rage; he is always on the verge of exploding, even to the point of risking self-exposure in the opening scene of the televised series by driving a stolen Mercedes into a crowd of poor people seeking employment opportunities. Bob Anderson, in contrast, epitomizes precisely the schizoid doubling Weinstock describes: the vicious slaughterer of random women and a child lurks just beneath the unassuming exterior of a public accountant, married husband of twenty-five years, and a respected and beloved father of a son and daughter. Their obvious differences aside, both Anderson and Hartsfield conform in varying degrees to Weinstock's definition of a killer "compelled by a demonic force within to commit monstrous acts. The result is a disconnection between external wholesomeness and his internal diseased state" (364).

Since the publications and subsequent film adaptations of *The Shining*, *Pet Sematary*, and *1922,* it is clear that Stephen King has long remained fascinated with secret selves—particularly *male* secret selves. We might posit that Jack Torrance, Louis Creed, and Wilfred "Wilf" James enter into acts of violence and lose their respective families and core identities as a result of rejecting multiple opportunities to confide in their respective wives, by journeying into dangerous places where women are deliberately excluded, and by engaging self-indulgent behavior that is kept private or shared only with other males. King is the legitimate contemporary heir to the masculine-centered gothic strain that produced *The Strange Case of Dr. Jekyll and Mr. Hyde* (1886); King himself confessed his debt to classic gothic fiction in *Danse Macabre*, "while my ball existed in the twentieth century, my wall was very much a product of the nineteenth" (38). Stevenson's Jekyll maintains a bourgeois exterior of highly successful physician and cultured gentleman. His revelation of the "Hyde within" comes as a result of his chemical efforts to make himself even more upright than his reputation already comports. Instead, Jekyll's well-intentioned experimentation with the "powders" unleashes Mr. Hyde, a dark, violent component of himself so much more powerful than the Jekyll-part that Hyde eventually assumes majority control and wrecks Jekyll's life. In his "Introduction" to the Signet Classic edition of *Frankenstein, Dracula*, and *Dr. Jekyll and Mr. Hyde*, Stephen King claims, "If we sweep aside the business of drinking the potion . . . we're left with the bleak tale of a good man's ruin as his 'lesser nature' gains the upper hand" (x).

Just as Jekyll hides the presence of Hyde in a Soho apartment and keeps his existence from his friends, Enfield and Utterson, over time, Bob has become a master at compartmentalization: after a killing, evidence of his violent identity is literally and metaphorically tucked away in secret underground storage, a symbol of his ability to repress the compulsions of his id: "'That's how I saw myself, and believe it or not, I still do. And I have the proof . . . a good home, a good wife, two beautiful children who are all grown up and starting their own lives. And I give back to the community'" (326). He blames his deceased high school friend, BD or "Beadie," for inciting his urge to prey on women that the adolescent boys labeled as "snoots," an etymological admixture of arrogance and superiority, associated always with attractive but "snooty" girls who manifest pleasure in their dominance over young males through rejection and humiliation. Bob has learned how to compartmentalize and direct his misogynistic reaction to the power of feminine sexuality; as was the case with Norman Bates in *Psycho*, Bob recognizes the feminine as an unreconciled allure that entices at the same time as he resents its potent clout. Like Hyde, Beadie contains a boundless fury that has existed for years quietly seething beneath the meek exterior of a successful middle-class accountant and exemplary family man. Evidence of Bob's alter ego remains submerged in a small souvenir box (ironically constructed as a gift to him from his daughter) hidden in "a secret hiding spot" underneath his workbench that contains the licenses and identification cards of victims used by "Beadie" to taunt the police. Film and novella borrow directly from *Jekyll and Hyde* in their use of a secret space as a metaphor for Bob's secret self. As King himself acknowledges in his discussion of the Stevenson novel in *Danse Macabre:* "On Jekyll's side, the side presented to the public eye, it seems a lovely, graceful building . . . on the other side—but still part of the same building—we find rubbish and squalor. Dionysus prances unfettered . . . the building serves as a nice symbol for the duality of human nature" (80). Inside the immaculate house that Bob shares with his wife Darcy, as Detective Ramsey notes, "everything has a place and everything is in its place," but in the darkened garage-workshop, "Beadie" lurks in bondage porno magazines mixed among Darcy's "misplaced" women's publications. Bob fears that if his wife finds this cache hidden in his workshop, his marriage as well as the tenuous balance he has maintained distinguishing his separate selves might collapse. No amount of good work will counterbalance his acts of violence and depravity, despite his denial that "someone else murdered those women."

Stevenson was scrupulous in maintaining the Victorian chastity of both his good doctor and even the "damned Juggernaut" that "trampled calmly over a child's body and left her screaming on the ground" (33). Not only is Stevenson's novel male-dominated, but its few women characters also occupy strictly minor, peripheral roles. Hyde has two brief physically abusive encounters with a street prostitute and the aforementioned girl child at three o'clock, but neither does he sexually assault nor murder women. These elements would arrive later by way of Hollywood's exploitation, each new film iteration upping the ante on Hyde's deviant sexuality and transforming him into a serial rapist/killer resembling more London's infamous Jack the Ripper than Stevenson's less sensational monster. It is a curious fact that nearly all of the dozens of cinematic adaptations of *Jekyll and Hyde* tend to include women in highly visible roles: either as love interests for Dr. Jekyll, or as objects of sexual assault for Mr. Hyde, and often as a combination of both. Bob/"Beadie" represents a culmination of the Jekyll/Hyde cinematic tradition: while he appears as a suburban American approximation to Jekyll's Victorian gentleman, his Hyde persona takes him to places by now familiar in the Hollywood pantheon, but far darker and more disturbing than Stevenson was willing to explore.[1] Although he epitomizes the surface idyll of a domestic Jekyll when he interacts with Darcy, his two grown children, and business affiliates, Bob turns into a "creepy" Mr. Hyde when he is out on the road hunting "snoots."

Like Jekyll, Anderson is both quietly ashamed of and compulsively drawn to his "lesser nature" and its deleterious consequences. Stalking his most recent victim in the film's opening black and white sequence, we trace a long tear descending from Bob's right eye—perhaps indicating a sad resignation that he remains "powerless over his nature"? Or does it emerge from some residue of his "Bob persona" still capable of grieving over the imminent waste of this poor woman who has done nothing to deserve her terrible fate? On an "even dozen" occasions, he has employed bondage, vicious torture, and violent murder as a means for expressing the dark side of his nature. The fact that Bob always utilizes forms of torture, binding and biting his women victims so aggressively, indicates his desire not merely to establish dominance over them, but also to cause sadistic discomfort and pain before releasing them to death.[2] Bob thus emerges as a quintessential illustration of Weinstock's concept of "disconnection"; he truly believes the specious rationale that he offers to his wife: "I didn't kill those women. It was another person inside my head." His own bifurcation helps to explain how and why for so many years he has treated his wife with such deference and affection— "he had never laid a hand on her, except to caress" (301)—because she is the mother of his children, a being he worships as totally separate from "a slut reading a slutty novel," his characterization of the single woman caught reading the novel titled *Bring Me to My Knees* in a late-night diner whom Bob stalks, or the buxom divorcee living next door. Bob's sexual dualism and its extreme two-sidedness is of course at the center of his behavior, but the film's far subtler and more engaging element is the manner in which his domestic passive-aggressiveness contains *both* elements of this duality.

Although handled primarily through body language and telephone conversations, Darcy is established as the unequivocal nucleus of the film as well as her nuclear family: her children consult with her (and not Bob) about their problems (Petra's wedding plans) and achievements (the first big client to sign with Donnie's fledgling advertising agency), while Bob is also shown constantly deferring to her in an effort to solicit her pleasure and approval. Bob accedes to her superior knowledge in the field of numisma-tology, acknowledging "you're the expert." Her status as the matriarch of the Anderson family only strengthens after she uncovers his "Beadie" self. Given "Beadie"'s violent compulsion to dominate women other than Darcy, it is interesting that, sexually, his "Bob" persona craves that she assume the female-dominant position in bed ("I'm on top, just the way you like it, right?" she mocks ironically at the very moment she kills him), and that he is also aroused observing their coupling through a large bedroom standalone mirror (for which he seeks permission to employ during their lovemaking scenes). It is clear that sexually with Darcy, the "Bob-part" of his libido seeks the role of a submissive "bottom," stimulated voyeuristically by his wife's efforts as she labors "on top" toward their mutual orgasms. "Beadie"'s victims share characteristics of a masculine aggressiveness, especially in their perceived sexuality, that Bob lacks. At the same time, however, the dualism at the core of Anderson's nature blurs in his efforts to surveil and manipulate Darcy through passive-aggressive means, such as checking in on her each night he is out of town, stalking her in her own bedroom when she thinks she is alone, and leaving her a plethora of condescending notes all over the house (e.g., change the oil in her car, how to park it in the garage, does she really need a sleeping pill, eating chocolate will end up "on her butt"). Male sexuality is always a complex admixture of oftentimes contradictory responses to sex and women, but Bob's is particularly contrary.

The verbal foreplay that precedes Bob and Darcy into their bedroom on two separate occasions in the film is noticeably puerile and repetitive, and certainly deserving of critical interrogation. Most long-term sexual unions employ, to some degree or another, intimacies and language inimitable to their particular relationship. However, the emphasis on the Andersons' ritualistic pre-coital dialogue in the form of Bob's mock-playful groveling that he is a "good boy" so that he might gain approval to be "Mama's naughty little boy," and thereby "might get lucky" sexually, all the while Darcy twirls coquett-ishly in and out of his fumbling embraces, points to a markedly immature and unstable bond in the context of a twenty-five-year-old marriage. The infantile self-referencing of himself as a "naughty boy" is some sort of attempt to make himself lovable despite his "peccadilloes," since in his psychosexual space his felony crimes against women are conveniently compartmentalized into the exclusive domain of "Beadie." Their well-rehearsed sexual dance is extremely uncomfortable to witness in light of this repression, especially occurring as it does because Bob initiates and pursues this infantilizing fore-play on both occasions. It transcends playful banter to underscore a range of contrary and possible performance anxieties in the bedroom—and with Darcy as a woman. Further still, its patterned repetition stimulates a ritualized return to and reliance on the severe bifurcation of females into categories that gave ultimate rise to "Beadie": where women are divided into "snoots," requiring violent retribution, or mother surrogates (Bob concedes to Darcy when she reprimands him for burning his mouth on hot pizza, "Mother knows best"), who must be cajoled, placated, and idolized. The closer we examine Bob's attitude towards her, however, the more it is possible to see how these two contrasting images of women fuse together psychoanalytically. Bob reveals once again to be only a slightly more socially adept version of Norman Bates in *Psycho*, suffering from the same compulsive dialectic to curry mother's approval at the same time as he scorns her ultimate knowledge and authority. Raymond Bellour advances a psychoanalytic treatise that proves operational for both films: "Mommy, mummy: the mother's body, fetishized to death, so to speak, becomes the body that murders [and is murdered], in keeping with the desire awakened in the eye of the subject possessed by it" (324).

While outwardly he is sexually and emotionally deferential to his wife at home, both in and out of the bedroom—obsequiously adhering to the "Kindness Matters" piping on a white throw pillow that resides at the top of their marital bed, inveigling Darcy for permission to be a "naughty little boy" when aroused sexually, obeying her directive to serve her pre-coital glasses of "fizzy water with a wedge of lime" in exchange for sex—the "Beadie" side of his personality, rapaciously violent with the random women he slaughters, also infiltrates his polished efforts to influence his wife's behavior. Even though he asks for exculpation from her for his crimes, his own attitude towards them is never sincerely repentant nor humbled. In fact, quite the opposite: he assumes an air of insolence while rationalizing his criminal acts; treats discussion about the tortured rapes and deaths of twelve women as casually as eating a pudding cup or having pizza for dinner; he spies on Darcy through her computer's search history; drives home to confront her at three-thirty in the morning because her voice sounded suspiciously "thick"; and informs her that while he "wouldn't lift a finger" to defend himself against the authorities, "you and the children" would suffer the dire social approbation consequent to his arrest. What he wants more than anything from Darcy is to intimidate her into a silent collusion, and, in exchange, Bob promises to repress "Beadie" so they can go on with their superficially good marriage. Once Darcy finds out his secret, Bob seems released, on some level, from his passive-aggressiveness, and assumes control in their relationship through the fear he now instills in Darcy. It makes me wonder if Bob has always viewed Darcy as one of the "snoots," given the upper hand she wields in their marriage. Is his unmasking as "Beadie," then, the means by which he finally gains control, a control he has been incapable of asserting in his Jekyll-like Bob reality? Is Darcy's discovery of his acts of violence and depravity the mechanism by which he finally assumes command?

Guided by Stephen King's screenplay, his first page-to-screen adaptation since *Pet Sematary* (1989), the film emphasizes the "Sophie's Choice" dilemma that aligns Darcy Anderson with another one of King's female chroniclers of masculine depravity, Dolores Claiborne: knowing the truth about the extracurricular sexual exploits of their husbands and the fathers of their children, is it possible, as Bob pleads, "to forgive and just turn the page"? Not only does it prove impossible for them to overlook these masculine violations, but they also conclude that their husbands must be stopped immediately because "he would do it again. He would hold off as long as he could, but sooner or later 'Beadie' would gain the upper hand" (336). After her sobering conversation with Vera ('Truth') Donovan, Dolores is made to realize that running away with her imperiled daughter is not an option; she has little money, even less knowledge of the world outside Little Tall Island, and her husband will track them down easily. Also, Claiborne fears that whatever level of incest her husband has already foisted upon their daughter will soon escalate, if it hasn't already, into full intercourse, so she needs to act fast and decisively. Sensing these truths intuitively, that their respective husbands are out of control and can no longer be trusted, each woman works through the initial shock and mortification of their betrayals to access a dark psychology of their own. As it often does in the Stephen King universe, culpability has seeped into the deepest corners of American life and its most intimate familial spaces.[3] What proves most interesting in both of these situations is that neither Dolores nor Darcy ever considers going to the authorities and supplying them with evidence to charge their respective husbands with felony crimes. Why do both women reject the option of police involvement, deciding instead to risk their own freedom and peace of mind by commissioning themselves their husbands' respective homicides? Maybe these male transgressions prove so intimate and egregious that neither woman can bear the humiliation of confessing it, especially to strangers who most likely would be men, such as detectives Holt Ramsey in *A Good Marriage* or John Mackey in *Claiborne*. Or the idea of their children suffering the shame that would attend their fathers' trials and punishments is perhaps another motivation behind their choices. Most plausible still, however, is that both women appear driven by their own righteous indignation as desecrated wives.

In the "Afterword" to the *Full Dark, No Stars* collection that includes *A Good Marriage*, King informs us that he wrote the novella "to explore the idea that it's impossible to fully know anyone, even those we love the most" (368). This is most obviously apparent given the secreted actions of Bob Anderson, who is somehow capable of remaining a fully functioning husband in spite of also being a vicious serial killer. But what truly needs to be acknowledged is that his good wife is likewise capable of transforming herself into "the monster's wife" (334). Although Darcy assures her husband that she will keep the secret of "Beadie" if he "makes a solemn promise" to give up his past behavior and they "never talk about this again," it is clear in both film and novella that she uses her proffered silence and, by extension, collusion, as a means for buying more time to form a plan. He certainly continues to conduct his life as if their status as a perfect couple remains unsullied and his wife has granted him a second chance at marital redemption. Defying audience expectations, the largest and best portion of the film does not center on Bob and his divided selves, but rather on the self-torment his wife is forced to undergo alone in their home, as Darcy comes to identify personally with her husband's bondage harem of dead women, and his dark history seeps into her psyche. She eventually realizes she can no longer compromise her own morality (and sanity), stated forcefully in the novella where she envisions an afterlife confronted "by a ghastly receiving line of strangled women branded by her husband's teeth, all accusing her of causing their deaths by taking the easy way out herself" (312). Film audiences observe Darcy's level of suffering as she creeps anxiously around familiar rooms and stairwells in the middle of the day, checking behind doors, nervously calling out Bob's name, watching from an upstairs window while her husband ogles their female neighbor outside, jumping at the sound of a newspaper hitting her front door, and especially in the hallucination of a television newscaster who speaks directly to her about the crimes her husband has committed and her responsibility to act upon this knowledge. In fact, on numerous occasions Darcy imagines her husband performing acts of violence against *her*—a carving knife left deliberately on the bedroom nightstand, smashing her head into a closet mirror. Thus, the intruder in her home appears to emanate from inside her own psyche as much as from the shared burden of "Beadie"'s crimes. And because her knowledge of these transgressions is second-hand, gleaned from the Internet and television, Darcy is left with visualizing their occurrence via her haunted imagination—"wondering if he had kissed *them*" (335)—while her former degree of domestic security and complacency is abruptly eroded, "her mind going around and around, now thinking of the victims, now thinking of her children, now thinking of herself, even thinking of some long-forgotten Bible story about Jesus praying in the Garden of Gethsemane" (314).

It is in the filmic projections of her stimulated dreamscape that the audience witnesses the deepest level of Darcy's personal suffering and the forging of an emerging empathy with Bob's murder victims. In the first of these, she awakens in bed because she pictures Bob strangling her in a way that connects her directly to her husband's succession of slaughtered women. In yet another dream, Darcy awakens after her husband smashes her face into a closet mirror while he, like Bluebeard, blames *her* curiosity for their predicament: "You just had to look, didn't you?" In the last of these nightmares, which is the one that ultimately convinces her to act, she discovers her daughter, Petra, bound and naked on her knees in their basement, juxtaposed in the exact position as Bob's quarry that Darcy views on the Internet, red bite marks on her torso, awaiting Bob's further awful ministrations. It is significant that Darcy juxtaposes Petra into this nightmare: the dream highlights the fact that her daughter is approximately the same age as Bob's prey and that Darcy is being charged with a responsibility to act on their behalf. Further, Petra's presence in the dream brings Bob's work home, literally into their basement, revealing in Darcy's subconscious a level of domestic defilement that includes the potential for father-daughter incest in addition to physical torture and murder. From the moment the couple begins to discuss "Beadie," Bob tries to manipulate his wife's response by reminding her of how their secret knowledge, if it was ever revealed to the public, would affect their children. The subliminal breakdowns in Darcy's inner psychology chip away at her own efforts to construct any personal barriers against her husband's horrific history; in fact, quite the opposite occurs because the potency of her imagination forces her into inhabiting "Beadie"'s parallel universe where Darcy finds herself—and her daughter—tied inextricably to Bob's "snoots." In her decision to act violently against her husband, Darcy overcomes the passive-aggressive skills her husband uses in an attempt to ensure her silence. Instead of merely shielding the status quo of her family or concealing the mouse hole of her husband's secret sins, however, Darcy expands outward beyond the confines of her life and home by recognizing an obligation to protect future women she will never meet.

Since the 1990s, the King cinematic world has centered much of its creative energies on describing American domestic relationships in monstrous disarray. Films such as *Dolores Claiborne, Bag of Bones, Rose Red, Rose Matter*, and *Gerald's Game* join *A Good Marriage* as studies of masculine violence perpetrated against women and girls. Violent sexual predators roam every one of these various cinescapes, and it is against them that the most compelling of King's heroines must battle, psychologically and physically. In contrast to King's males who typically are pictured operating alone in these films, the struggles of these wives and daughters are not isolated: Claiborne submits to a dark mentorship under Vera to rescue the former's daughter from incest; in *Gerald's Game*, Jessie Burlingame connects with Punkin, an interactive psychic extension of her younger self, and Ruth, an old college friend, to guide her imaginatively out of her own husband's attraction to women in bondage, and into a new definition of selfhood; while in *Bag of Bones,* Jo's spiritual aura, Sara Tidwell's revenge, and Mattie's ghost all work together to protect Mattie's young daughter, Kyra, from Max Devore's relentless machinations. The main way in which women in King texts and their adapted movies come to possess integral, independent lives is through reemploying violence. They subscribe to Hilary Neroni's position on violent women in contemporary American cinema who employ force that "does not necessarily erupt spontaneously or as an irrational response to a situation, but rather [use] violence to play a very specific role in creating individual and social identities" (41). Elsewhere in this volume, Patrick McAleer contextualizes Neroni's larger thesis in his argument that "King does find it to be plausible to engage in acts of violence if, perhaps, the alternative is essentially to enable more violence and destruction on the other end of the equation." Indeed, true independence for so many King wives and daughters occurs only after they have completely detached themselves from the various male relationships that have held them captive and move on to create alternative social bonds devoid of men. *A Good Marriage* is filled with the same existential questions and conflicted knowledge that King women experience in the face of perversity and aggression generated by wayward husbands and fathers. Darcy eventually acts from a position where shock and shame translate into bravery and an identification with her husband's anguished victims; Darcy murders her husband, like Dolores Claiborne, to protect potential future victims of his oppression at the same time that she revenges the women she never knew personally, but with whom she has come to share a kind of intimate solidarity.

Darcy's empathetic connection with Bob's victims technically commences at the moment she recognizes the same goldfish earrings he presented to her for their twenty-fifth wedding anniversary on a posted photograph of one of his murdered victims. Both Darcy and the dead woman were born under the astrological sign Pisces, a powerful water sign typically represented by fish. Naturally, once recognized, Darcy never again is seen wearing them, but on the day when she attends her husband's funeral, she throws both earrings into the grave on top of his casket. Petra chastises her for not putting them *inside* the casket before it was closed and lowered into the ground, especially since her mother admits "these are very special to me," but Darcy knows she is acting on the behalf of more than just herself. She owes a secret responsibility to the initial owner of the earrings, countering the dead woman's violation in a surrogate revenge; at the same time, the gesture also serves as Darcy's final dismissal of "Beadie" and Bob, sending both her husband and his alter ego into eternity burdened with this avatar of their earthly transgressions.

It turns out that in the commission of her husband's murder—especially since it requires a close physical struggle to suffocate him with a plastic bag and dishrag when the fall she orchestrates fails to kill him outright—Darcy summons a level of violent determination that proves to be every bit as efficiently compartmentalized as her husband's. In the final scene of the film, Darcy is pictured alone but definitely moving on with her life, devouring chocolates without criticism and perusing coin magazines as if Bob had been only a minor domestic problem she has since resolved. Darcy's cold efficiency and lack of remorse so offended Brian Tallerico that he dismissed

The shared earrings. From *Stephen King's A Good Marriage*. Dir. Peter Askin. Reno Productions, Screen Media Films, 2014. DVD. Screenshot captured by author.

the entire film because "the BTK [killer was] more interesting than the wife who you need to root for in her effort to stop him." There is some element of truth in Tallerico's critique, mirrored as it is in the many negative reactions from others who reviewed the film on Netflix's site.[4] The single time I taught this work to undergraduates, one of my students scorned it as a "made for the Lifetime channel" effort, predictable and overwrought. However, such criticism tends to undervalue the steep reaction curve that Darcy must undergo as a result of her lurid discovery, forcing her into a place where, if she is serious about containing her husband's serial murdering, she must harden her feelings against him. She is even disposed to committing another homicide by using a pillow to smother Detective Ramsey in his hospital bed to shield her children from criminal exposure and prosecution. The detective precludes her worries when he blesses the violent end of her marriage: "You did the right thing" in dispatching Bob. In final judgment, it is Darcy who becomes the truest keeper of secrets, emerging as a Mrs. Hyde: the history of Bob's killing spree dies with him, of course, but so too does the revenge murder she orchestrates on behalf of his past (and possible future) female victims and his desecration of a good marriage. The discovery of Bob's "Beadie" secret transforms Darcy's life, and not just because she is made into one of their victims. Like "Beadie," she becomes a highly efficient killer herself: taking care to clean up evidence of Bob's murder before calling the authorities and assuming the role of the grieving wife at her husband's gravesite. The birth of this film's Mrs. Hyde certainly reintroduces one of Stephen King's most obsessive characters: the violent female, drawn out by toxic men. In his fiction, the transition from wife and mother to Mrs. Hyde is a necessary and productive one. Darcy's choice, so similar to Dolores's in disguising the truth of Joe's homicide under an "accident of misadventure," serves as a reminder that women, and even loyal wives of many years, are capable of being just as diabolical as men, and just as adept at hiding the secret consequences of their own "female explorations."

NOTES

1. As Brian Aldiss opines, Stevenson's novel "is too cerebral, too bloodless, for the movies. We have to be shown Fredric March or Spencer Tracy, or whomever, consorting with prostitutes, wielding the stick, being cruel" (qtd. in Wolf 114).

2. King informs his readers that the inspiration for *A Good Marriage* had its origins in the infamous case of Dennis Rader, the BTK (bind, torture, and kill) serial killer from Wichita who "took the lives of ten people—mostly women, but two of his victims were children—over a period of sixteen years" (King, "Afterword" 368). While Rader mocked police and arrogantly dared them to find him, Rader's family remains emphatic that no one in their home knew anything about the killings prior to the husband-father's arrest in 2005; indeed, four months after the history of his actions were revealed, his wife was granted an emergency divorce while his children refuse to visit him in prison.

3. In her assessment of *Dolores Claiborne*, Colleen Dolan argues that "King does not portray Dolores as a murderer, but rather an avenging angel . . . who has also died an emotional, spiritual, and intellectual death from abuse, then rises from this death to become strong and whole again" (163, 161). I would imagine that Dolan would likely apply the same interpretation to a reading of Darcy's character in *A Good Marriage*. While I agree essentially with her position, it is important to point out that Dolores is more problematic than the "archetypal phoenix woman" (161) Dolan makes her out to be. All the flashbacks that occur in Hackford's film belong to Dolores herself, except, of course, the final one that Selena experiences on the ferry prompted by Dolores's taped history of familial events. The intensity and frequency of these flashbacks indicate that Dolores remains haunted by selected images of her past. We watch these flashbacks commence when Claiborne is forced to return to the house and property she shared with her husband, the unexpected visit from her daughter, and another similar Mackey criminal investigation. These combine to suggest the awakening of restive ghosts from her violent marriage and a reemergent level of guilt arising from her role in Joe's "death by misadventure" that Dolores has been able to repress until the recent loss of her protectress, Vera, and Dolores's return to the scene of her husband's "accident." Legal protections for battered women entered the U.S. legal code only in 1994, which means that in 1963, the year of eclipse, Dolores Claiborne would not have had a legal precedent upon which to justify killing her husband. This explains her obvious lack of interest in defending herself against Mackey's wrongheaded investigation into Vera's death and her concluding admission of guilt to Selena that it is finally "time to pay the piper." No such similar ambivalent

thoughts, however, appear to burden Darcy about her role in the commission of her husband's "accidental" fall.

    4. https://dvd.netflix.com/Movie/Stephen-King-s-A-Good-Marriage/80014887.

WORKS CITED

Bag of Bones. Dir. Mick Garris. Screenplay by Stephen King and Matt Venne. Perf. Pierce Brosnan, Melissa George. Nice Guy Entertainment, Sennet Entertainment, 2011. DVD.

Bellour, Raymond. "Psychosis, Neurosis, Perversion." Trans. Nancy Huston. *A Hitchcock Reader*. 311–31. Eds. Marshall Deutelbaum and Leland Poague. Ames, Iowa: Iowa University Press, 1986. Print.

The Dead Zone. Dir. David Cronenberg. Screenplay by Jeffrey Boam. Perf. Christopher Walken, Martin Sheen. Dino De Laurentiis Corporation, Paramount Pictures, 1983.

Dolan, Colleen. "The Feminist King: *Dolores Claiborne*." *The Films of Stephen King*. 155–65. Ed. Tony Magistrale. NY: Palgrave-Macmillan-Springer, 2008. Print.

Dolores Claiborne. Dir. Taylor Hackford. Screenplay by Tony Gilroy. Perf. Kathy Bates, Jennifer Jason Leigh, Christopher Plummer. Castle Rock Entertainment, 1995. DVD.

Edmundson, Mark. *Nightmare on Main Street: Angels, Sadomasochism, and the Culture of the Gothic*. Cambridge, MA: Harvard University Press, 1997. Print.

Frost, Rebecca. "A Different Breed: Stephen King's Serial Killers." *Stephen King's Contemporary Classics: Reflections on the Modern Master of Horror*. Eds. Philip L. Simpson and Patrick McAleer. Lanham, MD: Rowman & Littlefield, 2015. 117–32. Print.

Gerald's Game. Dir. Mike Flanagan. Screenplay by Mike Flanagan, Jeff Howard, Stephen King. Perf. Carla Gugino, Bruce Greenwood. Intrepid Pictures, 2017. DVD.

King, Stephen. "Afterword." *Full Dark, No Stars*. 365–8. NY: Scribner, 2010. Print.

King, Stephen. "*Big Driver*." *Full Dark, No Stars*. 133–245. NY: Scribner, 2010. Print.

King, Stephen. *Danse Macabre*. NY: Berkley Books, 1982. Print.

King, Stephen. "The Gingerbread Girl." *Just After Sunset*. 42–126. NY: Scribner, 2008. Print.

King, Stephen. *A Good Marriage*. *Full Dark, No Stars*. 281–364. NY: Scribner, 2010. Print.

King, Stephen. "Introduction." *Frankenstein, Dracula,* and *Dr. Jekyll and Mr. Hyde*. v–xiii. NY: Signet Classic, 1978. Print.

King, Stephen. *Misery*. NY: Viking, 1987. Print.

King, Stephen. "Strawberry Spring." *Night Shift*. NY: New American Library, 1976. Print.

Neroni, Hilary. *The Violent Woman: Femininity, Narrative, and Violence in Contemporary American Cinema*. NY: SUNY Press, 2005. Print.

Psycho. Dir. Alfred Hitchcock. Screenplay by Joseph Stefano. Perf. Anthony Perkins, Janet Leigh, Vera Miles. Paramount, 1960.

Stephen King's A Good Marriage. Dir. Peter Askin. Screenplay by Stephen King. Perf. Anthony LaPaglia, Joan Allen. Reno Productions, Screen Media Films, 2014. DVD.

Stevenson, Robert Louis. *The Strange Case of Dr. Jekyll and Mr. Hyde*. 1886. Toronto, Ontario: Broadway Press, 2000. Print.

Tallerico, Brian. Rev. of *A Good Marriage*. 3 Oct. 2014. https://www.rogerebert.com/reviews/a-good-marriage-2014. Web. 21 June 2020.

Underwood, Tim, and Chuck Miller, eds. "Stephen King Interview with *Playboy* Magazine." 24–56. *Bare Bones: Conversations on Terror with Stephen King*. NY: McGraw-Hill, 1988. Print.

Weinstock, Jeffrey Andrew. "Invisible Monsters: Vision, Horror, and Contemporary Culture." *The Monster Theory Reader*. 358–73. Ed. Jeffrey Andrew Weinstock. Minneapolis, MN: University Press of Minnesota, 2020. Print.

Wolf, Leonard, ed. *The Essential Dr. Jekyll and Mr. Hyde: The Definitive Annotated Edition of Robert Louis Stevenson's Classic Novel*. NY: Plume, 1995. Print.

Chapter 3

The Mad Lady

Racial and Sexual Violence in Mick Garris's Bag of Bones

Phoenix Crockett and Stephen Indrisano

Bag of Bones is a 2011 two-part miniseries adaptation of the 1998 Stephen King horror novel of the same name. Directed by Mick Garris, a popular director of King adaptations, and written by Matt Venne, it has since aired on the A&E network in two parts as well as on Britain's Channel 5 as a single film. Since the premiere, which drew over six million views in two parts and was the most watched broadcast of both evenings (Seidman 1), the film has been viewed hundreds of thousands of times on Youtube. The film starred former Bond actor Pierce Brosnan and scored an aggregate twenty-one percent on the popular film critique site *Rotten Tomatoes* as of October 2020, a score which conveys general audience distaste. Why, then, might an adaptation of a best-selling novel, helmed by an accomplished director attached to more successful adaptations and featuring a well-known lead actor, have received such spotty critical reception? While there are numerous potential reasons for this low score, one salient concern is the portrayal of violence and trauma within the film: *Bag of Bones* deals with graphic, racially motivated sexual violence in a way that is fundamentally exploitative. In addition, the decisions to depict certain instances of violence and not others based on the source material do not serve the adaptation. Further, the narrative and structural elements of the piece surround and draw attention to filmic tropes about hate crimes, with specific emphases on racial and sexual violence, leading to a narrative that plays into several racist tropes and histories.

Because *Bag of Bones* is one of King's lesser known novels, and the adaptation is one of the lesser known adaptations, a synopsis may be helpful in understanding this critical reception. Mike Noonan is a beloved author whose wife, Jo, is killed in a bus accident. He suffers from nightmares and hallucinations and decides to move into the couple's second home on Dark Score Lake in a small territory called TR-90, Maine. Many of these visions have a surreal sexual element to them and involve Sara Tidwell, a prominent African American jazz singer who lived in TR-90 decades earlier. He befriends a young woman named Mattie and her daughter Kyra, whose father attempted to drown her years ago and was shot by Mattie (Garris 00:00–45:00).

Maddie's father-in-law, a man named Max Devore, has opened a vicious custody case against Mattie, and Mike steps in to help. He learns that his grandfather and several other men—including Max Devore—participated in the brutal sexual assault and murder of Sara Tidwell. The men drowned Tidwell's daughter, Keisha, to avoid being jailed for the crime. As a result, Sara Tidwell cursed the men's descendants to drown their own daughters until their bloodlines end, explaining TR-90's dark paternal past, as well as Mike's ongoing role in Kyra's life (Garris 45:00–127:55).

After Noonan learns about the town's history, Max is found dead by suicide and there is a brief moment of hope for Mattie and Kyra. During a small backyard party to celebrate the end of the custody battle, however, Mattie is shot and killed by a man under the employ of Max Devore. Mike escapes with Kyra, but is chased to his home by Mattie's killers. Noonan is guided by the ghost of his late wife to find and destroy the remains of Sara Tidwell in order to end the curse. He succeeds by pouring lye on Tidwell's bones, saving Kyra once and for all. In an epilogue, he adopts her (Garris 127:55–162:00).

There are elements to this plot which are both compelling and in-line with some of King's most recognizable tropes. It is the story of a famous author and city-type, placed in an unfamiliar context and compelled to thwart malevolent supernatural elements. There are serious structural and filmic issues with the adaptation, however. The pacing is odd, with long, low-action sections punctuated by sudden bouts of sweat-inducing violence. While this format may have theoretically contributed to a sense of Gothic dread, any tension built up by the sudden acts of violence is dispelled by frequent commercial break transitions. Even without the presence of the advertisements themselves, these transitions continually cue the audience that there will be a break in the story, thus interrupting the underlying tension essential to Thriller cinema. The acting, as well, works against building tensions with moments of unintentional comedy wherein Brosnan fails to portray fear with any gravity. Zack Handlen, writing for *The A.V. Club*, puts this succinctly in his 2011 review of the original T.V. presentation: "King's protagonists tend to be solid everyman types, generally uncomfortable in displays of serious emotion, which means that every time emotion does surface, it's intense and shocking. What this translates to on screen is Brosnan looking like he's going to burp, fart, and sneeze simultaneously every ten minutes or so. Sometimes he yells at his laptop" (Handlen 4). This is in stark contrast to some of the more beloved adaptations of Stephen King works, such as *Dolores Claiborne* (1995), *Gerald's*

Game (2017), and *The Green Mile* (1999), which deal with similar themes of trauma, sexual violence, and race in America (Magistrale 24).

Dolores Claiborne deals with domestic violence and sexual abuse in an earnest way that does not ask the audience to pass judgements, only to bear witness. Its strength as an adaptation is due in no small part to matching the theme and tone of the original novel, which acknowledges sexual violence as traumatic, but does not use said trauma as a source of spectacle. *Gerald's Game* deals with the horrors of sexual violence with carefully written and directed scenes that dismay the viewer; like *Dolores Claiborne*, however, it manages to portray the depths of emotion associated with sexual trauma without crossing into gawking territory. Neither *Gerald's Game* nor *Dolores Claiborne* utilize camera perspectives from the point of view of the attacker in their depictions of sexual violence, and while *Gerald's Game* depicts the onset of an act of incest, the sequence ends upon the victim's realization of what is happening. In contrast, the sexual violence in *Bag of Bones* is shown in its entirety, with multiple detail shots of the victim's bare legs, the full motion of the rape, and multiple blows to the face and head.

The Green Mile, while controversial for its racial depictions, success-fully threads the same needle as *Dolores Claiborne* and *Gerald's Game*. The racial violence in *The Green Mile* is grounded in realism, and the audience is not expected to be thrilled or titillated by the racial trauma on display. Furthermore, the sexual violence which occurs in *The Green Mile* occurs fully off screen. It is worth noting that not all filmic representation of racially motivated and sexual violence in King adaptations are successful. *It* (2017) muted the racial violence inherent to the source material, and analyzers of the film *The Shawshank Redemption* have constructed arguments of both praise and concern surrounding the depiction of sexual assault in prisons (Kermode 38). To place the violence of *Bag of Bones* in the Stephen King adaptations canon, it is necessary to unravel and reflect on the exploitative nature of the violence in the film, the context of the violence in the film, and the tropes and conventions that mire the film's portrayals of sexual violence in a history of racist exploitation.[1]

To fully understand the racial aspect of exploitative violence in *Bag of Bones*, it may be useful to examine other black characters in King's collected works. King's portrayal of non-white characters has been controversial. One frequent criticism of King's black characters is their tendency to exist solely to benefit white characters, such as the slow and forgiving John Coffey in *The Green Mile,* the paternalistic Dick Hallorann in *The Shining*, and the saintly Mother Abigail in *The Stand*. These characters are often used as examples of the Magical Negro trope, which is here defined as a black character whose main narrative purpose is to come to the aid, often supernaturally, of a white protagonist (Farley 2–3). These characters stand in contrast to more complex black characters, such as Mike Hanlon from *It*. Hanlon is powerful without being magical, vengeful, parental or, arguably, violent, and his character arc is not motivated solely by his relationship to white characters. Outside of filmic adaptations, King's canon contains other complicated portraits of black women as well, some of whom are notably violent. Detta Walker in *The Drawing of the Three* is a black female activist in the American south in the 1960's who has an alternate personality who is pugilistic and uncouth, and her racial portrayal is dicey and debated. Seven years after *The Drawing of the Three,* King wrote the brilliant character Gert Kinshaw for *Rose Madder.* Gert is a black woman with power, intelligence, and sensitivity to her identity, who interacts with white characters without subservience; she is the apex of positive black portrayal in the King canon. Sara Tidwell exists within this canon in a unique role, as both a villain and a character defined by her relationship to white characters. Like John Coffey, Mother Abigail, and Dick Halloran, Tidwell exhibits magical powers; unlike these Magical Negro characters, Sara Tidwell, while certainly supernatural, is vengeful rather than benevolent. Unlike Mike Hanlon or Gert Kinshaw, however, Tidwell does exhibit harmful stereotypes. Throughout *Bag of Bones*, her more stereotypical aspects combine with the violence within the story to create a particularly racialized exploitative form of entertainment.

The interplay between racist tropes and exploitative violence in media is longstanding and thoroughly intertwined. Though we will discuss both in greater detail below within the context of *Bag of Bones*, when we refer to racist tropes we are broadly referring to stereotypes about racial groups as codified through the media. In America, these tropes can often be traced to the theatrical tradition of blackface minstrel. Jennifer Bloomquist writes in "The Minstrel Legacy: African American English and the Historical Construction of "Black" Identities in Entertainment":

> [Minstrel] comedy hinged on gross misrepresentations of what the actors determined to be (southern) Black culture, including singing, dancing, and delivering comedic speeches. In the early days of minstrelsy, more often than not, the actors had little or no real contact with African Americans, so their version of Black culture was almost entirely grounded in racist stereotypes. Early minstrelsy was used as a tool to further malign Blacks and to promote justifications for slavery. . . . Even after the traveling shows faded into obscurity by the turn of the twentieth century, the farcical and damaging construction of Black identity in minstrelsy was co-opted by vaudeville shows and early film. (Bloomquist 28)

Thus, when we refer to racially exploitative violence, we are referring to violence depicted with the intent to titillate or shock which in some way plays into, relates to, or reinforces these racist tropes. Not all of the violence within *Bag of Bones* is specifically racist or exploitative, but the occasions wherein violence edges into exploitative territory break down across gendered and racial lines.

This is evident from the opening of *Bag of Bones*, which includes a montage of drownings of several young girls shot from below, intercut with scenery of evergreens and a cemetery, all set to a jarring, discordant score. This upsetting sequence is followed by an abrupt shift in tone as the film's plot begins. The audience is shown a heartfelt moment between Brosnan (as Noonan) and actress Anabeth Gish (as Jo). This emotional whiplash will come to characterize the film's uneven treatment of violence. Within *Bag of Bones*, there is a fatal bus crash, an attempted drowning, and a fatal shooting, all of which are given a standard, tame television movie treatment: the wounds are left out, blood is used sparingly, there are plenty of closeups to curtail the scene, and reactions from characters are appropriate. It is worth noting that the bus crash that kills Jo Noonan, complete with slow-motion crying and swelling music, replaces a different fate in the novel, wherein Jo suffers an aneurysm. While the reason for this change is not immediately apparent, it does seem likely that the visual of a character being hit by a bus may be more "dramatic" than the invisible threat of sudden brain injury. In this way, we can get a sense for the priorities of Venne's adaptive changes: make the violence more digestible for T.V. audiences, while providing a thrill.

Another instance of notable changes between violence in King's source text and Venne's screenplay is the attempted drowning of Mike Noonan. While Venne and Garris' depiction of the scene is true to the source material, there is actually more than one attempted drowning of Mike Noonan in the novel. Drowning is among the most notable motifs in the novel, which carries over into Garris' *Bag of Bones* in the multiple drowning scenes throughout the movie. This begs the question, how did Venne decide which drownings to include and which to cut? Noonan certainly faces this kind of violence fewer times in the adaptation than in the novel, but the same cannot be said for the jaw-dropping opening sequence, nor for Kyra, who is in constant danger of being drowned throughout the film. Again, we see Garris and Venne leverage a highly visible form of violence for the purposes of raising audience tension. While the threat of violence—even against children—is not necessarily exploitative as a tension-building tactic, it bears mentioning within the context of *Bag of Bones*. What purpose is served by curtailing some violent acts and embellishing others? Why include the violent deaths of multiple children, while cutting similar violence against the protagonist? Whose trauma is palatable for audiences?

One final example of modulated violence within *Bag of Bones* is the death of Mattie Devore. In the source text, the backyard celebration shooting is a messy, chaotic affair more akin to the death of Bonnie and Clyde than the clean, efficient violence committed in the film (King 498). Unlike Jo's death at the beginning of *Bag of Bones*, here we see an instance of a decrease in violent spectacle; not only do fewer characters die in this sequence than in the source text, but the bodily depiction of Mattie Devore's death is sanitized for television. Perhaps the changes here are to avoid the more troubling aspects of a bullet-riddled dinner party. One could speculate that there was network pressure to tone down Mattie Devore's death, or that the diminished violence was in-line with regulations. One could speculate, in point of fact, any number of reasons to diminish the portrayal of Mattie Devore's death. There is, however, a singular act of violence within *Bag of Bones* which is so explicit, so unflinching in its depiction, and so important to the very structure of the story, that by comparison Mattie Devore's death may as well have been filmed for a different movie entirely. The violent, racially motivated and sexually traumatic death of Sara Tidwell complicates the decision to tone down Mattie Devore's violent death, because it makes visible the double standard at play in *Bag of Bones*: some violence is fair game for entertainment purposes and some is not, regardless of its intensity. Were the violent scenes from the novel muted in the miniseries to make emotional space for the violent hate crime that occurs, or was decision making regarding violence simply inconsistent? In terms of thematic and structural importance, all scenes in *Bag of Bones* lead back to the one hundred and twenty sixth minute of the film: the rape and murder of Sara Tidwell, which is nearly as difficult to watch as it is to describe.

A crew of men follow Tidwell into a wooded area, and the sadistic Max Devore holds her down and begins beating her while hurling racist rhetoric about what he is owed, sexually, based on her apparently salacious lyrics during her vocal performances. The beating shows real hits that land with realistic sound editing, and blood that is clearly made of a different substance than the blood used during the bus crash scene. Devore calls his cronies to hold Tidwell down while he removes her underwear beneath a purple dress. He implores her to beg for forgiveness, using the word "bitch" repeatedly. The camera zooms out and shows, for fourteen seconds out of the next thirty, the actual thrusting of the rape, which is extremely rare in both television and film. This scene is divided between that image and the image of Tidwell looking into her young daughter's terrified eyes. The daughter is then carried off by one of the men and drowned. The camera films from both below the water, showing the young girl's terror, and from above, which depicts the mechanics of the act, including the whip of the child's spine and the attacker looking away from his crime. After being struck with a rock once, Tidwell sits up and delivers an awful screech and a long, breathless hex. The camera pans back and forth between the paling faces of the white men. The final hit of the rock is much quieter than the others, the music fades out, and Tidwell's body hits the ground unceremoniously (Garris 127:08). The men bury her body under Devore's watchful eye. To say that this scene is exploitative is to say that choices were made to evoke emotional reactions from the audience at the expense of the group(s) represented, and it *is* at Sara Tidwell's expense; the viewer feels almost as if they are violating her privacy due to the graphic nature of the scene.[2]

The exploitation of the scene is not just evidenced by the emotionally charged elements but by inconsistent decisions regarding what is normally shown on prime time television. While gun violence, abuse, and other disturbing images have been fair play for decades, this depiction of sexual assault, as well as a lynching, is unusual (Rafter 16). In the years between 2000 and 2012, less than a dozen complaints were filed with the FCC about scenes depicting sexual assault, and not all of them resulted in fines (Complaints Regarding 10–80). Only three complaints were made regarding lynching and hate crimes, perhaps because they are not specifically monitored by the FCC. It is worth noting that *Bag of Bones* does not appear in any public FCC report, and that the notable cases appearing in the sources listed had many times more viewers than this broadcast (Parrot Analytics). Why, then, was this scene so intentionally graphic? It easily could have been brushed over or toned down, as was Mattie Devore's death, though there is merit to the idea that it is important to depict traumatic events that happen to people realistically, as in *Gerald's Game* and *Dolores Claiborne*. Nothing about the tone or content of *Bag of Bones* elsewhere matches this ethic. The host network, A&E, is no stranger to upsetting images, being a channel most notable for crime television, but most of the A&E complaints from the decade in question were for swearing. There are also examples of A&E removing scenes of sexual violence during re-runs before and after *Bag of Bones*, such as the assault of Dr. Melfi in *The Sopranos* (Steinberg 12–14). Reruns of *Bag of Bones,* which are extremely rare, do not remove the scene. Much of the media coverage surrounding the miniseries consisted of praise for the series and joy over A&E's significantly boosted ratings after the first airing, in which case the scene in question either did not achieve an emotional response, which is hard to believe, or it did what it was intended to do, which was to make millions of watchers feel negative emotions and then attempt to resolve them in a strange plot of ghosts and revenge.

The violence within *Bag of Bones* ties into tropes and filmic conventions which have cultural import far beyond the logistical hurdles of bringing a thriller to air on prime time television. One of the central theses of *Bag of Bones* is that the source and subject of violence—who performs violence and who is victim to it—are not arbitrary. The motivating force behind much of *Bag of Bones* is the discovery of, and defense against, a curse. As Darryl V. Caterine notes in his 2014 essay, "Heirs through Fear: Indian Curses, Accursed Indian Lands, and White Christian Sovereignty in America," curses against predominately white, Protestant New Englanders have a deep history in American literature which can be traced to the early 1800s, with specific meanings and implications (40–41). From the inception of the Indian curse trope, fictional and apocryphal curses held similar uses as the "early national jeremiad that shamed Christian readers for not living up to their own ethical principles and exhorted them to rectify their behavior in the future—if not in their dealings with Native Americans, then at least in the company of other whites" (Caterine 42). This lineage, Caterine writes, continues through the works of contemporary authors (including Stephen King, who uses the Indian Burial Ground trope in his 1983 best-seller, *Pet Sematary*) as "invariably part of a larger discourse about national origins in a culturally inscribed American nature" (54).

In *Bag of Bones*, we can see some parallels between the Indian Curse as outlined by Caterine and the curse which befalls TR-90 as cast by Sara Tidwell. Just as the early Indian Curse existed as a moral indictment of the Puritans, Tidwell's curse upon the residents of TR-90 is an explicit indictment of the racist violence perpetuated and tolerated by the town's white residents. This apparently anti-racist sentiment is undermined, however, by the cultural association between those who lay curses and a non-white racial "Other." Members of white society, whether they be Puritan New Englanders or contemporary White American citizens, are invariably the subject of these kinds of supernatural violence; this racial aspect persists in both the book and filmic adaptation of *Bag of Bones*. Sara Tidwell, having watched her daughter be drowned in the lake, invokes the central curse: "You and your kin are cursed! You and your sons are going to do to your daughters what you've done to mine. With your own hands, you will murder your daughters. And with their own hands, your sons are going to murder their daughters. A curse on you and yours until you're all gone!" (Garris 126:29–127:05).

While this moment certainly has thematic importance within American racial theory, its primary function is to entertain within the specific narrative form of the thriller. While there is a notable lack of consensus about the exact defining characteristics of thriller media, Kuhn and Westwell's *A Dictionary of Film Studies* posits that across thrillers "the aim is to startle, shock, scare, and surprise the spectator—responses generated narratively by means of twists, turns, and retardations in the plot and manipulations of point of view, editing, and offscreen space" (Kuhn and Westwell 1). The rape and murder of Sara Tidwell serves multiple purposes within the thriller structure: it is the informational payoff, clarifying why there are supernatural events occurring in TR-90; it is a flashback, placing us into a new and interesting point of view; it is a shocking act of violence, designed to elicit an emotional reaction from the audience; and it is a moment of supernatural dread wherein a curse is invoked. These genre factors intersect with the racial histories inherent to curses in American media, as well as the implicit and explicit racism of Tidwell's lynching, to form a scene wherein the audience is encouraged to be upset and entertained by the rape of a Black woman and the drowning of her daughter, as well as frightened by her justified rage at the hate crime which ends her life.

The moment of Sara Tidwell's rape is further complicated by her continual sexualization throughout *Bag of Bones*. Tidwell's jazz vocal performances are riddled with innuendo, with such lyrics and emphases as, "She *laid* . . . her eyes on him" and "He took her *in* . . . for a small poured wine (sic)" (Garris 123:14–123:27). The cinematography of Tidwell's performances is also purposefully sensual, framing shots with her shaking hips in the foreground, or with slow pans up her body. There is an element of racialized sexualization to these shots, which is commented upon within the text itself. When Devore and his co-conspirators ambush Tidwell, he gloats: "You think you can sing the way you do and get away with it, huh? You think you and *your kind* can boil our blood and not give us what we want when you're done, huh?" (Garris 124:28–124:34).

This confluence of factors makes Sara Tidwell both monster and victim, seductress and sexual object. She is to be both feared and pitied. Like the mythic "disappearing Indians" described by Caterine, Tidwell's lynching is portrayed as a moral failing of the town itself. Tidwell's righteous anger is understandable to the audience, but however sympathetic her motivations may be, Tidwell's curse ultimately casts her in the role of the vengeful spirit, in need of being "put to rest." Just as we cannot ignore the racial difference between Tidwell and her attackers, we cannot ignore the object of Tidwell's violence throughout the film: white women and girls. Specifically, the narrative arc of *Bag of Bones* ends with Mike Noonan protecting the young Kyra from Tidwell and those who would carry out her curse. Kyra gives Tidwell a name: the Mad Lady.

Here, too, it becomes useful to examine the cultural context of *Bag of Bones*. Much like the racialization of Tidwell's sexuality, there is an uncomfortable racial aspect to Tidwell's association with anger. The stereotype of the "angry black woman" has been well documented, and its influence should not be ignored within the context of popular media. California State Professor Wendy Ashley, an expert on racial stereotyping in American culture, defines the "angry black woman" stereotype succinctly: "the myth of the angry black woman . . . characterizes these women as aggressive, ill tempered, illogical, overbearing, hostile, and ignorant without provocation" (27). At first glance, this stereotype may appear to be irrelevant to the internal logic of *Bag of Bones*; after all, Sarah Tidwell fits into the more specific horror trope of the vengeful spirit which involves explicit provocation. However, further examination of Tidwell's motivation after her death provides ample evidence of an "ill tempered" and "illogical" quest for vengeance. As is repeatedly noted in the movie, Kyra had nothing to do with Tidwell's death, and any anger directed at her is, at best, "illogical."

The question to be answered, then, is not so much, Is the character of Sara Tidwell in some ways racially stereotypical, but rather, what does it matter that Sara Tidwell's character is in some ways racially stereotypical? The answer lies in the demographic and market-based data discussed at the beginning of this essay. *Bag of Bones* was written, directed, performed, and consumed by majority white Americans (Nielsen Academic Request 1.9) and its central monster—Sarah Tidwell, the Mad Lady—is mainly frightening from a white perspective. These audience and artist demographics provide a potential answer for one of the questions we posed earlier in this essay: Whose trauma is palatable for audiences? Given the overwhelmingly white racial makeup of the audience, the stereotypical aspects of Tidwell's character, and the notable downplaying of violence against Mattie Devore, the answer would seem to be black trauma. It is notable as well that, regardless of the filmic choices on display in Garris' adaptation, any faithful adaptation of King's *Bag of Bones* would include the "happy" ending of Sara Tidwell's ghost being forcibly put to rest, her remains disinterred and destroyed. Tidwell's rape and murder, as well as the murder of her child, are violent tragedies, but the "righteous" course of action in *Bag of Bones* is for this hate crime to be ultimately forgotten and not affect the white residents of the town. While King is not a writer typically interested in telling straightforward moralistic stories, it is hard to ignore that the symbolism of destroying Tidwell's body, and thus her legacy and curse, is written to be the salvation of not only the town of TR-90 but also of a young white girl, the last in a series of other young white girls to die because of Tidwell's black curse.

The work of adapting violent literature to film and television is, necessarily, fraught. Mick Garris' *Bag of Bones* adaptation had to contend with structural, filmic, and performance-based choices around the depiction of Tidwell's rape and murder. The miniseries would have had to take into account the standards of A&E, the desires of King's fanbase, and more mundane day-to-day hassles such as production schedules and budget constraints. Additionally, there is room for debate around what exactly constitutes an ethical depiction of racialized sexual violence at all. What constitutes a socially acceptable depiction of sexual violence has changed drastically over time, as well: *Bag of Bones* was released in 2011, five years after the creation of the #MeToo but still five years before its widespread cultural proliferation. The sexual and racial violence in Garris' *Bag of Bones* is ultimately exploitative not only for the filmic choices discussed in this essay, but due to the story structure of the base material itself. Could Garris have produced an adaptation which handles the racialized sexual violence more sensitively? Almost certainly, but not without fundamentally changing the structure of the source material in addition to changing the cinematography, pacing, and tension-building techniques utilized. If fundamentally changing the plot, characters, and genre scenes are all required to adapt *Bag of Bones* in a way which is neither exploitative nor racist, then the final question arises: why make an adaptation at all?

NOTES

1. In this essay, "exploitation" will not refer to the exploitation subgenre of film, but rather to the use of specific tropes and images whose function is to reproduce real-world trauma, racism, and sexual violence for entertainment value.

2. There is an argument to be made that the violence on display is so extreme as to fall into the realm of splatterpunk or exploitation genres. While it is outside the scope of this essay to describe the exact genre boundaries of splatter and exploitation cinema versus the broader construction of thrillers, an important distinction should be made: in splatter and exploitation cinema, violence usually contains a slapstick or camp element of unreality (Kovacs 88), which is not the case in this sequence. Violence in *Bag of Bones* is filmed as 'real' violence.

WORKS CITED

Ashley, W. "The Angry Black Woman: The Impact of Pejorative Stereotypes on Psychotherapy with Black Women." *Social Work in Public Health* 29:1 (2013): 34. Doi:10.1080/19371918.2011.619449.

Bag Of Bones (A&E): United States TV executive insights updated daily - Parrot Analytics. (2018). tv.parrotanalytics.com/US/bag-of-bones-a-e. Accessed November 25, 2020.

Bloomquist, J. "The Minstrel Legacy: African American English and the Historical Construction of 'Black' Identities in Entertainment." *Journal of African American Studies* 19:4 (2015): 25.

Caterine, D. "Heirs through Fear: Indian Curses, Accursed Indian Lands, and White Christian Sovereignty in America." *Nova Religio: The Journal of Alternative and Emergent Religions*, 18:1 (2014): 37–57. Doi:10.1525/nr.2014.18.1.37.

Complaints Regarding Various Television Broadcasts Between February 2, 2002 and March 8, 2005 / March 2, 2008 and March 8, 2010 (n.d.)., 2020, www.transition. fcc.gov/eb/Orders/2006/FCC-06-17A1.html / www.fcc.gov/general/obscene-profane-indecent-Broadcasts-notices-apparent-liability. Accessed November 2020.

Farley, C. J. "The Old Black Magic," *Time,* November 27, 2000.

Garris, Mick, director. *Bag of Bones.* A&E, 2011.

Handlen, Z. (2011, November 12). *Bag of Bones*. [Review of the media Bag of Bones, dir. Mick Garris] *A.V. Club*, tv.avclub.com/bag-of-bones-1798170818.

Kermode, M. *The Shawshank Redemption* (London, UK: British Film Institute, 2009).

King, S. *Bag of Bones*. New York: Scribner Classics, 1998.

Kovács, S. "Exploitation," *Sight and Sound (London),* 51:2 (2003): 88.

Kuhn, A., and Westwell, G. "Thriller." *A Dictionary of Film Studies* (2 ed.). www.oxfordreference.com/view/10.1093/acref/9780198832096.001.0001/acref-9780198832096-e-0721?rskey=ZD7BUB&result=1. Accessed December 2020.

Magistrale, T. *Hollywood's Stephen King*. New York: Palgrave Macmillan, 2003.

Nielsen Bulk Data 2011. (n.d.). *spec. Academic Request, Demo.*

Obscene, Profane & Indecent Broadcasts: Notices of Apparent Liability. (2015, October 08). Accessed November 25, 2020.

Rafter, N. "Crime, film, and criminology: Recent sex-crime movies." *Theoretical Criminology*. 2007. Doi:1362480607079584.

Rules & Regulations for Title 47. (2017, December 21), www.fcc.gov/wireless/bureau-divisions/technologies-systems-and-innovation-division/rules-regulations-title-47. Accessed November 25, 2020.

Seidman, R. (December 13, 2011). "Sunday Cable Ratings: Kourtney & Kim Top 'Housewives Atlanta' + 'Boardwalk Empire,' 'Bag of Bones,' 'Homeland,' 'Dexter' & More." TV by the Numbers. Archived from the original on January 7, 2012. Accessed January 2021.

————. (December 13, 2011). "Monday Cable Ratings: Rams/Seahawks Down, But Still Tops + 'Pawn Stars,' 'Bag of Bones,' 'Closer,' 'Rizzoli & Isles,' 'WWE RAW' & Much More." TV by the Numbers. Archived from the original on January 7, 2012. Accessed January 2021.

Steinberg, J. (2006, May 09). *Sopranos* Undergoes Cosmetic Surgery for Basic Cable. www.nytimes.com/2006/05/09/arts/television/09sopr.html. Accessed November 2020.

Venne, M., & Unknown. "Bag of Bones Screenplay." 2011, www.scripts.com/script-pdf/3482. Accessed August 25, 2020.

Chapter 4

Cujo, the Black Man, and the Story of Patty Hearst

Sarah Nilsen

The impact of human violence and cruelty on nonhuman animals has played a central role in the writings and films of Stephen King. As a Stephen King fan recently noted on the Goodreads discussion board, "Has anyone noticed that King kills off at least one animal (usually a dog) in almost all of his novels? I was just wondering if anyone else caught on to this and might have an idea why he does it. Perhaps unconsciously?" (Goodreads). King has often noted the childhood origins for his interest in horror and its link to the violent encounters between humans and nonhuman animals. He has repeatedly singled out *Bambi* as a primary source. In a 2014 *Rolling Stone* interview, when asked what drew him to writing about horror or the supernatural, King responded: "It's built in. That's all. The first movie I ever saw was a horror movie. It was *Bambi*. When that little deer gets caught in a forest fire, I was terrified, but I was also exhilarated. I can't explain it" (Green). In a 1980 essay for *TV Guide*, written while King was writing his novel *Cujo*, King again explained that "the movies that terrorized my own nights most thoroughly as a kid were not those through which Frankenstein's monster or the Wolfman lurched and growled, but the Disney cartoons. I watched Bambi's mother shot and Bambi running frantically to escape being burned up in a forest fire (King, *TV Guide* 8). And in his 2006 *Paris Review* interview, he retells the origin story again: "I loved the movies from the start . . . I can remember my mother taking me to Radio City Music Hall to see *Bambi*. Whoa, the size of the place, and the forest fire in the movie—it made a big impression. So, when I started to write, I had a tendency to write in images because that was all I knew at the time" (Rich). The fact that *Bambi* premiered at Radio City Music Hall in 1942 and King was born in 1947 makes it unlikely that his first film going experience was at Radio City Music Hall, but King certainly considers *Bambi* central to his development as a horror writer.

King's early encounter with the threat of death experienced from the perspective of animals, explains the lasting impact of *Bambi* on many viewers, young and old. King understands fundamentally how the use of nonhuman animal characters and their "creatureliness" creates anxiety in the viewer about their own fear of death. The cultural anthropologist Ernest Becker described in *The Denial of Death* (1973) how the terror of our own mortality leads us to deny our nature as animals. "Mortality is connected to the natural, animal side of his existence; and so, man reaches beyond and away from that side. So much so that he denies it completely. As soon as man reached new historical forms of power, he turned against the animals with whom he had previously identified—with a vengeance, as we now see, because the animals embodied what man feared most, a nameless and faceless death" (92). King's childhood recognition of the mortality represented by nonhuman animals was coupled with an obsession with killing and death. As he reveals in his famous *Playboy* interview, "I was terrified and fascinated by death—death in general and my own in particular . . . death as a concept and the people who dealt out death intrigued me. I remember I compiled an entire scrapbook on Charlie Starkweather, the Fifties mass murderer . . . I used to clip and paste every news item I could find on him, and then I'd sit trying to unravel the inner horror behind that ordinary face . . . I wavered between attraction and repulsion, maybe because I realized the face in the photograph could be my own" (Norton).

As the film critic Pauline Kael perceptively noted, "It is one of the para-doxes of movie business that the movies designed expressly for children are generally the ones that frighten them the most. I have never heard children screaming in fear at any of those movies we're always told they should be protected from as they screamed at *Bambi*" (225). While children viewers screamed in horror over the many scenes of animals being killed, the main villain in *Bambi* is man. King, in his *TV Guide* essay, addresses his recogni-tion of the horror that is unleashed by forcing his readers to face their own mortality through a recognition of their creatureliness. Discussing the impact of TV on children, he states that "[i]t is not possible to know everything that will frighten a child—particularly a small one—but there are certain plot elements that can be very upsetting. These include physical mutilation, the death of an animal the child perceives as 'good,' the murder of a parent, a parent's treachery, blood in great quantities, drowning, being locked in a tight place and endings that offer no hope—and no catharsis" (King, *TV Guide*10). King's childhood imaginative space was populated with images of human and nonhuman death and killing, and novels and films are permeated by his early recognition of the cognitive terror humans experience by forcing them to confront their own mortality.

THE ORIGINS OF *CUJO*

King's essay for the *TV Guide* was written while working on his one novel, *Cujo*, that has a dog as its eponymous hero and villain. *Cujo* is the story of a beloved family dog, a St. Bernard, who develops rabies from a bat and becomes a murderous killer. King based the story on two different incidents involving a St. Bernard dog. In a 1983 radio interview, King explained that he had read in the local Portland, Maine newspaper about a child who had been "savaged by a Saint Bernard and killed" (Underwood 114). The main creative seed for *Cujo* was King's personal and violent encounter in the Spring of 1977. In the origin story for the novel, King (in multiple interviews) recounts his encounter with a St. Bernard when he stopped to get his motorcycle repaired at a remote garage in rural Maine. His recollection and retelling of this encounter are noteworthy for the ways in which class, violence, and creatureliness intersect into a potentially significant act of violence. The garage was located in an area whose class based social differences were apparent to King and yet he chose to seek out the mechanic because he had heard of his mechanical abilities. Having just received his first sizable earnings as a writer after the blockbuster success of his novel, *Carrie*, King, like Vic Trenton in *Cujo*, had moved into a comfortable middle-class lifestyle. At the time, he and his family had moved to Bridgton, Maine, which King describes as a "resort town," while the repair shop was in a "really rough country. There were a lot of farmers just making their own way in the old style." King characterizes the owner of the garage as living an "old style" life, and further explains that, like Joe Camber, he looked almost like "one of those guys out of *Deliverance*" (*Stephenking.com*). Like the "guys in *Deliverance*," King associates the rural community with people lacking cultural awareness, living like animals closer to the earth, and displaying an animalistic demeanor that in *Deliverance* leads to rape and death. King sees this rural community and its excessive linkage to the animal world as a bodily threat to middle-class normality and closely linked to the popular perception of nonhuman animals as aggressive and unruly. King explains that when he took his bike out to the middle of nowhere, "this huge Saint Bernard came out of the barn, growling. And I was retreating, and wishing that I was not on my motorcycle, when the guy said, 'Don't worry. He don't bite.' And so I reached out to pet him, and the dog started to go for me" (*Stephenking.com*). In response to the dog's threat, the mechanic told the dog to get down, and then gave him "this huge whack with a steel wrench." According to King, "It sounded like a rug beater hitting a rug. The dog just yelped once and sat down. And the guy said something to me like, "'Bowser usually doesn't do this, he must not have liked your face.' Right away it's my fault" (Rich). Arriving in a rural setting, with a physically threatening *Deliverance*-like guy, King was immediately put into attack mode by the St. Bernard's unexpected and unpredictable behavior.

King's fear and vulnerability signaled his own challenged masculinity in this working-class, rural, male environment where he was immediately made to feel like he was "at fault" for not knowing how to handle a dog. "I remember how scared I was because there was no place to hide. I was on my bike but it was dead, and I couldn't outrun him. If the man wasn't there with the wrench and the dog decided to attack" (Rich). But rather than having this battle over classed masculinities occur in the novel and film, King transformed the victim of the attack to a wife and child, thereby transferring his own feeling of fear and trepidation about being the victim of a working-class, rural assault, onto his fictionalized wife, while the husband character (and surrogate King character) remains untouched by the Camber's and Cujo. So, King, in his writing of *Cujo*, takes his experience of feeling doubly emasculated because of his fear of a pet dog and his inability to fix his own vehicles, and imagines his wife now becoming the victim of working-class animal rage and violence. He further links the attack of Donna to feelings of emasculation concerning his own creatureliness because of her infidelity. The origins of the *Cujo* novel and film are linked to the fear and anxiety that comes with questions of masculinity due to class differences and the way in which they impact human and nonhuman relations. The challenge to King's masculinity that the dog encounter unleashed was transformed in the novel and film into the victimization of a wife, who has cheated on her husband, by a dog that because of rabies became a nonhuman killing machine. When Vic first encounters Cujo in the novel, he "saw a huge dog emerging from the barn. For one absurd moment he wondered if it really was a dog, or maybe some strange and ugly species of pony" (17). Donna and Vic are immediately fearful of Cujo and the threat he poses for their son, who is drawn to the dog. As Cujo picks Tad up by his Spider-Man t-shirt, and Tad puts his hand into Cujo's mouth, Vic "was amused, but his heart was still beating fast. For just one moment there he had really believed that the dog was going to bite off Tad's head like a lollipop" (18). The filmmakers were unable to make the four St. Bernards cast in the role of Cujo behave aggressively enough on screen, so they resorted to using various mechanical St. Bernards and a Great Dane mix, Harry, whose "ability to snarl on command had earned him mad-dog roles in *Amityville Horror* and numerous television productions. Harry spent 13 weeks bulging his eyeballs and foaming at the mouth inside a specially constructed St. Bernard suit that covered his entire body" (London). King, therefore, transfers his own fear of death in the face of the St. Bernard by exaggerating the physical threat that it embodied and making the target of that threat a more vulnerable, female victim. King relates "when something really fired over in my mind . . . [W]hy didn't somebody come and rescue her? . . . Where is her husband? Why didn't her husband come rescue her? . . . What happens if she gets bitten by this dog?" (Rich). King, through a reversal of his original encounter, becomes the hero and his wife the victim, due to her infidelity. Furthermore, the original catalyst for his fear, the threatening *Deliverance*-guy with his crude, working-class, manner, becomes devoured and killed—they pay the most violent price for Cujo's rage and King's threatened masculinity.

CUJO: FEMALE SEXUALITY AND THREATENED MASCULINITY

Cujo, the novel, consists of a parallel structure that intercuts between two struggling marriages. Donna and Vic Trenton's upper-middle-class, suburban marriage has begun to fall apart because of Vic's anxiety and fear about the loss of his ad agency and possibly his marriage. King, in his *Playboy* interview in 1983, describes, in similar terms, his own experiences as a young father and struggling writer.

> Even though I was only in my mid-20s and rationally realized that there was still plenty of time and opportunity ahead, that pressure to break through in my work was building in a kind of psychic crescendo, and when it appeared to be thwarted, I felt desperately depressed, cornered. I felt trapped in a suicidal rat race, with no way out of the maze. But what did worry me was the effect all that was having on my marriage. Hell, we were already on marshy ground in those days, and I feared that the quicksand was just around the bend. I loved my wife and kids, but as the pressure mounted, I was beginning to have ambivalent feelings about them, too. On the one hand, I wanted nothing more than to provide for them and protect them—but at the same time, unprepared as I was for the rigors of fatherhood, I was also experiencing a range of nasty emotions from resentment to anger to occasional outright hate, even surges of mental violence that, thank God, I was able to suppress (Norton).

As a pencil pusher (like King), Vic is incapable of aggressively acting to save his business or his family. Vic's impotence in the face of failure reinforces Donna's own fear of losing her sexual desirability as she ages. Further, her social isolation as a stay-at-home mom in a new town causes her to seek out an escape from a lifeless and passionless future. By choosing to have an affair with the local handyman, Steve Kemp, she hopes to rediscover the youth and joy she had enjoyed before becoming a mother and wife. King's own anxiety about the status of his own marriage during these years can be linked to his father's own infidelities and abandonment of his family when he was two years old. According to King, "my mother once told me, he was the only man on the sales force who regularly demonstrated vacuum cleaners to pretty young widows at two o'clock in the morning. He was quite a ladies' man, according to my mother, and I apparently have a beautiful bastard half-sister in Brazil. In any case, he was a man with an itchy foot, a travelin' man, as the song says. I think trouble came easy to him" (Norton). The target of Cujo's rage is not the handyman, Steve; Donna's betrayal of her spouse and family leads to the unleashing of a monstrous rage, Cujo, thus causing her son's death (in the novel) and the permanent fracturing of her marriage. As King relates, "I'd never risk my wife's affection for some one-night stand . . . I wouldn't dare cheat on her!," but he does transfer the feelings of "a range of nasty emotions from resentment to anger to occasional outright hate, even surges of mental violence" (Norton) that being a father created within him onto the cheating Donna. The film reduces the parallel structure of the novel to a battle between the monstrous rage of Cujo and Donna's battle for the survival of her child and herself.

The Trentons' struggling marriage is juxtaposed to Charity and Joe Cambers: rural and working-class, their marital relationship is defined by Joe's continual physical and verbal abuse of Charity. Joe's violent and toxic masculinity reaches a turning point when Charity realizes that her son, Brett, is becoming more and more like her husband. Joe has decided that as a rite of passage into manhood, Brett should join his friends at their deer camp to learn how to hunt. Charity is extremely isolated in a rural environment and Joe's constant threat of physical violence has made Charity's life unbearable and the possibility of a future together inconceivable. Unlike Donna, who chooses to have an affair as an escape, Charity purchases a winning lottery ticket. Charity's decision to remain faithful in a violent marriage is rewarded with financial gain, and the convenient killing by Cujo of her husband and his toxic friend.

CUJO AS A FORCE OF MASCULINE VENGEANCE

The monstrous killing dog that Cujo becomes is birthed from two murderous, avenging fathers. It is not the rabies virus, but the supernatural male, avenging rage that imbues him, making him into a bloodthirsty killer. As a composite vessel of human rage, King selects a nonhuman domesticated animal that is at once man's best friend and capable of killing that man. With the selection of Cujo, a canine, as the avenging force, the rationality of a human killer is stripped to the most brute and base animalistic form of rapacious and devouring death. The first spirit of male rage that occupies *Cujo* is the monstrous Frank Dodd. The novel opens with an evocation of Dodd, the Castle Rock deputy sheriff in King's novel, *The Dead Zone* (1979), who was also the "Castle Rock Strangler," responsible for the rape-strangling murders of children and women for several years. Dodd's victims varied in age and background, but they were always raped prior to being strangled. The monster is called back to life in *Cujo* and enters Tad's closet, after Donna's fateful decision to cheat on her husband and then reject her illicit lover. Throughout the novel and film, Tad is terrorized by the Outsider male who eventually coalesces into the raging Cujo.

While the male targets of Cujo's violent revenging spirit of death—Joe Camber and Sheriff Bannerman who had discovered that Dodd was the "Castle Rock Strangler"—are quickly and brutally slaughtered and devoured by Cujo, the attack on Donna and her son is much more structured and sustained. The plot of the film sets up Donna as a stay-at-home mom in an unhappy marriage who has taken on a lover to enliven her existence. The catalyst that ruptures the status quo of her life is not her decision to have an affair, but rather the termination of that affair that leads to the emasculation of her lover, whom she mocks and then bluntly rejects. Donna's double betrayal is what leads to the violent and sustained attack by Cujo on Donna and her son as they struggle to survive. While the malevolent spirit of Dodd is directed towards the killing of Sheriff Bannerman, the spirit that attacks Donna is directly linked to Cujo's namesake, William Wolfe. Wolfe (his name signifying the non-domesticated, unfeeling canine forefather) was a member of the Symbionese Liberation Army (SLA), his code name was "Cujo," and he was involved in the kidnapping of the 19-year-old heiress, Patty Hearst with whom he had a sexual relationship. Wolfe, like Hearst and Donna, were all white, middle to upper middle-class, educated, seemingly average Americans, who appeared on the surface like anybody's child, but their placid middle-class façade appeared to hide behind it a terrifying and threatening core. Like the Manson girls, and Hearst, Donna only becomes truly alive when she resorts to violence by killing Cujo after his unrelenting assault on her. Many commentators noted during the Hearst trial the discrepancy between Hearst's pathetic appearance during the trial and her image as Tania (her chosen SLA code name), urban guerrilla. As Shana Alexander explained, "The tiny, dowdy, downcast creature at the defense table bore no resemblance to any of the famous newspaper photographs." When Hearst's lawyer introduced in court the *Newsweek* photo of Hearst as Tania, "all of a sudden this picture comes around of a vibrant young woman who's *alive*, feeling, showing her emotions, attractive, lipstick on, a big smile" (Alexander, 531). The media generally had lumped Patty with the Manson girls, inviting readers to see her as the bizarre product of a highly sexualized feminism run amok, and her attraction to phallic weaponry as an expression of an energizing, but deeply disturbing, "sexual awakening." "Patty Hearst embodied a cultural nightmare about the violent potential inherent in all women and about the power of promiscuous sex to unleash that violence" (Browder, 54). Tellingly, Donna waits throughout most of the film and novel for a male hero, who never appears, to rescue her. It is only after her child is dying that she fully develops the will to live. Like Donna, Hearst had decided during her kidnapping that she "would not die, not of my own accord. I would fight with everything in my power to survive, to see this through" (Graebner, 18). By stepping out of the Pinto/closet, Donna also finally comes alive by confronting her own mortality when she alone vanquishes the animalistic forces of male vengeance and death represented in Cujo.

Hearst's kidnapping led directly to the horrific killing of most members of the SLA, including Donald DeFreeze (Code named "Cinque"), the leader of the SLA and Wolfe by the Los Angeles Police, who were burnt to death when the house they were hiding in caught fire during a shootout with the police. Soon after their killing, Hearst released a eulogy stating that Wolfe/Cujo was "the gentlest, most beautiful man I've ever known. We loved each other so much, and his love for people was so deep that he was willing to give his life for them. The name 'Cujo' means 'unconquerable.' It was the perfect name for him. Cujo conquered life as well as death by facing and fighting them. Neither Cujo nor I had ever loved an individual in the way we loved each other, probably because our relationship wasn't based on bourgeois, fucked up values, attitudes and goals" (quoted in Toobin 190). After Hearst's capture and during her subsequent trial, she dramatically denied having a relationship with Cujo and accused him of raping her. King's decision to make Cujo the star of his novel signals his own obsession with the kidnapping and trial that was transfixing most of America. And it links together, even unconsciously, the various masculine terrors that joined together in King's imagination: the aggressive St. Bernard, the men of the SLA, and Donna Trenton's abusive affair with Steve Kemp.

While living in Boulder, Colorado and after completing the first draft of *The Shining* in January 1975, King began working on *The House on Value Street*, a fictionalized version of the story of Patty Hearst. King had done some research for the idea the previous year and while living in Colorado was attempting to write a draft of the novel. King recalled that "[i]t seemed to be a highly potent subject, and while I was aware that lots of nonfiction books were sure to be written on the subject, it seemed to me that only a novel might really succeed in explaining all the contradictions. The novelist is, after all, God's liar, and if he does his job well . . . he can sometimes find the truth that lives at the center of the lie" (*Danse Macabre* 397). Was the truth at the heart of the center of the lie, Hearst's love of Cujo? After six weeks of writing, unable to get the story to work, King put it down, but the story of Patty Hearst would influence several of King's novels, including *The Stand*, which King began work on soon after. According to King, "[*The Stand*] was to be a roman a clef about the kidnapping of Patricia Hearst, her brainwashing (or her sociopolitical awakening, depending on your point of view, I guess), her participation in the bank robbery, the shootout at the SLA hideout in Los Angeles—in my book, the hideout was on Value Street, natch—the fugitive run across the country, the whole ball of wax . . . one day while sitting at my typewriter I wrote—just to write something: The world comes to an end but everybody in the SLA is somehow immune . . . [Later] I wrote Donald DeFreeze is a dark man. I did not mean that DeFreeze was black; it had suddenly occurred to me that, in the photos taken during the bank robbery in which Patty Hearst had participated, you could barely see DeFreeze's face. He was wearing a big, badass hat, and what he looked like was mostly guesswork. I wrote A DARK MAN with no face and then glanced up and saw that grisly little motto: ONCE IN EVERY GENERATION A PLAGUE WILL FALL AMONG THEM. And that was that. I spent the next two years writing an apparently endless book called *The Stand*" (Winter 54–5). A similar kind of plague finds its way into *Cujo*; it can be read as the rabies virus that transforms Cujo into a monster. And the cause for the unleashing of that virus is a darkness rooted within an avenging male rage.

Like Donna's decision in *Cujo* to have an extramarital affair to escape the tedium of her monogamous relationship with her husband, for many commentators, the key to Patty Hearst's violence lay in her sexual awakening (Browder 182). Patty Hearst was simultaneously a victim and an aggressor embodied in one woman. She was terrifying because her victimization made her an aggressor. As Shana Alexander described her at the time, "Though some saw her as a victim, most Americans then saw Patty as an ungrateful child, a sexual and political adventuress who probably had set up her own kidnapping. She quickly became a female hate object, a modern witch" (Alexander 183). Donna's betrayal of her husband becomes even more problematic when she decides to end her affair with her lover, Steve. No longer sexually satisfied by him, Steve immediately responds with violent anger and retaliation against her. But that retaliation is only a precursor to the hyper-violent attack by Cujo (both the dog and the spirits of Wolfe and Dodd). In this way, Donna's entrapment in her Pinto creates a parallel to Patty Hearst's closet cage, where both women are forced to undergo severe mental and physical tortures in the provocation of an instinctual masculine rage. Donna's violent battering inside her tiny Pinto forges a link to the physical abuse Hearst underwent during the early days of her captivity by the SLA. In fact, the image the viewer has of Donna ravaged by her ordeal suggests a similar kind of personal violation to what Patty underwent—bound and gagged inside a closet whenever she was not being sexually assaulted, restrained from access even to a toilet. Many Americans, however, suspected that Hearst (nee Donna) enjoyed the sexual promiscuity that she experienced during her capture and conversion into a "urban guerrilla." A psychiatrist, Joel Fort, hired by the prosecution in the Hearst case, argued a highly sexist thesis that her closet rapes, prolonged incarceration in such a small space, and her subsequent conversion to the cause were masochistically satisfying. He testified that "[i]t also seemed plausible to me that she got horny frequently. She's been sexually active since the age of fifteen, which I consider very healthy. I think if you'd had a period of deprivation and isolation for a few days or a few weeks, you'd want to have sex all the more—for pleasure, for companionship, and so forth" (Browder 184–85). Similarly, in *Cujo*, Vic's impotence is pointed to as a cause for Donna seeking out sexual gratification with Steve, and yet, even Steve is incapable of satisfying her.

CUJO AS A SYMBOL

King does not excuse Cujo's killer behavior as a product of his being a predator, and, in fact, prior to being bitten by a rabid bat, the dog is the epitome of goodness. Yet the rabid Cujo functions as a powerful symbol of the marital discord within the Trenton and Camber families, and the impact of Donna's affair on the family. During the time of her infidelity, Vic's career becomes seriously threatened because of a tainted cereal that causes children to vomit blood, Tad begins seeing monsters in his closet, and Donna's lover, in a rage over her desire to end the affair, destroys the family's home, concluding his violation by masturbating onto the connubial bed. The clearest manifestation of Donna's punishment for her affair is Cujo, a family pet gone mad with rabies who relentlessly attacks her physically resulting in the death of Tad (in the novel, but not the film). The rabies, contracted by accident as Cujo benignly chases a rabbit, signifies the violent forces in the King universe that foment random chaos, such as Vic's company's tainted cereal, the sudden disruption of a newspaper heiress' life, the random rapes and murders of Frank Dodd. As King explains, "[W]hat I do is like a crack in the mirror. If you go back over the books from *Carrie* on up, what you see is an observation of ordinary middle-class American life as it's lived at the time that particular book was written. In every life you get to a point where you have to deal with something that's inexplicable to you . . . whether you talk about ghosts or vampires or Nazi war criminals living down the block, we're still talking about the same thing, which is an intrusion of the extraordinary into ordinary life and how we deal with it" (Rich).

Not only does the family suffer for Donna's sexual escapades, but Cujo also undergoes a horrific, physical collapse full of pain and suffering as the rabies virus takes over his body. Spewing blood and foaming at the mouth, his body begins to decay, he descends ever deeper into madness, and pieces of his flesh begin peeling off his body as he wages an extended attack on Donna. King's use of Cujo as a symbol of the destruction and violence created due to Donna's infidelity is typical of the ways in which animal symbols are used in literature and film. More specifically, Cujo appears to contain all the masculine rage of Donna's lover after he is spurned. As Josephine Donovan argues, "In literature, one of the most common devices that exploit animal pain for aesthetic effect is the animal metaphor, or, more specifically, that animal 'stand-in' or proxy where the animal is used as an object upon which to project or act out human feelings" (206). The majority of the novel and the film is centered on Cujo's attack on Donna and Tad as they sit for several days in their Pinto waiting for someone to rescue them. Set during the heat of the summer, Donna and Tad are slowly dying from dehydration while Cujo enters the final stage of rabies and experiences the horrific process of a painful and agonizing death. While in the novel, King frequently explains the suffering that Cujo is experiencing as the rabies virus spreads, in the film, the audience is denied any access into his inner torment and pain, and so he becomes a superhuman and relentless killer, who willingly flings himself against the Pinto in order to kill Donna. Because the film version also reduces the complex emotional crises that Donna is experiencing to a cliché rendering of spousal infidelity, Cujo's obsessive assault on Donna is directly linked to her infidelity, thus amplifying her guilt and negating Cujo's suffering. As Donovan explains, "In all of these stories animals figure only insofar as they amplify or symbolize aspects of the human characters' relationships or situations; the moral reality of the animals' own suffering is elided . . . the moral reality of the animals' suffering is overridden in the interest of creating an aesthetic effect" (206). And there is no greater aesthetic effect in this film than the protracted violent assault on Donna and Tad as they remain locked in the Pinto dying of dehydration as Cujo experiences an utter destruction of his body, ending with an exuberant and deadly beating by Donna. A horrendous act of animal cruelty that is justified due to Donna and Tad's suffering. Gary Arnold, in a *Washington Post* review of the film, remarked, "Although the material is conventionally manipulated to provoke horror by exploiting Cujo as a mad dog—a four-footed Jaws as a shameless matter of fact—moviegoers are likely to feel too appalled at the way a sick animal is systemically neglected" (Arnold).

CONCLUSION

There seem to be two "plagues" that were unleashed in King's imagination via the Hearst kidnapping: the superflu that nearly exterminates the human race in *The Stand* and the rabies virus that a playful St. Bernard would contract five years later in *Cujo*. In both cases the "plague" is linked to a similar hypermasculinity that comes to dominate both texts. In *The Stand*, that energy revolves around Randall Flagg, whose authoritarian power is unleashed simultaneous to the emergence of the superflu: "It was almost time to be reborn. He knew. Why else could he suddenly do magic?" (184). *Cujo*'s "plague" coalesces into the monstrous masculinities of Donna's lover, Steve Kemp, the rapist-murderer Dodd, the brutality of the SLA males in their treatment of Patty Hearst, and the rabid male St. Bernard. Behind both *The Stand* and *Cujo* it is possible to read the spirit of Patty Hearst's kidnapping—especially the prolonged violent terror and physical abuse she is forced to undergo—forming a parallel with Donna Trenton's own closeted hours of torture trapped inside her broken Pinto and under siege by a rabid, out-of-control force of masculinity.

WORKS CITED

Arnold, Gary. "*Cujo*: A Really Bad Dog," *Washington Post* (August 16, 1983).

Becker, Ernest. *The Denial of Death*. NY: Free Press, 1973.

Becker, Ernest. *Escape from Evil*. NY: Free Press, 1975.

Browder, Laura. *Her Best Shot: Women and Guns in America*. Chapel Hill: University Press of North Carolina, 2006.

Bunner, Richard K. "News of Old Revolutionaries Reopens Heartbreak." *The Morning Call* (February 10, 2002).

Donovan, Josephine. "Aestheticizing Animal Cruelty." *College Literature* 38:4 (Fall 2011): 202–217.

Goodreads. Stephen King Fans discussion. https://www.goodreads.com/topic/show/282669-animal-killings (accessed 1/14/2021).

Graebner, William. *Patty's Got a Gun: Patricia Hearst in 1970s America*. Chicago: University Press of Chicago, 2008.

Green, Andy. "Stephen King: The Rolling Stone Interview." *Rolling Stone*. (11/6/14): 72, 74–9.

Gupte, Pranay. "Why Did a 'Harmless' Dog Kill Boy? Officials in Suffolk Seek the Answer." *New York Times* (April 26, 1974).

Kael, Pauline. *Going Steady*. Boston: Little, Brown & Co., 1969.

King, Stephen. *Cujo*. NY: Gallery Books, 1981.

King, Stephen. *Danse Macabre*. NY: Berkley Books, 1983.

King, Stephen. "A Master of Horror Stories Has Some Provocative Thoughts about Tots, Terror and TV." *TV Guide*, June 13, 1980. 7–8, 10.

King, Stephen. *On Writing: A Memoir*. London: Hodder & Stoughton, 2000.

King, Stephen. *The Stand: A Novel*. NY: Anchor Books, 2012.

Lehmann-Haupt, Christopher. "Books of the Times: Manipulated Terror Not the Usual Rules." *New York Times*, C21. August 14, 1981.

London, Michael. "A Pack of Bogus Bernards Helps Give 'Cujo' Its Bite," *Los Angeles Times*. (August 19, 1983): pg. H1.

Rich, Nathaniel, and Christopher Lehmann-Haupt. "Stephen King, The Art of Fiction." *Paris Review*, 189: 178 (Fall 2006). Accessed 1/14/2021.

Toobin, Jeffrey. *American Heiress: The Wild Saga of the Kidnapping, Crimes and Trials of Patty Hearst*. NY: Doubleday, 2016.

Underwood, Tim, and Chuck Miller, eds. *Bare Bones: Conversations on Terror with Stephen King*. NY: McGraw-Hill, 1988.

Winter, Douglas E. *Stephen King: The Art of Darkness*. NY: Dutton, 1984.

Chapter 5

King of Pain

Exposing the Raw, 'Unpleasant Truth' of Stephen King's Use of Extreme Violence in Doctor Sleep

Mary Findley

Stephen King is no stranger to the use of violence in his novels and films, and King fans have come to expect as much. After all, how successful would *Carrie* have been without the telekinetic firestorm that took out most of Bates High School's junior and senior prom-goers? Or how frightening would *It* have been if not for Pennywise's appetite for children? And let's face it, *The Shining* would have fallen flat if not for Jack Torrance's bouts of domestic violence and murderous rage. It's true that violence and horror fiction have a long history together and King scholars, as well as King himself, have long contended that his works are life-affirming as they reveal the "Dionysian side of the world and human nature to help its audience cope with the horrors of real life and to explore their legitimate fears" (Davis 3). However, there comes a point when even the most hardened horror scholar draws a line at the gratuitous use of violence against children, most notably when the violence borders on kiddie torture porn and serves little purpose other than for overt shock value, which is the direction King's latest works affirm and suggest his future works are headed. Though praised as a compelling follow-up to *The Shining* and a story of redemption for the adult alcoholic Dan Torrance, King's use of extreme violence against children in both the novel and film *Doctor Sleep* exposes an "unpleasant truth"—a disturbing pattern in King's fiction that has escalated from the sacrifice of childhood innocence, as seen in his earlier works, to a promulgation towards the normalization of America's culture of violence, especially as it relates to the most vulnerable population—children.

King's films and novels have a long history of violent content, but until recently, little was known about King's actual position on violence. In January of 2013 he published a little-known 25-page essay as a Kindle Single titled *Guns*, the first detailed insight into his thoughts on the subject. What appears to be an attempt at an honest discussion about gun violence in the wake of the Sandy Hook school shooting, the essay soon falls flat. Instead of offering concise thoughts on the topic at hand, it ultimately offers a conflicting and contradictory message that eschews gun violence and simultaneously embraces the idea that America does *not* inhabit a culture of violence—even though it is the prevalence of violence that called the essay into being. The essay begins with a diatribe against the media's handling of school shootings which, as King suggests, minimizes the real human tragedy at the heart of any such event which is, of course, the senseless death of children. It then discusses the plot of his novel *Rage*, details a number of potential copycat crimes in which *Rage* was found among the belongings of the teen shooters, and explains King's reason for pulling it from publication. "My book did not break Cox, Pierce, Carneal, or Loukaitis, or turn them into killers," he states. "They found something in my book that spoke to them because they were already broken. Yet I did see *Rage* as a possible accelerant, which is why I pulled it from sale. You don't leave a can of gasoline where a boy with firebug tendencies can lay hands on it" (King, *Guns* 7). This admission clearly posits his novel, *Rage*, as a possible influence in such acts; one that King feels a moral obligation to rectify. This is cemented by his decision to pull the novel from publication. His thoughts on this, followed by his clear actions to pull the novel from publication, indicate that he understands the influential nature his works may have in the real world, especially when embraced by "broken" people. King clearly feels an obligation to hinder the possibility of such violence, or at least remove the works he feels could influence it. However, later in the essay he denies a culture of violence exists in America by saying: "Let me be frank: The idea that America exists in a culture of violence is bullshit. What America exists in is a culture of Kardashian" (King, *Guns* 12). If America exists primarily in a culture of materialism, excess and superficiality, which is suggested by a reference to Kardashian, as opposed to a culture of violence, then why the worry about the influence his works may have in the hands of the wrong people? In short, the duality of King's message here, which points to gun violence, especially against children, as a real concern with no solution in sight, is paired with the odd idea that America doesn't actually exist within a culture of violence. While confusing, to say the least, *Guns* offers an important insight into the machinations of violence in King's fiction—especially *Doctor Sleep*. Able to acknowledge that his works may pose a violent threat to children on the one hand, King fails to accept the violent culture that pervades American reality. His idea of violence is limited to the use of guns—to school shootings or, at the very least, this is where he seems to draw the line. His inability to understand, accept and acknowledge the true culture of violence against children is, perhaps, why King's violence towards them in his works is increasing to the extreme with no accountability for its use.

At its core, both the film and the novel *Doctor Sleep* offer a familiar and underwhelming plot. Centered around Dan Torrance, the formerly tortured child of *The Shining, Doctor Sleep* shines a microscope on Dan Torrance in light of the unresolved trauma he experienced years ago at The Overlook Hotel. Now a wandering and homeless alcoholic with a penchant for loose women and bad choices, the adult Dan eventually discovers sobriety through the 12 steps of AA, but it is only through Abra Stone, a tween with a shine to rival that of Dan's as a child, that he truly overcomes his past trauma and discovers meaning and purpose in his life. Together they set out to destroy a band of gypsy vampires known as the True Knot that torture, murder and feed on the essence, or steam, of psychic children. Originally called to this dangerous adventure by Abra's voyeuristic dream and psychic connection to the violent death of an 11-year-old boy named Bradley Trevor, Dan soon realizes that Abra is being hunted by the True Knot and intervenes in an effort to save her life and destroy the True Knot once and for all. Together they succeed, and in the process, Dan conquers his own demons, and gains redemption by overcoming a generational life of addiction and abuse.

If not for the culture of extreme violence against children that pervades this narrative, *Doctor Sleep* would be wholly unremarkable—a cookie-cutter King plot of adult redemption from a dysfunctional childhood by fighting evil and, well, losing a few kids along the way. We have seen this before. It is as predictably King as it can get. But one thing makes this narrative remarkable—his extremely graphic, over-the-top torture and gratuitous violence towards children. It is true that King has historically used violence against children in his works, but never to this extent. This story begs a question few King tales ever ask: Is the redemption at the end of this story worth the sacrifice within it? The gratuitous and extreme violence leveled at Bradley Trevor, the 11-year-old tortured and murdered at the hands of the True Knot, and suggested towards countless children in the story—is a violence so extreme that it elevates *Doctor Sleep* as a stand-out in King's canon. The violence here not only qualifies as horror's definition of torture porn, "a genre of horror films in which sadistic violence or torture is a central aspect of the plot," but goes one step further and gains its own distinction as "kiddie torture porn"—a term not yet coined but fitting what King is up to here: the sadistic violence or torture of *children* as a central aspect of the plot (CollinsDictionary.com). While yes, King has targeted children for violence in the past, this particular level of gratuitous torture and violence is not typical of King's past works, but it *is* indicative of his current work and suggests the problematic and disturbing direction his works are headed. This is clearly seen with the *The Outsider,* published in 2018, five years after *Doctor Sleep,* which features the rape and mutilation of yet another 11-year-old boy, Frankie Peterson, and the 2019 publication of *The Institute,* which centers around the torment of innocent children at the hands of adults.

In examining the foundation for the the film adaptation of *Doctor Sleep,* the novel begins with a rendering of the violence both Danny and his mother, Wendy, lived through and seemingly escaped when The Overlook Hotel burned to the ground. While leaving physical injuries and scars on Wendy, the scars left on Danny are psychological, ongoing and far more damaging. While time eventually heals Wendy's wounds, 8-year-old Danny's psychological trauma and threat of physical violence is ongoing. The evil entities of The Overlook Hotel follow him, and Danny is left to protect himself with little, other than the advice of Dick Halloran, to guide him. Two years later, while Wendy is well on the road to physical recovery, 10-year-old Danny is still dealing with real physical and psychological threats. Horance Dewent, yet another Overlook ghost, makes an appearance and Danny must lock him in a box within his mind to stave off harm. The novel's opening sets the tone for the events to follow, which focus on Danny's journey to overcome the ghosts of his past and find redemption. Though the novel also leads the reader into King's dark underworld of child kidnap, torture and murder, it at least begins by setting the focus on the young Danny Torrance and his long road to redemption. The 2019 film, however, begins on a different note.

Directed by Mike Flanagan, the film *Doctor Sleep* also starts with a rendering of violence, but one that sets a different tone and is far more ominous than that of the novel. The continued haunting of Danny Torrance by the Overlook's ghosts take a backseat to the imminent violent threat of Rose the Hat and her band of merry wanderers. The film opens with an aerial camera view that spirals down to the top of a camper as its door swings open to reveal a young girl, Violet, who is no more than 5 or 6. This stylized opening, complete with an auditory heartbeat, suggests the viewpoint of a hawk descending upon its prey and places the audience as both voyeur and predator. The prey here is young Violet. As Violet leaves her mother's side to pick flowers the camera follows behind her, placing the audience in the position of silent stalker. It follows in this position until she comes to a view of Rose the Hat, sitting on a stump and singing down by the water's edge. She is holding a beautiful bouquet of wildflowers. For a moment, the audience becomes one with Violet as the scene is seen from her perspective, but the camera quickly shifts to a front view of Violet, showing her curiosity at the scene before her. This shift in camera angle repositions the audience and places the viewer in the role of protector, standing between Violet and what awaits her. There is a moment of reckoning here where the audience understands the imminent danger and wishes to intercede, only to be quickly repositioned as stalker when the camera moves behind and follows Violet to the water's edge. The camera pulls out just enough to reveal the seemingly innocent scene, yet also reveals the space Violet places between herself and Rose the Hat, showing Violet's hesitancy and fear. At this point the audience is a voyeuristic participant, complicit in the stalking of this child and unable to stop the events that are about to unfold. The next camera angle cements this position as it switches to Rose's perspective, showing the hesitancy and nervousness on Violet's face as Rose offers a flower with an outstretched arm. As Violet reaches for it, Rose pulls her arm back slowly, manipulatively drawing Violet within inches of her grasp. Pulled in close, the audience is now enticed to accept its role as willing participant in the manipulation of this child.

The intensity of this scene continues. When distracted by the True Knot members forming around her, which is shown in quick cuts between the forest and Violet's worried face, Rose commands her attention by performing tricks from her magic hat. At this point the camera positions the audience as one of the members of the True Knots. The viewer is watching the scene unfold, often seeing portions of both Rose and Violet in the frame even as perspective shifts between them. This indicates that the scene is from neither character's perspective, but from that of those gathering to watch. Rose offers one trick, designed to test Violet's "steam" ability. She asks her to identify the color of the flower in her hat. The camera shows Violet's concentration as she correctly guesses purple, before it switches to the growing crowd encircling her. Violet's fear is palpable, yet the audience cannot intercede. Rose once again demands her attention back by forcibly saying "Violet!," echoing both her name and the color of the flower, as she puts it in her mouth and eats it. Dueling camera angles continue to include both Rose and Violet in the frame, and expose the girl's horror that Rose ate the "special" flower, only to be juxtaposed by Rose's joy at taunting the child by saying, "Honey, it's the special ones that taste best." The camera then moves to an aerial view, coming full circle from the scene's opening, the perspective of a Hawk watching its prey as the True Knot descends upon Violet (*Doctor Sleep*). Though only 3 minutes and 17 seconds in length, this opening offers a distinct and notable difference from the novel. Instead of focusing on the backstory of Danny and Wendy's violent past, as well as Danny's continued struggle against the ghosts that haunt him, the opening here sets the tone for only one thing: the manipulation, abduction and violent death of children—of which the audience is complicit.

At first blush both of these openings may seem typical of King's works and his treatment of children. In "Inherited Haunts: King's Terrible Children," Tony Magistrale articulates the importance and multi-faceted roles King's

children play in his fiction, often functioning as a door into a broader interpretation and understanding of his works. He states that "King's children, like
those found in Dickens' novels, illustrate the failings of adult society. The
destruction of their innocence accomplishes more than a simple restating of
the universal theme of the Fall from Grace; it enlarges to include a specific
critique of respective societies and cultures as well" (49). Magistrale goes on
to explain that some "represent the nucleus of familial love," which enables
healing to occur in dysfunctional family relationships, while others "represent the principle of good in a corrupt world" and still others, namely King's
destructive teenagers, like Arnie Cunningham from *Christine,* function "to
wreak destruction on anyone or anything weaker than or different from themselves," thus offering a glimpse into the creation of the dysfunctional adults
that often appear in his work (49). Sara Alegre agrees and points to the fact
that "King's sacrificial children are heirs to Henry James's Miles and Flora
in *The Turn of the Screw* (1898)," thus giving King's treatment of children a
literary heritage (106). For all intents and purposes, the children of *Doctor
Sleep* can easily be dismissed as part of King's and horror's literal history.
However, Alegre defines an issue with King's use of children that is often
overlooked: "Writers like King no doubt use the child to portray the faults
of the adults, but in the process they offer adult readers disturbing images of
victimized and victimizing children" (105–106). This, she notes, creates "an
ambiguous position regarding the relationships between children and adults.
Despite his apparently siding with the unprotected children, King's child
characters are often exposed to a high degree of abuse that may not be wholly
justified by this criticism of the American family" (106). This couldn't be
more true when considering the high degree of abuse and torture used against
the children in *Doctor Sleep*. There is, quite frankly, no justification for it and
it sets the stage for that crucial question: Is the redemption of Dan Torrance,
the adult, worth the brutal, gratuitous, and violent sacrifice of these children
in the name of entertainment?

     Although the openings of both set different tones, each goes on to include
disturbingly detailed scenes of gratuitous violence and torture of children.
These scenes are often combined with a euphoric state of sexual ecstasy,
which adds another layer of complexity to the use of children in this manner
for the sake of entertainment. Even before Abra psychically witnesses the
cruel and torturous death of Bradley Trevor in the novel, King offers the death
of Richard Gaylesworthy, a psychic child described as a "good boy, a lovely
boy" with parents who were "good Baptists," as a bit of foreplay for what's
to come (193). Despite the functioning family dynamic of the Gaylesworthy
family and the prevalence of a psychic ability that often protects children in
King's fiction, Richard Gaylesworthy is afforded no protection by King. He
disappears and his body has "long since rotted away beneath the gone-to-seed

back field of an abandoned farm" (193). Even nature's reproductive power has flourished over the bones of this child. Though the details of his death at the hands of the True Knot are purposefully left out, the euphoric influence his steam has on its members as they consume the last known essence of this innocent child is troubling due to the sense of sexual excitement it elicits. As his steam envelopes them and they physically take it in, it causes several to "hyperventilate and swoon to the ground" (193). Rose the Hat feels herself "swelling physically and sharpening mentally," knowing full well that "Crow would come to her camper, and in her bed they would burn like torches," while others, like Snakebite Andi and Silent Sarey forgo privacy, "kissing deeply" with "Andi's hands plunged into Sarey's mouse-colored hair" (193–194). This juxtaposition of the death of a child directly resulting in a state of sexual ecstasy and orgy-like euphoria for adults complicates the narrative for the reader as they try to come to terms with the shock value King has placed as an offering: the death of children causing sexual euphoria. Crossing the lines of cultural taboo, the overall effect of creating a sense of dread and hatred towards the True Knot runs the risk of being lost here. Instead of turning the reader against The True Knot, the reader finds him or herself standing at the edge of a cliff, questioning the writer that offers this up as entertainment with reckless abandon and a lack of moral regard that was so prevalent in the pulling of *Rage* from publication for the fear of its influence. That 'broken people' exist as real monsters ready to kidnap, murder and use children for their own sense of sexual gratification is no secret. They exist and victimize children every day. Perhaps this is the point King is trying to make. It follows suit with the inherent theme his readers have come to enjoy: the idea that people are the real monsters in the world. But this is a point that has been aptly made ad nauseam in the fiction that predates this novel. Are we here again? Because nothing new is offered in this narrative, other than the shock value of how this is served up and plated for the reader, one must question its use.

In general, the heart of the violence in both the novel and the film *Doctor Sleep* resides in the dual torture of both 11-year-old Bradley Trevor and Abra Stone. This occurs as Trevor meets his fate at the hands of the True Knot. While violent enough as a solitary scene, King forces young Abra to psychically witness Trevor's death, bringing the mallet of violence down on both children. Explicit in its own right, the novel unfolds the horror in a way that is later capitalized on in the film. In the novel, Trevor is duped by Barry Smith, kidnapped, duct-taped and taken to the grounds of an isolated, abandoned ethanol processing plant, a symbolic setting for what is about to transpire. Much like ethanol is "a colorless volatile flammable liquid which is produced by the natural fermentation of sugars," Trevor undergoes extreme violence and torture that transforms him into nothing more than a colorless steam to be consumed by the True Knot—a natural process for them (Merriam-Webster. com). And, as King reminds the reader, he is just one of "thousands of other unfortunate children" that have suffered a similar fate at the hands of the True Knot (199). From here King details the scene: a weeping, duct-taped child begging for his life as the True Knot gathers around him like wolves around a helpless animal, or a hawk attacking its prey. As Trevor begs and asks if they are going to hurt him, Rose-the-Hat smiles and taunts him by saying, "As little as possible," all-the-while holding a "short and very sharp" knife behind her back, knowing that pain purifies steam (200). King goes on to describe the scene as a "makeshift operating theater" and notes that "the boy lasted a long time. He screamed until his vocal cords ruptured and his cries became husky barks" (200). At one point Trevor can only whisper and he begs to be killed. This is met by a "comforting smile" from Rose the Hat with the assurance of the word "Soon," which indicates the opposite (200). Later, Abra recounts in a psychic vision how the True Knot ignored his screams as they licked his blood off their palms.

The 2019 film, which King signed off on—giving his consent to the final cut—further complicates this scene and King's violent treatment towards children. In a scene that lasts nearly three full minutes, Trevor is carried from the van screaming, kicking and actively fighting for his life. Not duct-taped, he is, instead, laid in the dirt with each arm and leg tied by rope, angling him in a splayed position as Barry dons the baseball glove and taunts him with how good he was. Once again, the camera angle places the audience in role of active participant, watching Trevor struggle with Barry as he exits the van, then using the aerial angle to place the audience as predator, as he is splayed and tied. When he asks if they are going to hurt him, Rose-the Hat, straddled atop him, responds "Yes," informs him that "pain purifies the steam," then stabs him, eliciting a scream that causes a wisp of steam to rise from his mouth (*Doctor Sleep)*. Once again, the purposeful placement of the camera in this scene puts the audience in a precarious position. Rose is viewed from Trevor's angle as she taunts him with the placement of the knife in her hand. She is above him, and the camera reveals this as her presence takes up the frame as a larger than life figure—a purposeful maneuver ensures his vulnerability is not merely viewed, but experienced by the audience. What is more disturbing is the moment in which Rose inhales the steam and passes it, mouth to mouth to other members, creating an uncomfortable atmosphere of sexual intimacy that no child should witness. This moment, the start of this sexually euphoric and symbolic orgy, is captured from Trevor's perspective. From there, each plunge of the knife, splatter of blood and release of steam from Trevor causes heightened sexual pleasure, carrying the True Knot away on a wave of euphoria as the camera switches between Rose's perspective, Trevor's perspective, and that of active viewer. Every emotion is experienced by the audience—Rose's joy at torturing him, his fear and pain as he is sense-lessly stabbed, and the True Knot's sexual euphoria as participants.

Complicating this scene even more, the camera cuts to an aerial view of Abra, vulnerably sleeping in her bed. Once again, the audience is a predator, viewing her from above as she psychically connects to the torture of Trevor. As she sits up, clearly terrified at what is unfolding in her mind, the camera is face-to-face with her, at eye level. As she shakes, eyes wide in terror, she mouths the words "Help" to the only one there to assist her—the audience. But once again the viewer is leveled as mere voyeur, predator and stalker, which is affirmed with yet another aerial view as she throws herself back on the bed, thrashing in fear.

Though it can be argued that the brutality, torture and violence in this scene is needed because it is the engine that drives the narrative—it is the inciting incident that causes Abra and Dan to hunt down the True Knot and eventu-ally destroy them, the truth is that this is literally overkill. The narrative for the novel *It,* for example, was driven by the same general subtext—the disappearance and murder of children; however, the reader of the novel or viewer of the film is never brought into a gratuitous play-by-play blow of the manner of death. Georgie's arm is ripped off by Pennywise in the 2017 remake of *It* while he reaches for his boat in the gutter, and though violent and horrifying in its own right, the violence stops there. The audience is never placed in a position of accountability for Georgie's safety, or as a par-ticipant in Pennywise's pleasure. Pennywise is happy in his conquests, but the happiness does not depend on the release of physical pain and suffering alone. In both the novel and film versions of *It* the disappearance and death of children is enough of a reason to destroy the monster, and enough for the reader to become invested in the story. If the nexus of King's work is to tell the "unpleasant truth," then King's inclusion of drawn-out detail, torture, and sexual gratification as *Doctor Sleep* offers up a sad truth, and one that King himself may not be ready to consciously admit: that America *does* exist in a culture of violence, especially against children, and it is becoming normalized at an alarming rate—partly at his hands.

Another detail that further complicates King's stance on violence and chil-dren, is the decision to cast Snakebite Andi as a 15-year-old sexualized minor in the film, as opposed to an overweight 32-year-old woman as portrayed in the novel. A history of being repeatedly raped by her father from the ages of 8 to 16 before putting a stop to it by popping his balls with a knitting needle before plunging it into his eye, the Andi of the novel has enough life experience behind her to stand her own ground and make her own decisions. When kidnapped by the True Knot and confronted by Rose, Andi is given a choice—join them and live a long life, or be dumped at the side of the road with a wiped memory and the loss of her gift to put people to sleep. She is still under the duress of being kidnapped but at least she is an adult with a choice in front of her. For the Andi of the film it's a different story. Only 15, she is at a movie with an assumed pedophile. Though able to put him to sleep, take his money and leave her token snakebite mark on his face, she is still an exploited child. She is then kidnapped, by the True Knot, turned into one of them, made an accessory to the kidnap, torture, and murder of other children, and made to participate in the sexual orgies that take place at such events. Though she gave her consent to be turned, Andi's consent is inconsequential because she is a kidnapped minor under duress and unable to give such consent.

As if this isn't bad enough, both the novel and the film feature an all-out gun fight in a public park where Andi is ultimately shot and killed. This stands in stark contrast to King's disdain of school shootings and gun violence towards children. From King's own perspective as discussed in *Guns,* it is not okay, on the one hand, to leave a novel in publication because it features a crime related to gun violence against children in a high school and is a possible accelerant, but it *is* permissible, as the reality of his fiction suggests, to leave a novel in publication that features the kidnapping of a 15-year-old minor, turns her into a marauding vampire, makes her complicit in the torture and murder of other children, engages her in euphoric adult orgies, then shoots her—all in the name of entertainment? She is the exact age of the high school kids whose deaths King tries to avoid by pulling the publication of *Rage.* What, exactly, is King's stand on this issue? There is much to discuss in regards to King's treatment of Andi in the film version of *Doctor Sleep* but perhaps it is more aptly served through a feminist lens of critical theory. At the very least, Andi's ultimate end in the film stands in stark contrast to King's assertions in *Guns.*

It can be argued that the redemption in *Doctor Sleep* is worth the sacrifice of offering up the overt kidnap, torture, and murder of children as a means to sexual gratification because the True Knot is eventually destroyed, thus saving other innocent children from the same fate faced by Bradley Trevor and the thousands of others left in their wake. Jonathan Davis states that "the appeal of King's fiction to his readers rests in the fact that it constantly raises the question of morality; it recognizes the pervasiveness of evil, but it also aims to prove that the forces of good, when formed behind a collaboration of human hearts to enforce good, will almost always reign over evil" (36). In this light the destruction of the True Knot and Dan Torrance's redemption is enough to justify the sacrifice and torturous death of innocent children in this narrative. Dan Torrance and Abra did unite to enforce good and triumphed over the True Knot, and Dan triumphed over the trauma from his childhood, as well as generational abuse and addiction. But what about Abra? Though Dan's personal journey has afforded some redemption and the personal cycle of abuse and addiction that was prevalent in his life has been overcome, in King's fictional landscape here, this cycle hasn't been broken. The cycle of King's children potentially becoming dysfunctional adults due to violence and psychological harm is still very much in play for Abra. At the end of the novel she is a minor and her story is yet to unfold. All that is revealed is a typical teen rebellion against her parents. The end of the film also offers no clear closure or guarantee that Abra will grow to be a functioning adult. All that is known is that Abra has a gift. She is not a typical teen and King's kids, as we know, grow up with unpleasant truths of childhood violence, abuse and trauma that have clear consequences on the adults they become. But, should King have some sense of moral obligation towards this narrative?

Sara Alegre takes a slightly different approach to moral standing in King's fiction, stating that "King may put his finger on the dark areas of the American lifestyle but lacks an answer as to how American society could protect its own children from the horrors adults inflict upon them" (105). She asserts that his novels "address morally autonomous readers capable of understanding the boundaries between exploitation and denunciation in contemporary horror. King's implicit moral message—be good to your children—is addressed to them" (105). Again, a reasonable explanation grounded in theory that allows the reader and viewer to forgive the excessive violence against children presented here because each is capable of understanding the boundaries between exploitation and denunciation in contemporary horror. This reasoning, however, assumes that every consumer of horror fiction is a well-balanced adult capable of discernment and not a "broken" person with a penchant for violent tendencies. But even if Alegre's assertion is true here, not everyone will agree that the message of "be good to your children"needs to be delivered through reading about or viewing the drawn out kidnapping, torture, manipulation and violent abuse of the same.

In an opinion piece written for *The Washington Post* soon after the film's release in November of 2019, film critic Alyssa Rosenberg explains her reason for walking out of *Doctor Sleep* during the Bradley Trevor torture/murder scene. Her decision was not because she "didn't want to confront the fact that children are sometimes miserable, and that they are sometimes treated with profound indifference or even cruelly abused." Instead she walked out because as a mother tending to a small child, she was "simply not capable right now of treating violence and neglect toward children with the level of detachment that would enable me to consume those images as entertainment, or even as an attempt at edification" ("Go Ahead. Walk Out of that Movie"). And this strikes at the heart of the matter. King's escalating violence towards children is being offered up as entertainment, and his own criticism of the media's handling of school shootings in *Guns*, that they treat them like a cheap form of entertainment, is exactly what he is perpetuating in *Doctor Sleep* with the murder, kidnapping, torture and even shooting of his child characters. And most spectacularly of all, King is doing so with a free pass—without as much as a single essay to counter its truth and question its existence. Scholarship on King's children focuses largely on the role they play in the broader context of interpretation. However, this disturbing and escalating pattern of kidnap, torture and murder, which adds to the normalization of a culture of violence towards children in America, largely goes unnoticed. The extreme violence and abuse that happens to his children, like the detailed rape of young Sam Peebles in "The Library Policeman" in 1990, is overlooked and treated as normal collateral damage in a King narrative, and something that the future adult Sam Peebles must someday contend with. And if, by chance, King's children don't survive the abuse, torture and torment—all is well as long as the ends justify the means—as long as the final redemption in the narrative is worth the sacrifice. And the sad truth is that it isn't. Plating up violent and brutal depictions of child kidnap, manipulation, torture and death, and passing them off as entertainment is punishable by law if done-so without the pass of a publisher or production company with an MPA rating.

Instead of ridding his fictional landscape of dangerous gypsy vampires that torture and murder children, King has populated the real world with graphic images of the torture, murder, abuse and exploitation of children. Instead of protecting children from the "broken" people that could use his fiction as an "accelerant," he has served up a tasty dish of kiddie torture porn, further normalizing the culture of violence in America that King doesn't believe exists. If his works tell "unpleasant truths," as King contends, one must wonder what unpleasant truth is told in *Doctor Sleep.* Is it that a marauding band of vampires is murdering children for their steam? Is it that real-life monsters actually do exist? Or is it that the escalating use of violence towards children is being served up on a platter for the sake of entertainment? Whatever the reason, one isn't necessary an "asshole with no conscience" for throwing a blanket over the unpleasant truth. Blankets are also thrown over fires—to put them out.

WORKS CITED

Alegre, Sara Martin. "Nightmares of Childhood: The Child and the Monster in Four Novels by Stephen King." https://gent.uab.cat/saramartinalegre/sites/gent.uab.cat.saramartinalegre/files/v23%20n1-7.pdf. 2 Jan. 2021.
Collins Dictionary.com. https://www.collinsdictionary.com. 12 Feb. 2021.

Davis, Jaime L. "Monsters and Mayhem: Physical and Moral Survival in Stephen King's Universe." https://citeseerx.ist.psu.edu/viewdoc/download?doi=10.1.1.102 7.2151&rep=rep1&type=pdf 2 Jan. 2021.

Doctor Sleep. Mike Flanagan. Warner Brothers. 2019.

King, Stephen. *Guns.* Kindle Single. Philtrum Press (January 25, 2013).

———. *Doctor Sleep.* New York. Pocket Books. 2013.

Magistrale, Tony. "Inherited Haunts: Stephen King's Terrible Children." *Extrapolation,* 26:1 (1985): 43.

Merriam-Webster.com. https://www.merriam-webster.com/dictionary/ethanol. 4 Jan. 2020.

Rosenberg, Alyssa. "Go Ahead. Walk Out of that Movie." *The Washington Post* 7 Nov. 2019. https://www.washingtonpost.com/opinions/2019/11/07/go-ahead-walk-out-that-movie-if-its-not-you/

Chapter 6

Violence Persists

Muschietti's IT *Films and a Sadistic Status Quo*

Michael J. Blouin

Andy Muschietti's remake of Stephen King's epic *IT*—divided into segments, *IT* (2017) and *IT Chapter Two* (2019)—offers an extensive cinematic study of American violence. That is, the films pose a series of vital questions on the subject of filmic violence: are human beings inherently violent? Can we make sense of American History and its bloody character?[1] How should we respond when faced with acts of violence—ignore them or retaliate? And what exactly is the role of Hollywood—or, more broadly, the American culture industry— in sustaining this bloodshed? Over the course of the two films, Muschietti guides his audience through each of these inquiries, before arriving at something of an impasse. Muschietti's contributions arrive at a dead-end because they cannot quite figure out how to escape from the cyclical violence at the heart of King's narrative. The main reason that these films cannot escape from systemic violence: systemic violence constitutes King's plot *at its most foundational level*. American society, King reminds us over and over again in his fiction as well as his films, remains eternally driven to violence—a thesis that Muschietti's films demonstrate but ultimately disregard.

This chapter builds upon the thesis of *Stephen King and American History* (Magistrale and Blouin, 2020). As arguably the main character of *IT*, the city of Derry cyclically engages its citizens in savage, brutal behavior. The city's avatar, Pennywise (Bill Skarsgård), returns every twenty-seven years to steal children and inspire wayward residents to murder one another in manners most foul. Derry—a microcosm for the U.S.—appears to be caught in a hopeless entropic loop, drawn back forever into a state of violence. King's tale understands History to be deterministic in its ferocity, which is to say, propelled by a sort of sadism. Indeed, Paul Ricoeur observes that violence serves as "the very mainspring of [H]istory," as "the privileged mode with which the form of [H]istory changes" (224, 227–28). This mainspring fuels a wide variety of social change: "How empires rise and fall, how personal prestige is established, how religions tear each other to pieces, how the privileges of property and power are perpetuated and interchanged, or even how the authority of intellectuals is consolidated" (225). This deep mainspring explains why Derry keeps sinking back into the morass, its unwholesome essence visualized by the grotesque Barrens atop which the municipality sits. American History habitually strikes King's audience as a bleak metaphysical underpinning. The first film *IT* affirms such a grim outlook as we watch young Eddie (Jack Dylan Grazer) softly whistling the "Star Spangled Banner" before being horrifically attacked by a rotting leper. Elsewhere, a monument dedicated to the soldiers lost in the World Wars stands at the very epicenter of Derry, and it is upon this monument that we gaze upon young Henry Bowers (Nicholas Hamilton) as he awaits his prey. In these works, American society is erected literally and metaphorically upon a dreary slough into which centuries of innocent victims of violent crime have been dumped—hence the enormous pile of Derry's detritus later discovered in Pennywise's underground lair.

Perhaps we should begin by asking ourselves how History is "made." In Muschietti's films, History most often manifests as a signature—an excruciating etching, carved into the flesh. Consider the many historical sketches in these remakes: the unsightly mural in the alleyway near Quality Meats that depicts the brutal gang violence of the early twentieth century (Pennywise himself pops in and out of the image); the cruel prank pulled by the pharmacist's daughter when she writes "Loser" on young Eddie's cast; and, perhaps most viscerally, Bowers and his brood carving a bloody "H" into Ben's "cottage cheese" (Jeremy Ray Taylor) at the lover's bridge, where less antagonistic couples go to carve their initials alongside the initials of the ones they love. "Making one's mark" means something quite ruthless in the *IT* films. American History, then, is comprised of misguided monsters that wish to be remembered by crudely inscribing their names onto innocent surfaces. The audacity of the act, and the need to dominate that it reflects, is keenly felt by the audience as Ben writhes and wails under the penetrating scrawl of his abuser. The same can be said of Pennywise's missives, sprayed in blood on bathroom walls and under bridges. If we extend the violence of the signature out a bit, we might consider furious markings on other surface to be relevant as well, such as photographs or celluloid ("writing in light," as the saying goes). Through these burned signatures, Muschietti's films religiously memorialize Derry. Ben's walls are covered with unsavory newspaper clippings; one of the most important sites of the film remains the Derry Library, with its many (haunted) monographs. Pennywise himself moves freely in and out of the frame, as when he crawls out of the projector in young Bill's garage (Jaeden Martell). The purportedly innocuous signature—a desperate emblem, scratched into a screen to commemorate one's participation in American

History—"I was Here"—recalls the unsettling impetus of American History and its accompanying urge for eternal recognition. This perverse form of commemoration is ultimately what the Losers are doing when they cut their palms with shards of glass to signify their bond and then use the scars as a reminder of their shared History. Through signatures that are always-already scars of a sort, Muschietti's films bring the battlefield of History into focus.

Yet in another sense, these scars play an important role in *saving* the Losers—and so we cannot off-handedly dismiss them as just another expression of innate brutality. After all, Bill goes on to become a famous writer, and Muschietti's films do not appear to argue that film-making is itself a morally dubious activity (we will return to the self-reflexivity of *IT Chapter Two* in a moment). Relatedly, by providing the only signature in Ben's yearbook, young Bev (Sophia Lillis) lays the groundwork for future bliss. And Stan's final letter to the Losers—albeit replete with vague platitudes and maudlin sentiments—cements their sense of unity as well as their purpose moving forward. Part of the spectator's task, then, is to decipher "good" signatures from "bad" signatures, and to do so in a way that redeems History (instead of catering to its more vainglorious impulses). The *impossibility* of this proposal, however, underscores the sheer difficulty of eluding the cycles of violence that characterize American History. (As Tony Magistrale and I have argued, King's entire corpus reflects the difficulty of this endeavor.)

The impossibility of a "good signature" can be traced back to a basic (and enduring) premise: violence begets more violence. The recent *IT* films obsessively ask why violent actors do what they do. Maybe, the common response of the cultural warrior resounds, it's the video games that are teaching these kids to be so violent. The local arcade remains young Richie's favorite spot in Derry (Finn Wolfhard), where he plays the game *Mortal Combat* and tells Bill, during a spat, that he's "pretending it's you." Or perhaps the bloodlust of these adolescents can be attributed to parental failings: Bowers' authoritarian father, who shoots at his son's feet to cut him down (to make a "paper man crumble"), or Eddie's mother and her covetous affection, or Bill's father and his impatience with a grieving son, or Bev's father who assaults her (in more ways than one, the films suggest). These examples of model behavior could very well lead the children to lash out violently. Then again, the city's violence could be attributed to biology instead of culture—which is to say, nature instead of nurture. In one of the film's earliest scenes, young Mike (Chosen Jacobs) reluctantly utilizes a captive bolt pistol to slaughter sheep on his uncle's farm. To be more "responsible," he must learn to "do his part," to become an adult by destroying innocent animals for food. This naturalist lesson of survival—to kill or be killed—sinks in as the audience watches the young man (emotionlessly) conduct his killing business. You're either the bully or the bullied in this world. The captive bolt pistol therefore serves as a significant totem throughout the *IT* films, like when Bill—young as well as old (James McAvoy)—employs the weapon to dispatch his traumatic past. A pressing question remains: what is the audience meant to do with this totem? Are the *IT* films advocating for violence as a legitimate response to external threats? If not violence, what *is* the escape route from this larger entropic cycle?

What happens when characters try to make a "good signature" by putting away their respective pistols? Ben does not sign the love ode that he sends to Bev, so his love for her very nearly goes unrequited. Unwilling to "make History," he is forced into the margins. Since he initially refuses to make his mark on History, that is, to carve his name into that postcard and assert his feelings, the passive Ben appears condemned to watch Bill and Bev fall for one another. Without committing his signature to paper, Ben suffers through these films the fate of a poetic cuckold. Similarly, when the elder Eddie (James Ransone) cannot join his friends in killing their former friend's head-turned-spider, Bill lashes out at him, excoriating him for his weakness in the face of danger. Eddie's paralysis may explain why the film eventually singles him out to die: his momentary unwillingness to go with the group on their violent quest must be punished (*IT Chapter Two* thus strikes me as a morality play in favor of violent retaliation).

Muschietti's films summarily condemn the path of nonviolence. Young Bill scolds his friends, "Are you just going to pretend it isn't happening like everyone else in this town?" Perhaps most forcefully, the first film takes up the issue of bystander apathy—a specialty of Derry residents (including, as we have already seen, Eddie). The city's populace appears to be acutely incapable of intervening on behalf of victims of violent crime. While Pennywise sucks young George into the sewer drain at the beginning of the first film, the camera turns to a woman on her porch as she battens down her house for the storm. She gives off an air of being nonplussed to see a small child leaning into a sewer drain and subsequently does nothing to stop him. When all that remains of the boy is a streak of blood across the road, the woman still appears relatively unmoved and painfully silent. In another scene, when Bowers slices into Ben's abdomen while his cronies hold the boy down, an elderly couple drive by the incident without stopping to help. The second film continues to interrogate this idea, as the Losers must be coerced and cajoled incessantly into saving a younger generation of Derry youngsters. The elder Bill wrestles mightily with his obligation to protect the child that now occupies his former home. Pennywise eventually forces him to watch through a glass wall in a funhouse as the clown devours the child, thereby forcing him to experience the horrifying sense of impotence that accompanies the weak bystander. Pennywise himself loves to watch Derry residents as they attack one another; oscillating between the unbridled fury of an unleashed pit bull (or a shark, with his eyes rolled back and his enormous jaws extended outward) and the stupefied, drooling expression that punctuates his speeches, Derry's monstrous mountebank highlights *the violent undertones of nonviolence*. In many cases, Pennywise stands out as the apex apathetic bystander, indifferent to the plight of the people. And the consequences of this widespread unwillingness to intervene on behalf of strangers fall squarely on the shoulders of Muschietti's spectator. After all, isn't watching a horror film (on an experiential level) akin to bystander apathy?

In the group's climactic confrontation with Pennywise in *IT Chapter Two*, Muschietti makes the bystander effect even more keenly felt by deliberately referencing other film adaptations of King's work. Gesturing at Stanley Kubrick's *The Shining* (1980), an image of the young Bowers does his best Jack Torrance impression as he tries to barrel through a stall door and declares "Here's Johnny!" In the same stall, blood floods over the elder Bev (Jessica Chastain), calling to mind the ballroom sequence of Brian De Palma's *Carrie* (1976). Muschietti's metacommentary forces audience members to reconsider the legacy of Stephen King on film because if American History remains cyclical and bloody (as King's stories so often claim), and if countless adaptations of King's work keep feeding off of one another, there appears to be an important correlation: due to both their gruesome character and their status as spectacle, King's films perpetuate the entropic cycle of violence in question. Another Derry landmark stands out on this front—the local theater's marquee (in one of the final shots of the film, it reads *Nightmare on Elm Street 5*), which alerts us to the prominent role that cinema plays in sustaining the city's violent nature. The film being prominently screened is a late sequel—a form of postmodern self-referentiality that remains at least as claustrophobic as the rest of daily life in this backwater burg.[2] The horror film itself therefore supplements the fear and violence that drives so many citizens of Derry to their demise. One reason that the conclusion of *IT Chapter Two* remains more effective than the ending of the initial remake (1990) is because Muschietti's version manages to capture the frenzied feeling of King's rapidly expanding fictional universe. It tells the tale of how horror films circle back upon themselves and force participants (including spectators) into making "false" choices. For example, Pennywise corrals the elder Eddie and Richie into choosing which door to use: Not Scary at All, Scary, or Very Scary. This *illusion* of choice—in the end, all of the doors offered by Pennywise lead to nasty endings—speaks to the inner workings of the horror genre, and it recalls the Native American mantra that the elder Mike (Isaiah Mustafa) regularly intones: everything must abide by the limits of its form. Spectators, like the Losers, cannot elude the structural limits of this genre's mode of spectatorship. They too are given a series of false "choices" that offer them no escape from the torment of a sadistic ritual (in this case, habitual encounters with the genre itself). Muschietti's postmodern playfulness, in other words, reaches the conclusion that to evade the violent cycles of History, spectators must evade the confines of formulaic horror shows. By plunging victims into a state of stupefaction, the Deadlights—the cosmic force behind Pennywise's success—recreate the cinematic experience: slack-jawed, Losers like Bev and Richie are condemned to stare blankly at the screen before them, thus mimicking Pennywise's periodic posture as anaesthetized mouth-breather. The film ultimately suggests that to break away from this pattern of bystander apathy remains the only hope for salvation for the Losers.[3]

But doubling down on feelings of entrapment does not in itself solve the issue of violence and History. The method of escape from King's cyclical violence regularly proves to be *just as damaging as life inside the loop*. For instance, although Louis Creed in the initial film adaptation of *Pet Sematary* (1989) recognizes that he must not "play God" (and so he should learn to live without a plan), this revelation does precious little to defy the bloody norms imposed by late capitalism and the interstate highway system. The profit-driven trucks that murder his son continue to barrel through his idyllic space. If anything, the film's final lesson—that Creed should have resigned himself to this "crazy world" rather than claim absolute power for himself—actually upholds the dreadful logic of the trucks themselves (namely, a willingness to plow down innocent lives in the name of efficiency and profitability). Along the same lines, in Muschietti's *IT* films, Derry keeps replaying its violent past because precious few individuals can conceptualize an effective way to "move on." They keep returning to the three doors that Pennywise offers to them. But the films offer an equally convincing antidote to the crisis and so, ironically enough, they fall prey to the very tendency that they mock when they ridicule Bill for his bad endings (King makes a good-natured cameo as the owner of an antique shop that comments upon his own apparently inept conclusions). In a word, because they remain unable to imagine a truly non-violent path forward, *IT* and *IT Chapter Two* conform to the violent inner logic that they cannot exorcise through mere exposure.

Consider the scenes in which the Losers rally together (and what that union requires of them as well as the spectator). When the group rescues young Mike from Bowers and his gang, they enter into a "rock war" in which the two gangs throw rocks at each other from across a stream. In effect, the one thing that solidifies their bond is Bowers himself, which is to say, the glue that holds them as a unit proves to be their antagonistic relationship with the local bully. They only manage to "beat" the Bowers brood by becoming an equally menacing cohort themselves. Likewise, the Losers later coalesce around their collective beating of the human head/spider hybrid (a moment, again, in which Eddie fails to act and apparently seals his fate). And then once more, at the close of *IT Chapter Two*, the Losers realize that they cannot defeat Pennywise without adopting the mannerisms of the Bowers crew, and so they shape shift into "bullies," push the clown into a corner, and (literally) rip out his beating heart. It may strike the spectator as a bit odd that to defeat Derry's greatest monster—a monster that feeds upon "tasty" fear and stokes the flames of violence—the Losers must behave *just like It*: they belittle It, declare It to be "just a clown," and then use physical force to back the creature into a corner and assault It. Of course, the point here is certainly not to petition on behalf of Pennywise, since no sane viewer would ever condone the atrocities It commits. Rather, we must inquire into the counter-argument offered by these films (if one truly exists). Is the only way to defeat a bully by meeting the bully on his or her (or It's) terms? How else could the "rock war" have ended, if not by joining in on the bloodbath? (Of note, a bloody rock from the "war" later serves as the cherished artifact that Mike holds onto in order to remain ever vigilant against the return of Pennywise.)

We return to the captive bolt pistol, wielded by members of the Losers' Club in various important moments throughout both films. Most pointedly, both the young and the elder Bill seize this weapon to remedy their personal ills: the younger Bill uses the pistol to "kill" his feelings of guilt for Georgie's death, graphically shooting the ghost of his younger brother at the close of the first film; in the second film, the two versions of Bill stand off against one another, each holding the pistol in turn, with the elder Bill ultimately murdering his younger self so that he can "move on." The *IT* story always involves reckoning with trauma; like almost all horror narratives, it wrestles with the collective as well as individual memories that disturb traumatized subjects. But because Muschietti's *IT* films tarry at such great lengths with the concept of violence (where it comes from, who commits such acts, why people sit back and watch it, *et cetera*), and explore violence as a fundamental aspect of being human, we might ask why catharsis demands *even more violence*. Are spectators really expected to cheer when the Losers pick up their sundry weapons and behave just like Bowers (only somehow "righteous" this time)? Do the *IT* films affirm a mindset steeped in violence? Undoubtedly, critics can read the Losers as defending themselves. Since they do not throw the first stone, or draw the first blood, it remains difficult (but not impossible) to blame them for wanting retribution against their tormentors. Muschietti's films contend that humans remain violent beings. Force meets force; power necessitates power. This macabre loop recalls the foundation of Ovid's ancient mock epic, *Metamorphoses*—another narrative that claims violence to be the root of any and all personal as well as public change. For Ovid and Muschietti alike, humans appear born to destroy one another. In turn, we should not be surprised when the Ritual of Chüd fails to deliver an end to the bloodshed.

Certain that his group would succeed based upon the strength of its convictions, the elder Mike does not tell his friends that the Native American ritual that he proposes has never actually worked. His supernatural mumbo jumbo amounts to nothing. The only way to defeat a monster, *IT Chapter Two* concludes, is to act like a monster yourself. Holding hands and singing Kumbaya may be charming—even edifying—but it moves us no closer to escape from Pennywise, from Derry, or from the clutches of American History Itself.

Yet even as these films maintain faith in a system built upon violence, they gesture (less than convincingly, I would argue) at less sanguinary alternatives. I must account for these seemingly gentler, more humane moments if I am to confirm that Muschietti's *IT* films in fact augment the gory social order that predates them. Like the King novel from which they draw their inspiration, these films occasionally retreat into a pastoral mode by lingering lovingly on images that convey the beautiful simplicity of childhood (see, for instance, the numerous tracking shots from on high paralleling Rob Reiner's 1986 adaptation of King's novella, *Stand by Me*). When the gang plunges into the refreshing reservoir at the edge of Derry to "wash" themselves clean from doing battle with evil, the films lead spectators into believing that this fuzzy, redemptive world at the border is more "real" than the postmodern funhouse that comprises Pennywise's lair. In these romantic, placid waters, the logic goes, the characters caress and cavort, grieve and gallivant—a retreat that culminates in a saccharine underwater kiss between Ben and Bev at the close of *IT Chapter Two*. King's narratives regularly return to the nostalgia of small-town America in the 1950s as a sort of panacea for the horrors that he unleashes. But these waters are also acknowledged to be the backwaters of Derry; in effect. they are the final resting place for fetid fluids that clog the intestinal tract of Derry's digestive system. There is something not quite right about the heavy-handed righteousness of the reservoir. For one, this heightened sense of "togetherness" among the Losers *does not actually save the day*. The act of singing in a circle may close the first film, but it does not close the sequel; no, as we have already seen, the sequel decidedly *rejects* such a sentimental send-off by transforming the adult Losers into a murderous mob, galvanized by their hatred before shape-shifting into yet another iteration of the Bowers brood. (It is perhaps fruitful for us to contemplate at this point the very thin line that separates the Bowers crew from the Losers—in the end, after all, both small communities are exclusionary and resort to violence in order to maintain their own concept of orderliness.)

Nevertheless, the *IT* films want spectators to believe that they can alter the bloody signatures of Derry's History, as when Eddie scratches out his bully's signature on his cast that reads "Loser" and replaces the "S" with a big red "V." Through this editorial intervention, Eddie salvages his group from the rubbish bin of History and categorizes them as "Lovers" instead of "Losers."

The remainder of the first film uses Eddie's cast as a striking visual line within various shot compositions, meant to magnify a slew of heroic postures. Eddie's red "V" may well stand for "Victory." But it is still a signature and, as such, it still aggressively imposes its meaning over others. Just what exactly *is* "love" in these films? In their final conversation, Bill and Mike express their devotion by saying "I love you" to one another. Meanwhile, Richie returns to the lover's bridge to complete a heart sketch that he etched into the wood twenty-seven years prior, entering his friend's initial "E." Surely, Muschietti's audience is meant to assume that these devotional expressions— these well-intentioned marks of "love"—can overcome the names and letters written out of blind hatred, or in pursuit of "perverse" commemoration. But the story is not so simple. The potency of the Losers' fraternal "love" reso- nates only when it has been backed up by the promise (and execution) of violence. "Lovers" do not defeat Pennywise. "Love" emboldens characters into acting violently. Stan's sacrifice, in which he commits suicide because he knows he will hinder the group's fight, may be the closest thing to an expression of "love" that effects meaningful change in these films. However, Stan's self-sacrifice too requires a violent supplement: we witness the earlier shot of Stan in the bathtub, his wrists cut and bleeding profusely, his lifeless stare out into the future. Killing the self on behalf of one's friends may sound nobler, but it is nonetheless a violent deed. That is, Muschietti's adaptations recapitulate an otherworldly battle between good and evil (and it is a battle, let us make no mistake) without conceptualizing a very different route. These films lead always-already back to the same bloodstained choices that have, at least according to the logic of Stephen King's vision of American History, existed since time immemorial. The imagination of the films falls well short of Bev's desire "to run towards something—not away." In sum, because these films remain unable to construct a truly alternative perspective, violence con- tinues to beget violence.

Which brings us to the inexplicable voiceover of Stan's last letter to the Losers. Against swelling background music, Stan explains his choice to enact violence against himself (instead of Pennywise) and then launches into a sequence of disconnected platitudes. While Stan's logic of "taking himself off the board" may make tactical sense, it does not posit a functional alternative to the violent History of Derry—if all of the young people chose self-violence to violence against the other, Pennywise would "win" without contest. In a broader sense, Pennywise represents the Id of the city as a whole, and so the deaths caused by It are *always* a form of suicide. A powerful figment of the city's unconscious, the clown invariably signals a kind of collective self-harm. In response to this macabre reality, Stan's final "advice" for his friends offers precious little substance. "The thing about being a loser is you don't have anything to lose," he tells them. Although it sounds philosophical, what does the statement actually mean? That a lack of attachment propelled them to victory? (We might note the minor but important distinction added to Muschietti's version of *IT*: to explain or justify the willingness among the adult Losers to stay in Derry and kill Pennywise, the second film inserts the plotline that if they do not defeat the demonic clown, they will die premature deaths—an insertion that undermines the spirit of goodwill and benevolence in favor of apparently understandable selfishness. In other words, this change suggests that spectators only understand courage that stems from self-interest; it would be implausible for these characters to stand up for complete strangers.) Stan's missive goes on to remind the group, "Be Brave" and then "Believe." These feel-good platitudes may feign a sense of resolution, but they are essentially vacuous. Eddie was "brave" when he launched a spear into Pennywise, and he only does so because he "believes" in his own abilities. *Yet Eddie dies and the clown remains unscathed by his impotent attack.* The ending of *IT Chapter Two* provides a completely false impression of closure. Minus Stan's parade of lyrical clichés, the film's message could not be clearer: in the name of self-interest, rally your friends into battle, bully your enemies into submission, and violently vanquish your foe.

Audience members will be forgiven, however, if they do not immediately process the tacit endorsement of a violent worldview. For all of their outward mockery of King's inability to finish his novels successfully (a well-worn critique), Muschietti's films arguably arrive at an ending that remains even more dull and conventional than King's original. At the close of *IT Chapter Two*, Bill ostensibly overcomes his writer's block: "I think I know where I'm going this time," he informs Mike. Mike, in response, reports to his audience that "nothing lasts forever." The entity known as It has apparently been exterminated, and no further cycles will be necessary. A standard bourgeois "happy ending" wraps everything up in a relatively neat package: Bev and Ben are seen aboard a private yacht, blissful in their union; Richie, no longer ashamed of his sexuality, finishes the etching that he started twenty-seven years ago; even the ghost of young Stan finds peace, watching over his friends with a look of deep satisfaction. But as Stan's voiceover drones on, and the pastoral camera transcends the bounds of community into the skies above Derry, Muschietti's conclusion raises a number of questions concerning its initial thesis on violence. What are we to make of this surprising about-face into utopia? By placing Muschietti's adaptations into conversation with their source material, we recognize the sheer difficulty of resolving Derry's violent impetus. As I have argued elsewhere, despite the constant haranguing of its critics, King's novel *IT* provides one of the most thought-provoking endings of any of his works (for this reason, I would position King's Ovidian venture to be his strongest contribution to American literature to date).[4] Whereas Muschietti's films generally (but not exclusively) flatten out King's erratic timeline into a coherent chronology, King's novel jumps around with considerable abandon. If anything, King's text argues that trauma can *never* be overcome, not really, because the young long to grow up while the old wish to be young again. John Sears writes, "King's endings are conventionally apocalyptic, often . . . self-consciously drawing on mythic notions of cyclical return. More frequently, they tap more subtly into the ways Gothic endings deploy such returns as forms of perpetuation, resisting conventional closure and inviting instead deferral and extension" (209–10). Said another way, King's *IT* unsettles even itself. Unlike cinematic Ben's utopian musings, with his petition for "fewer walls," King's novel decidedly rejects utopia—that is, it holds true to its initial dialectical inclinations. In King's novel, there is no reason to believe that Bill won't simply forget everything once again and restart the battle with It. In contrast, Bill in *IT Chapter Two* remembers everything this time around, and so Mike (and the audience) can rest easy that there will be no additional sequels—at least, sequels that would follow the same cyclical logic. While the ending of King's text preserves the entropic loop of a violent American History—evil can never fully die, it acknowledges—Muschietti's films eventually posit a (superficial) solution. Unlike the novel, they *de-antagonize* Derry, which is to say, they aim to resolve, to heal, to plaster over the violent means of propulsion that have driven their entire narrative. The scars on their hands disappear, as Mike (literally) shuts the book on Derry's History. As such, Muschietti's films (unlike, I would argue, his source material) renege on their own argument that silly rituals and a mystical sense of wholeness cannot defeat the raw power struggle at their core. In their quest of syrupy sweet reconciliation, the films (impossibly) forget that violence stubbornly begets violence.

To assert that Pennywise, or his puppet Bowers, can only be defeated if antagonists mimic their behavior is to advance a grim social message. In their most revelatory (if unnerving) moments, the two *IT* films strip away the metaphysical baggage of "belief" and "common purpose" to expose the bare bones of a collision between competing forces. The only way to win a "rock war" is to pick up a rock; the only way to protect the group is to return every blow with an equally savage blow. Mike's greatest crime against his friends, then, is his reluctance to share with them the *failure* of the theatrical Native American ceremony. The second chapter must abandon the romanticized unity that closes the first film. *Nevertheless, Muschietti's films echo Mike's duplicity against the group by claiming to wiggle free from the underpinnings of violence.* As cinematic rituals, they too deny their own inconvenient truths about the antagonism of human experience. Even though they would cease to exist without an inherent drive to violence that defines individualism and community alike, *IT* and *IT Chapter Two* feign a faulty sense of resolution. They ignore the lessons of Ovid's mock epic at their own peril. They expose but then hide the reality that we are all shape-shifters, just like Pennywise—which means that we are all drawn from (and to) acts of violence, against others as well as ourselves.

One glaring omission proves this case: the decision in both films to underplay Richie's sexuality. The two films settle for extremely oblique gestures at the issue, like the scene in which young Richie is accused of being gay by Bowers' cousin or the scene in which the elder Richie frantically tries to stop Pennywise from exposing his "secret." Yet when Richie finally carves the initial "E" into the lover's bridge, apparently signaling to the audience that Richie has at last come to terms with his real identity, this "E" is hardly given the same resonance, the same self-assurance or vibrancy, as the letter "V" on young Eddie's cast. The audience can only assume that the letter "E" stands for Eddie, the departed friend. Moreover, the film's potential critique of violence against the LGBTQ community fades in favor of defanged fraternal bonds. Any sign of passionate sexuality is thus neutralized by the relatively banal memorialization of a dead comrade. There is no concrete reason to suspect that Richie was ever "in love" with Eddie. In Muschietti's adaptations, Richie's "secret" is never brought wholly to the surface and so it remains essentially invisible. This preference for suggestion, for invisibility, matters to us because Richie's potential challenge to his violent, heteronormative hometown could have carved out a genuine alternative to the bloody pathways in existence. If given full resonance, his carved "E" could have marked something truly different from the ugly "H" of Bowers. If a truly non-violent foundation remains to be discovered in these films—that is, any honest resistance to the toxic expressions of "love" in these films (expressions that double as brutality)—I would contend that this alternative must be tied to the ever-marginalized sexuality of Richie. Or, perhaps such an alternative resides in the marginalized love of Mike, one of Derry's few black men that must caretake the story of his (white) community in the attic of the local library. Could it be Mike's final "I love you" that offers us something different, something somehow less violent—sliding from Loser to Lover at last? Alas, these alternatives are given almost no shape whatsoever. Unable or unwilling to confront systemic racism (the "scarlet letter" that Derry scrawls onto Mike is parental drug use, a matter seemingly divorced from issues of race), Mike's final declaration of love lacks real teeth, since there can be no forgiveness without accountability. In his interview with Bill Hader, Marc Malkin writes, "While Richie doesn't discuss his sexuality in the film, Hader said of Richie, 'Hopefully, he has an understanding of, an acceptance of who he is'" (Malkin). The topic of sexuality is mostly implicit in the two films: for example, in the first film young Bill wears a Tracker Bros. shirt; in the novel, the Tracker Bros. are considered by Eddie's mother to be gay. The shirt signals a hidden connection

to queerness—but only the most eagle-eyed viewer who has extensive famil-
iarity with King's novel will catch the reference. Why does Hader's character
have to come to terms with being gay in the most obfuscated manner? Why
only "hopefully"? Why can't the acceptance to which Hader alludes find
its way into the film in a more concrete, definitive way? On the subject of
violence against disenfranchised communities, why can't the film—as Bev
suggests—run "towards," not "away from," something?

After all, the films do not hesitate to show extremely graphic violence
perpetrated against these outside groups. Audiences are subjected to singed
black hands, trying to claw their way out of a burning room as the infant Mike
watches, and the grotesque hate crime committed against Adrian, a gay man,
at the open of *IT Chapter Two*. We could even consider the camera's willingness to linger on Bev's sexual assaults. Why is it that these films spend so
much time gazing upon horrific acts of violence—yet the only "non-violent"
visions that they offer are decidedly weakened, as when Bev is objectified and
coopted into the highly normative fantasies of Bill and Ben, or when Mike
nearly perishes for his advocacy of a pacifist counterpoint to Pennywise, or
when Richie's "desire" materializes in an uncontroversial memorial to his
deceased friend? Put differently, whether it is due to a lack of risk-taking,
generic constraints, or the need to appeal to a broad audience (or all three
reasons at once), *the ideal of nonviolence gains no serious purchase in these
films*. Folding in upon themselves at their formulaic finale, Muschietti's adaptations foreclose the possibility of a sustainable escape from Derry's curse.
Violence persists. Still, against an impulse to resignation, we can cling to the
fact that traces of another worldview remain, lingering at the very edges of
these films. "Non-violence wishes to be the whole of action," Ricoeur muses.
Against all odds, in *IT* as well as *IT Chapter Two,* nonviolence (against all
odds) "wishes to make [H]istory" (223). In its wake, we must seek a way to
preserve healthy antagonisms without simultaneously retreating into vapid,
sun-soaked utopias and Stan's empty platitudes—which is to say, our communities must imagine a *non-violent antagonism*. Although we may be left
with such seedlings, Muschietti's films suggest that we cannot yet fathom a
future that is not merely a repetition of the past.[5] It is to this unexpected future
that we must now turn our joint gaze.

NOTES

1. Gary Hoppenstand and Ray Browne note of King's outlook, "Certainly one
prejudicial idea dominates (the American landscape): the notion that the American
experience is a positive experience. A serious examination of American [H]istory (and

the American popular literature that reflects that [H]istory) shows that nothing could be further from the truth" (8).

2. Like many adaptations of King's fiction, the film indulges in extensive metacommentary on itself as a typical King narrative: real clowns blur with simulated clowns (dolls; funhouse effects); Bev's father utters the infamous line from Stanley Kubrick's *The Shining* (1980)—"Here's Johnny!"—as the older Bev relives the literal bloodbath from Brian De Palma's *Carrie* (1976); and the Derry landmark round barn, which features prominently on Ben's postcard to Bev, is seen as the backdrop of one shot in the first *IT*—and, furthermore, Ben replicates it as a flimsy social studies project that he drops repeatedly upon meeting Bev for the first time. Overall, Muschietti's films revel in metacritique of the horror genre broadly (and the film adaptations of Stephen King in particular).

3. Muschietti's films are hardly the first adaptations of King texts to venture into this postmodern territory. Kubrick's *The Shining* famously paralyzes spectators within a rigged maze. Jan Mikael Håfström's *1408* (2007) similarly pontificates upon our entrapment within a web of King films by presenting a character hopelessly lost in a world of generic conventions. For an extended discussion of a self-enclosed sense of History and King's predictable narratives, see Fredric Jameson's "Historicism in *The Shining*," in *Signatures of the Visible*. New York: Routledge, 1992.

4. For an extended discussion, see Michael J. Blouin's *Stephen King and American Politics* (2021).

5. It is the sort of work imagined in Lee Edelman's influential book, *No Future: Queer Theory and the Death Drive*. Durham, NC: Duke University Press, 2004.

WORKS CITED

Blouin, Michael. *Stephen King and American Politics*. Cardiff, UK: University of Wales Press, 2021.

Hoppenstand, Gary, and Ray Brown. T*he Gothic World of Stephen King: Landscape of Nightmares.* Bowling Green, OH: Bowling Green University Press, 1987.

IT. Dir. Andy Muschietti. Screenplay by Chase Palmer, Cary Joji Fukunage, and Gary Dauberman. New Line Cinema, Vertigo Entertainment, 2017. DVD.

IT Chapter Two. Dir. Andy Muschietti. Screenplay by Gary Dauberman. New Line Cinema, Vertigo Entertainment, 2019. DVD.

King, Stephen. *It*. New York: Viking, 1986.

Magistrale, Tony, and Michael J. Blouin. *Stephen King and American History*. New York: Routledge, 2020

Malkin, Marc. "*IT Chapter Two*: Bill Hader on Richie's Sexuality, His On-Set Injury and Cast B12 Shots," in *Variety*, September 12, 2019. https://variety.com/2019/film/podcasts/bill-hader-it-chapter-two-richie-sexuality-1203333073/. Accessed online July 22, 2020.

Ricoeur, Paul. *History and Truth*. Evanston, IL: Northwestern University Press, 2007.

Sears, John. *Stephen King's Gothic*. Cardiff, UK: University of Wales Press, 2011.

Chapter 7

"Cut You Up into Little Pieces"

Ghosts & Violence in Kubrick's The Shining

Danel Olson

Snow that comes right inside a hotel door. A hotel that any of us might like to stay in, at first glance. A concerned mother; an intuitive, haunted, and mysteriously afflicted child. A father who becomes a workaholic. The White American male writer who is haunted by dreams and visions—a blind man who grows into a bewildered one. A man who has not been the father to his child that he sought or ought to be. A protagonist who may not have believed in ghosts before but now sees them. A worry about the child, and those messages shared by the child to other sensitives. The sudden appearance of an axe. Powerful people who stayed the night. Intimations of sexual trysts (for strangers, but not between the husband and wife). Routine murders, some suicides, and other half-forgotten deaths by unknown agents. Alcohol, anger, guilt, and visions of blood. Bathrooms not as private as one would suppose. Memory flashes of stylish parties. A Black employee who knows the inside horrors of the hotel, and protectively does not want anyone to go into a certain always-locked hotel room, and says as much, without anyone ever heeding him. The constant potential for fire. A window that might mean escape but might also mean death by fall. An MS which seems to be going capitally, but then may not be going so splendidly, after all. A creeping madness which finally lunges forward leaving the protagonist shaking and yelling like a Kabuki actor. The father and writer who ultimately becomes so incoherent that he swings and chases and smashes about the venerable and venereal hotel, and then dies. A film inspired by a work of Stephen King, though not by a screenplay authored by him. Elements that have the potential to be irresistible to any "true mystery and horror addict" among us.

So why has the aforementioned film—*1408,* directed by Mikael Hafstrom in 2007—no single academic study dedicated to it? Why are scenes from it not part of pop-culture consciousness, and why is the name of its protagonist,

Mike Enslin, obscure? How to explain why the Enslin Family remains unknown to the popular mind, while the Torrances of The Overlook haunt imaginations and all forms of international media? Kubrick's *The Shining*, sharing all the components introduced above with *1408*, inspires over a dozen critical volumes (by last count at Amazon and Google Books), along with hundreds of ever more inventive essays and even documentaries, all launched to air its riddles, raise its conspiracies, and enter and map its maze-like construction.

This is not to search and destroy *1408* for defects, or to quickly agree with Nicholas Adrian Prescott that its lead actor John Cusack was "offered too good a deal as an actor to refuse, and that he took the money and ran, . . . all in service of a film that you're likely to forget the moment the final credits' reflection fades from your eyeballs." In fact, Stephen King may not be simply unsuccessfully rehashing elements of *The Shining* in his *1408*, either. Audiences can admire *1408* as casually scary entertainment, even if it leaves few apparent horror-scars on viewers' minds. Many viewers must agree that *1408* is not mere repetition of the Kingly tropes because it earned $155 million at the box office against production costs of just $25 million (BoxOfficeMojo). We might enlarge the discussion to another film that Mary Findley closely interrogates in this volume that has many of those above elements, *Doctor Sleep*, the sequel to *The Shining*. We could ask why that film (costing $45–55 million just in production, without adding in its commercial campaign, and only earning a disappointing $72.3 million at the box office (*BoxOfficeMojo*) did not put a thorn of mystery in our hearts that we keep trying to dig out. For all of the millions spent on SFX to render the violence in both *1408* and *Doctor Sleep*, it might be difficult for many viewers asked to remember these films' most potent scene of threat (though admittedly some, like myself, might remember with disgust, and not so much terror, the True Knot's gang snuff-attack on the little baseball player for puffs of his expiring steam that they crave). Almost nostalgic to our eyes in its totally non-computer generated, wholly practical effects of violence, *The Shining*, like the TV adaptation of *It, Part I* in 1990, is still remembered and repeated in endless artifacts of our current culture, from animation, to games, commercials, operas, Halloween cakes (even some Divorce Party cakes). Jack's axe and the door he smashes and pushes his face through have a place in our imaginations that a winding dark stairway and long white fangs in *Dracula* have, or a laboratory and big black boots and neck bolts as in *Frankenstein*. If we were to ask viewers, what scene of violence was the most upsetting for them in *The Shining*, they might instantly raise at least three and then have to carefully choose the one. Was it the flood of elevator blood, the repeated sudden appearance of deceased twins,[1] or the scene where Wendy sobs but finally (and satisfyingly) whacks Jack with the bat, and Jack comes tumbling after?

Doubtless any scholar in this study on violence could offer ten critical pages of corroboration to show that *The Shining* is the most often cited movie of family horror, but that may not be necessary. It seems just as much a given as to say that Stephen King is still the living author most identified with carrying captive readers into the excesses and exhilaration and gory glories of modern horror. I find among my students that if I ask the origin of the line "Come out, come out wherever you are?" they do not say the fairy tale of a wolf and three little pigs, they do not say "Hide and Seek," they say, "Jack and Wendy from a bathroom in *The Shining*." The interest here is to offer some more unusual and less often cited reasons for *The Shining* to have such long reach in its terror—around the world and across generations and throughout media from cartoons like those obligatory riffs appearing on *The Simpsons, Bojack Horseman, South Park*, and *Bob's Burgers* (the episode "The Belching: A Masterpiece of Modern Burger" being my favorite) to a clutch of Pixar Movies either directed, produced, or co-written by Lee Unkrich or comedy skits like those of *Key & Peele* (Peele of *Get Out* fame) to commercials for Mountain Dew–No Sugar featuring Bryan Cranston, a terrified woman in a bathroom, an axe, and a flood of sickly green soda splashing out of the elevators and drowning the cameras. That does not begin to catalog all the filmic nods to *The Shining* in recent films of race, gender, or class-isolation, like, respectively, *Get Out, Sorry to Bother You*, and *Passengers*. I contend it is the way violence emerges in *The Shining* that aids the film's longevity and relevance for viewers and for filmmakers. Caitlin Duffy, in an appreciative evaluation of Noël Carroll's seminal *Philosophy of Horror; or, Paradoxes of the Heart*, notes that "Too often, critics will examine only the literature itself without asking why a certain genre is so popular and why, more specifically, horror and gothic plots are so continuously repeated and rewritten." I would like to engage with this under-asked question as applied to violence against one's will and against others' flesh in Kubrick's *The Shining*.

Some could argue, correctly I think, that the reason *1408* is not as remembered as *The Shining* is that it lacks struggle: its writer Mike Enslin is a numbingly popular one (his semi-formulaic series of books on haunted places are bestsellers). He is not fighting for attention for his art, and he has too much success, money, comfort, and power already to avoid seeming a little dull. Kubrick's nearly anonymous Jack Torrance never gets to that point: we know of no writing he has published, and in that fashion, he wisely contrasts with King's Torrance who has published in as notable a venue as *Esquire*. King's Torrance has at least the beginnings of a reputation to lose. Kubrick's Torrance has no writerly presence to lose at all. Enslin, however drab, is an author with a catalog of books in print, gives frequent bookstore readings, and has people seeking autographs and sending him mail. Jack, on the other hand, only has the opportunity of a lifetime in all those months to write a spectacular literary debut, or even a book of non-fiction about the crimes (and perhaps ghosts?) of the Overlook just as King's Jack threatens Ullman to do, or even a lucrative and unforgettable chiller like King's *The Shining* itself.

As this is a volume dedicated to the sources, operations, and revelations of violence in Stephen King's filmic adaptions—and characters' reactions to his body horror and mind terror—let us look inside the sublimely threatening nature of *The Shining* for its continued worldwide resonance. How does *The Shining* seed its violence in ways that can explain its captivating imaginations from Portland, Maine, to Portland, Oregon, and beyond? Physically and emotionally we all have immediate and traceable responses to violence in life and cinema. Anything that could harm us is always noticed first, and we can expect our pupils widening, mouths drying, adrenalin flowing, pulses quickening, and blood pressure rising. But *The Shining* is not satisfied in merely developing conventional scary-movie threats: it wants to play with us, and that engages our whole mind. It aims to shake us and the Torrances like rag dolls missing a couple of eyes: it masks its nature and unmasks it and masks itself again. The imagery of violence begins with Danny at its center. The ghosts make Danny their first target (mentally as early as his vision of a flood of elevator blood, and physically with the strangulation attempt of the woman said to be in Room 237). If the ghosts await Jack and Wendy's reaction to the "play" they have made of Danny's endangerment, then the film awaits us to signal when we would first bolt away from The Overlook and be Denver-bound. This Hotel and Kubrick both like to play chess, and like chess grandmasters, they have us and the Torrances as their pawns. Kubrick's first move (like the queen's gambit move in chess that gives up a piece to gain advantage later) is to allow the Torrances at first some sense of power: that a snowy time, a fantasy hotel, and complete privacy are all theirs, and that a healing bonding, a work-vacation of a lifetime, and a developed writing project are commencing. Perversely enough, rather than any of those wishes to come true, we in our theater seats find it far more intriguing to watch the ghosts playing and destroying all those dreamy expectations and the Torrances losing all their pieces.

There is an insightful line from legendary activist and polemicist Angela Davis where she concludes that slave cabins in American antebellum history were the one and only place that her ancestors were free from the master's gaze. Unfortunately, there is no such place for the Torrances, even if they should consider themselves to be free folk. It is the now-retired Pixar Director/Writer Lee Unkrich (who is also the Caretaker of TheOverlookHotel.com) who in discussing with me a preface for my anthology on Kubrick's *The*

Shining referenced a "spiking the camera" shot I never considered. After Wendy's understandable pleading that she and Jack take the half-throttled Danny down the mountain for care, and Jack's failed attempt to convince her or us that Danny's bruises must be proof that he has been busy trying to asphyxiate himself, Jack storms out. But as he angrily heads for the door, he shoots the corner of the room from where we are looking at him a direct hostile glance. It is a split-second look, and we imagine it says, "Do you see? Do you see the constant complaining I get from this irritating, skinny-assed, stupid, nickel-plated cold-cunt whining bitch I patiently endure year after year? Did it ever cross her mind for one moment that this could be the reason I can't *fucking* get my work done? *I'll be at the bar!*" The Gold Room bar is the place where we will see even more breaking of the Fourth Wall, and quasi-confessional takes with the ghosts. But this moment is an alarming one because it is an unfeigned communion inside one's bedroom with a sinister Hotel's denizens—where no one but your lover or spouse should be.

One of the surprises or omissions in *The Shining* scholarship, that critical land with mountains of illuminating studies along with widening torrents of strained conspiratorial readings, is how little research or thought goes into the ghosts' and the Hotel's psychology. If we were to assume both the ghosts and the Hotel have thoughts, agency, personalities, wishes, and drives, what would they be, and how would they act upon the Torrances? Roger Luckhurst, who has written so convincingly on trauma and torture, describes "the scenes around the events inside Room 237 [to be] the enigmatic core of the whole film" (57), and I would like to explore that room and the occupants further. Indeed, Luckhurst notes in talking of the twins, "can they really be Grady's daughters, who Ullmann states were eight and ten years old? Might they not signify something else, subliminally encoded? Of course! All ghosts are signs of broken story, and bear witness to silent wrongs" (47). Here I believe *The Shining,* as is appropriate for a film genre-challenger like Kubrick, fights the common trope of ghosts like, say, Hamlet's father, those spirits who wish to give a story of a contemptible crime, a free transgressor, and a plea that his son avenge him and kill his uncle. Nor do Kubrick's ghosts act like those of famed comic or dramatic films that came after his—from *Beetlejuice* (1988) to *The Others* (2001)—where the ghosts mostly want the incoming living new residents to get the hell out. Nor do Kubrick's ghosts act to promptly kill, either by a fright to our heart or a more direct, pre-emptive and physical assault.

WHAT DO THE GHOSTS WANT? TO COME
OUT AND PLAY JUST WITH YOU

Isaac Bashevis Singer once remarked that we may not believe in ghosts, but they believe in us, and even admitted to their presence in his Nobel Prize banquet speech. Singer also observed that that character analysis might just be the highest form of human entertainment, and if so, detecting the ghosts' motivation in *The Shining* might be said to be a worthy challenge to puzzle out. Maybe phantoms want too many things. Stanley Kubrick has argued himself that at least some of the ghosts present in the film are real in the sense they are not simply hallucinations of Jack, Wendy, and Danny. The revenants have agency. Indeed, when Michel Ciment asked Kubrick in 1980, "So you don't regard the apparitions as merely a projection of his mental state?" Kubrick unequivocally answered that, "For the purposes of telling the story, my view is that the paranormal is genuine. Jack's mental state serves only to prepare him for the murder, and to temporarily mislead the audience." The most obvious example that the paranormal is authentic in the film is how Kubrick and co-screenwriter Diane Johnson craft the scene where Grady can open the walk-in pantry lock behind whose heavy door the injured Jack has been stashed by Wendy. We quite clearly hear Grady taunting Jack for letting his family get the better of him, and we hear the unmistakeable click of the opened door. What slices deeper than the reality of the ghosts for the living characters, though, could be the film's question of gain from them. What violent arrangements by Jack can be secured through the paranormal realm? He wants the phantom alcohol they can bring to the bar, he wants to get even with his wife for holding a grudge, he wants to erase the past, and he is possessed enough by a past persona and with the idea of killing his family, that he can escape everything. Unconsciously or consciously, he wants the deep pleasure that he supposes comes, according to Laura Van den berg's own ghost novel of a widow who may have driven over her husband dead in *The Third Hotel* (2018): "The break, that exhilarating moment of long hoped for upheaval: that fulfillment of a sometimes avowed, sometimes disavowed desire to see power at last unmade, laid finally to waste and torn limb from limb—and our structures of dominion and domination replaced finally and forever with Utopia, if only for the already dead" (78). This hunger for another utopia also stems from the manipulation by the rich of the poorer as rigorously investigated by Fredric Jameson and Tony Magistrale. The ghosts of the rich are really asking Jack, What are you willing to do to get money, liberation, and women (other than Wendy, naturally)? Jack enters most fully into the ghostworld of the Roaring Twenties (instead of his son and wife, too), as Magistrale evinces, because Jack most wants what the 1920s offers adult male WASPS: booze, flappers, unquestioned freedom, and an embarrassment of riches without an embarrassment of one's (retreating) ethics. Pale penis privilege in a pink phallus palace. Just like The Overlook in its good old days! There is just this unstated question from the spectres that hover in the Gold Room: How fully will you let us exploit and manipulate and possess you, if you might get what you want? Phantomic promises to remedy his injured patriarchy and power—with "Perhaps a bit more," as Delbert Grady offers—seems one of the ghosts' best games of play in The Overlook, but the issue is deeper than this.

Horror literature records how ghosts love to infest the minds of the living—they possess them, they trick them, they mock and imitate them, they whisper to them, they awaken them in the middle of the night with a bump and a howl. Ghosts routinely make visitors to houses unhinged, as they have recently in Netflix remakes of both a Henry James ghost tale "The Turn of the Screw" (from *Doctor Sleep*'s director Mike Flanagan and retitled as *The Haunting of Bly Manor* in 2020) and a Shirley Jackson novel (again from Mike Flanagan with *The Haunting of Hill House* in 2018). The undissected heart of this question, though, is why they do this. It seems a truth universally acknowledged, to follow the logic of Jane Austen, that a Ghost in possession of a good hotel, must be in want of a Life, though few articles treat it. Some amusing articles are written by psychologists joking about what goes on with spectres. Writing for the professional journal *Association for Psychological Science,* Lisa Feldman Barrett and Daniel J. Barrett admit that "Scientists still know frighteningly little about the emotions of ghosts. Even trivial questions such as 'Do ghosts perceive fear?' are at an embarrassingly early stage of inquiry." But that question is one we can pursue. If ghosts have no longer a fear of death, is that something which, true to our perverse human nature, they begin to miss once it is gone? I would like to argue that it is, and that the missed emotion of fear is one factor, among others, that fuel ghostly interest and attentions on the Torrances.

If Jack wants his family dead, why does he not simply axe them to death in their sleep at night or during an afternoon nap, as proper madmen have done throughout history? Axe murderers can have a hard time catching victims, especially most or all of the members of a family, as the large weapon, the apparent lack of trees thereabout, and some grunting or drooling of the perpetrator tends to disclose motive prematurely. Thus in real life the victims are often dispatched by axe while in repose, as happened in these well-publicized American cases: to the prostitute Helen Jewett in New York City in 1836; the Harlson Family in Nebraska in 1878; the eight murdered servant girls in Austin from 1884–1885; the father and stepmother and a guest of the infamous Borden family in Fall River, MA; the six members of the Moore family and two houseguests in Villisca, Iowa in 1912; the five members of the Licata family in 1933; and the "scores of murders of entire families, committed from 1898 to 1912, occurring in Oregon, Kansas, Florida, Arkansas, and other American locations" which one team ascribes to serial killer Paul Mueller, the so-called "Man from the Train Murderer," who would use the blunt edge of an axe to bludgeon families as they slept in homes near railway junctions (Bill James and Rachel McCarthy James). After much searching, I can safely say that chasing people with an axe in the waking hours is a fairly rare attempt at slaughter in real American life, though a fat lot of good this crime fact does for Hallorann. Something is amiss and off-script from history in Jack's hunt. Still, heaving an axe around seems one way to let them know your murderous intent, your readiness for the kind of asylum Jack Nicholson found in *One Flew Over the Cuckoo's Nest* (1975) just five years before, and to enjoy some sadistic pleasure at seeing how prepared for a grave the family might be, to give them a taste for what body horror really is: not only the desecration of the physical but a torture of the mental, the reducing of people to unrecognizable, almost inhuman bits of flesh.

I would like to reconceptualize the idea, though, that the Torrances are simply becoming hollowed out and more like the ghosts, or at least one that Jack is. It seems that the ghosts are also becoming more like the Torrances. One of the questions in many ghost movies is whether the ghosts realize that they are deceased, or are they in a slow dance of puzzling out their deaths, as in *The Others* (2001) or in *The Sixth Sense* (1999) or even in *Carnival of Souls* (1962)? If The Overlook ghosts know—by hearing what is playing on the hotel's TV along with conversations of living guests during the resort's active season and with discussions of their death by the manager Stuart Ullman— that the Torrances are caretaking no earlier than 1978 (judging by the January 1978 date of the *Playgirl* Jack reads in the lobby), then at least some of these spirits must realize that they have died, and presumably they are no longer suffering the fear of death as mere mortals do. They may remember the hour of their death, the means of it, and how others properly mourned them, or did not, which often leads to the arrival of ghosts in literature and film. Perhaps these phantoms, like the rest of us and like many characters in King's fiction, simply want what they cannot have. They want to be alive in the way we are, which includes feeling the dread and fear that the living do, fierce emotions over how fragile our hold on life always is. Thus, the one thing ghosts do not suffer, assuming they are that kind that know of their death, is a fear of the unknown hour of death. If it is violence that the spectres do, it is (at least partially) all done in the name of being alive again. And who can blame anyone for wanting to be alive again? They are the sons and daughters of death, but they are longing for life itself—the stuff unpredictable, unscripted, unrepeating, and ripe with new possibilities and twists. These ghosts, without their favorite "caretaker here," move only in the depressingly fixed direction that many of King's most violent characters do: in "repetitive loops in which the future is only ever the reiteration of a self-destructive past" (Magistrale and Blouin 133). Screenwriters Kubrick and Johnson are suggesting there is some inability to imagine new things after death, a repetition-compulsion seemingly locks spirits into never escaping the old patterns they had in life. With the arrival of the Torrances after Closing Day, spectres start responding to their rhythms. The Torrances are moving this tortuous and inquisitive Hotel in some direction, as opposed to the typical reading that the Hotel constantly controls Jack.

Curious and distinctly distant from visitants' behavior in traditional literature and film, *The Shining* ghosts seem not to be obsessed with telling the whole of an untold story, redressing wrongs, sketching murders, or identifying perpetrators. They know the future has no cure for their past. They are not the traditional sort of ghoulies. They enjoy a soiree and want to see what new party favors the Torrances bring. Kubrick's 1980 interview with Vicente Molina Foix (not published in English until 2019) sheds pearly light on this ghostly difference or rupture from tradition. Kubrick vows, "Never attempt to explain what happens, as long as what happens stimulates people's imagination, their sense of the uncanny, their sense of anxiety and fear. . . . Be building on the imagination (imaginary ideas, surprises, etc.) . . . There's a great satisfaction when it's all over not having been able to have anticipated the major development of the story, and yet at the end not to feel that you have been fooled or swindled" (462). As we know, Stephen King claims to have felt swindled by the auteur's ending, junking it as a swipe from an original *Twilight Zone* episode (King does not specify, but we can imagine he means the mannikin-becomes-alive episode "The After Hours," written by Rod Serling, and airing first on June 10, 1960, almost 20 years earlier to the day before *The Shining's* debut). However, Kubrick himself recorded with glee the shock of New York audiences on seeing the photo of Jack on Independence Day and knew best to trim his ending back to a smiling tuxedoed Jack. Kubrick's changing the usual ghostly modus operandi keeps audiences awake, not letting us fall asleep on the old tropes as if upon a sofa of hoary horror. But in one way Kubrickian ghosts are traditional. They savor blood. For instance, one of the visions in Danny's head is of the twins butchered by an axe, but not stacked yet neatly in a guest room yet like a cord of wood as Ullman reported to in Jack's pro forma interview, so we see what blood would have awaited the hungry ghosts.

Once the blood of the latest residents starts to drip or splash in *The Shining*—with Jack whacked by the bat and falling down the stairs or cut by Wendy's butcher knife a bit later, and especially following the death-by-axe of Hallorann, the ghost activity rises. As Hallorann's blood congeals, the ghouls start chanting; Wendy sees skeletons; and spirits smile, toast, drink, and fellate. But Kubrick doesn't allow the revelry to go quite so far as we might wish, before we see Jack return as the real monster. The ghosts may well be imbibing what blood they find to more wildly activate themselves. They are thus like the ghosts of Homer's *Odyssey* (including Odysseus's mother) hungry for a taste of blood, or right up to the latest literary novel, like George Saunders' Booker Prize winning *Lincoln in the Bardo* (2017), largely populated and voiced by ghosts who are so conscious of the blood of the living. In Saunders' completely original narrative, even the Holy Ghost just wants blood: "What IT wants, it seems for now, is blood, more blood, . . . even as those three thousand fallen stare foul-eyed at me, working dead hands anxiously, asking, 'What end might this thing yet attain, that will make our terrible sacrifice worthwh—'" (Saunders 310). Indeed, in much of Saunders' fiction we spy hungry ghosts—in "The Wavemaker Falters" (1993), "Sea Oak" (1998), "Brad Carrigan, American" and "CommComm" (2005),"Esc ape from Spiderhead" (2010), and "Ghoul" (2020)—even if this author is always held in the highest literary sphere, and never ghettoized (or elevated in my eyes) by being shelved in the bookstore's "Horror Section." Like Saunders' ghosts, the phantoms of *The Shining* are more like real people—you can imagine how callous and casually dominating they were in real life by meeting them in death. Saunders, in mysterious, unsettling Kubrickian fashion, lets the ghosts have their say, and they often want blood. Indeed, in "CivilWarLand in Bad Decline," the ghosts follow *The Shining*'s lead by spying on the living, and even trying to intervene with the living (kiss them, give them punishing marital advice, shock them, and unite with them once the protagonist dies). The point is that the dead always rush to wherever blood is spilt, seem to sniff and dance at first in it, but in reality they are re-enacting the past of their slaughter, and then they beg for more. The blood is the life—for us in our world as it is for them in theirs. Like Mr. Grady, in Saunders' tale Mr. McKinnon sliced his wife and two daughters to bits, though McKinnon did it with a scythe. Quickened by the blood of the living and passing over the field where the family murders transpired over 100 years before, "He's shouting for forgiveness. He's shouting that he's just a man. He's shouting that war made him nuts. . . . The Mrs. starts screaming about the feel of the scythe as it opened her up. The girls bemoan their unborn kids" (Saunders 24). Like Jack, Mr. McKinnon aims to be absolved or forgiven of his wrong-doing at first and forswears alcohol after the primal injury to Danny which is the shadow over the book. But the shadow grows longer: when Danny's neck is bruised, Wendy's suspicious of Jack attacking him again ("You son of a bitch! You did this to him, didn't you? How could you?"), and the ghosts are standing by ready to serve, more than able to exploit an innocent Jack with his rage over being accused again. According to Jack's memory of the incident to Lloyd the Bartender, he yanked the "little bastard" he loves with a few pounds too much of pressure/inch a couple years before. It sounds like a physics problem to work out, and not the angry attack on a small child by a drunkenly wheeling parent out of control. Men suffering similar past humiliations over their behavior sometimes use a reframing of the incident as he does here, but in conjunction later with violence against Wendy to make her sob, to make her seem like she is the unstable one, now incapable of coherence or clear memory. How can a witness of trauma be accurate if she is crying and unable to utter her case on the stairway, Jack may ask with a sneer? Bashing women is routinely used as Jack plans, which Simon Winlow and Steve Hall found in their study of violent working-class men in the UK, to take "control of painful and humiliating memories, rewriting the past and rehabilitating the self from its previous failures." Besides this correspondence, what stuns us from Saunders' story is the news that everyone starts to "shine" once they die, seeing past, present, and future at once, as with the protagonist in "CivilWarLand in Bad Decline." When you die, according to Saunders, you possess "perfect knowledge":

> I hover above him as he hacks me to bits. I see his rough childhood. I see his mother doing something horrid to him with a broomstick. I see the hate in his heart and the people he has yet to kill before pneumonia gets him at eighty-three. . . . [And] I see the man I could have been, and the man I was, and then everything is bright and new and keen with love and I sweep through [my killer] Sam's body, trying to change him, trying so hard, and feeling only hate and hate, solid as stone. (Saunders 26)

If Jack Daniels signals the earthly waters of oblivion and release and forgiveness for Jack Torrance, the fresh blood of the Overlook's visitors announces memories, actions, and feelings to the ghostly denizens of that hotel—and they know what is going to happen in the end to Jack and to Wendy and Danny. We recall from chapter seven of Freud's *The Interpretation of Dreams* that the dead sipping blood in dreams and in *The Odyssey* are trying to recall who they were and who they were connected to and what they were doing—and blood allows them to articulate all this. Those urges are compared by Freud to living patients contending with what is contained in their unconscious as it bleeds out through hypnosis and their dreaming life. Less developed from Freud is the belief that their consuming blood or their act of dying lets them see into the future and into others' agonies. After his fateful wandering of the maze and freezing to death, who can say what Jack sees now inside us?

Fascinatingly, the ghosts in *The Shining* also seem to be energized by the blood in a sexual way.[2] By the time Halloran is axed to death but before

Wendy discovers his body, she will glimpse a gentleman (perhaps Kubrick's version of Harry Derwent who the film does not otherwise develop) gifted fellatio by a lover in a bear suit. Their door is oddly open for such an intimate moment, and while they seemed fairly occupied with each other, they do hold Wendy's gaze for a second longer than is decent, as if to float the suggestion of a three-way, to which she has not time as her wobbling knife and running away suggest. After this scene she discovers the body of Dick, and then running from that corpse, she is saluted by the flirty older gent of fractured skull in fine tux who looks at her with a leer and approvingly toasts, "Great party, isn't it?" Then she enters the room of the cobwebbed skeletal partiers still waiting for their champagne, and finally the elevators of blood nearly overcome her. The ghosts have really come out to play now. But have they have not been playing with the Torrances all along, especially in a voyeuristic way? Earlier, before any blood was spilled, the ghosts were watching and intruding upon Danny, taking heightened interest, Wendy surmises in the novel, due to his "shine or life-force or spirit" electrically powering the hotel out of "its old semi-sentient state" (King, *The Shining* 1022). In the same intense chapter of divided loyalties, Danny reaches to free the bolt that locks his father into the pantry at the same moment Wendy takes that small hand and "pressed it between her breasts," asking herself the haunting question: "If [the Overlook] absorbed Danny . . . into itself—what would it be then?" (1022). When Danny makes his circular, fated return to the snowy Overlook as a grown man in *Doctor Sleep*, his Mom's inescapable question is raised again: the spirits will still be there, along with his father as barman, and the Hotel gets a charge from him once more.

PLAY THE TORRANCES LIKE A VIDEO GAME

Survival Horror video games in their salient, *Shining*-like features have evolved from their earliest versions like *Sweet Home* (1989), *Alone in the Dark* (1992), the original *Resident Evil* (1996), *Silent Hill* (1999), *Resident Evil 4* (2005), *Stay Alive* (2006), *Dead Space* (2008), *Deadly Premonition* (2010), *Devotion* (2019), *Dreams* (based on *The Shining* film, 2019), to *Maid of Sker* (2020). Perhaps Kubrick's film in some ways anticipated the advent and directions of survival horror game craze by almost a decade, but these games also tell us something vital about the violence in *The Shining*, concentrating it to its barest elements. The games' plots can be simple, as in some ways *The Shining*'s plot is simple—just three living people in a haunted hotel slowly going crazy as the ghosts around them close in. So much of the history of the hotel is not revealed in Kubrick's version but savored and developed in King's, especially through the prologue and via the scrapbook.[3] In Survival

Horror video games very little is explained about the horror's origin, and the game can be enshrouded in the mist or snow or darkest night where the character can barely see what is hiding around them. Third, key in such games is that the avatar has (at least before the game-changing *Resident Evil 4* came out) very limited or crude weapons, and if the player has a gun, very little ammunition. Fourth, there are mazy corridors with limited escape. Last, a *Shining*-like feature is well explained by game designer Richard Rouse III: There is "a power imbalance of some kind where the forces of evil are vastly more powerful than those of the hero, making the eventual victory or survival of the hero all the more impressive" (224–225). It seems that the ghosts act both like game designers and game players in Kubrick's *The Shining*. They have inherited the plot of a haunted house and all the tropes that go with it from earlier novelists, but the revenants rise to the occasion by shaping the game with their own idiosyncratic dark designs.

Perhaps The Overlook ghosts, like the spectres in Steve Rasnic Tem's novel *Deadfall Hotel* (2012) where a caretaker and his daughter manage a hotel of ghouls and Ramsey Campbell's "The Entertainment" (1999) where a lost wanderer happens upon elderly people in an institution that grow phantomic and more demanding, mostly want to feel the pang of being alive again, and to carry on their Roaring Twenties party spirit with a few witnesses to show off their powers, and of course to harness any sensitive's spark to make everything come even more alive—and to be alive means to have the possibility of change. Feeding off fear is what they do, too. I notice how it is the play-obsessed eerie twins who are largely interested in Danny, for obvious reasons. They want a fellow kid to play with, and possibly torment by doing the torturous things little girls do to boys like hauling out dolls to play with, in their case possibly sprung from coffins. Mostly, the ghosts want to be entertained. This is their resort, and for them, there is no better season at The Overlook. Every ghost story seems to have both a bondage to and a breaking free from the constraints of merely chronological time. On the one hand, the ghosts seem cemented to the spot of their affairs and demise; on the other hand, they are visiting us, reappearing at no scheduled time, years and years after their traumas, but whichever the case we the living supply their viewing pleasure. Like a video game we play starring ghosts, they react to our steps, our defenses, and our eventual paths chosen. All the possibilities that open from our arrival make a break in the loop they exist in (and even if Jack is a re-incarnation for them, something new about his family develops every time he comes). Through the film we get a glimpse of the moral wilderness prevailing in The Overlook over decades of debauchery and cover-ups, but we are still like fresh visitors in awe of the puissance of the place, not knowing of *all* its depravities but wanting to. Possibly the Overlook shocked in its day as the mansions and pleasure islands of financier and pedophile Jeffrey Epstein and his procurer Ghislaine Maxwell do—along with their high-ranking guests in finance, science, royalty, and politics. When we look inside at Epstein's pleasure domes, at places in Miami where a French model scout Jean-Luc Brunel sent three twelve-year-old-triplets for Epstein as a gift to assault on his birthday (according to 2015 court records), when we consider what is left and what is torn away and what untold secrets the hidden cameras recorded in Mr. Epstein's blackmail treasury that flitter like ghosts wanting out, we get an Overlook shudder. We cannot resist writing on this Hotel. Against all good advice, we will keep stealing into rooms we were warned against, just like Danny.

NOTES

1. Joining the Shining Twins actresses Lisa and Louise Burns in 2015 at The British Library's most popular exhibition, "Terror and Wonder: The Gothic Imagination," and walking over to an Italian restaurant with them afterward, I had no idea how much they would teach me about ghosts and haunting that evening, concepts which feed this essay. The long dinner began with much chianti and concluded with a little limon-cello, and them standing on either side of me on the tube just before midnight (though I imagine myself steady, in fact, quite sober). They and their warm brown eyes left me with a question on that cool January night: "How do we know that you are not the ghost, wanting to dine with us forever and ever and ever?" The answer is maybe I am.

2. The everything's-for-sale and we-will-take-it-all ethos of "all the best people" whom The Overlook hosted is well-described in our own time by Jeffrey Epstein-accuser Virginia Roberts Giuffre in a civil suit brought by the U.S. Attorney's Miami office in 2015. Giuffre remembers that the Harry Derwent–styled Jeffrey bragged after he met them that they were 12-year-olds and flown over from France because they're really poor over there, and their parents needed the money or whatever the case is and they were absolutely free to stay and flew out. He was so excited about the entire event, replayed over and over again over the next course of weeks how cute they were and how you could tell they were really young. Laughing the whole way through, Jeffrey thought it was absolutely brilliant how easily money seduced all walks of life, nothing or no one that couldn't be bought (*New Zealand Herald*).

3. The horrors of *The Shining* also comprise what you don't see. What sits with Jack besides an ashtray and Kubrick's own manual typewriter on that massive writing table is The Overlook's Scrapbook, so deeply revealed in King's novel and barely glimpsed in Kubrick's film, an ominous but barely understood presence. We remember King's Scrapbook of gangland-style murders, rich women's half-covered up suicides, and other notorious tragedies. However, the film's Scrapbook prop covers other sorts of crime beyond high society. Surprising few analyses of the Scrapbook exist, besides a short article that its former director Richard Daniel wrote for an English newspaper and BFI, along with an illuminating 2020 piece by Ian Christopher for

SensesofCinema.com. However, Director Daniels' staff took out the Scrapbook for me to read one afternoon inside the University of Arts-London's Stanley Kubrick Archive. The distressing surprise I found was that approximately half of the stories record the deaths of children, and most of the articles are copies from Colorado newspapers between the 1920s and 1940s. There are other stories—some of the pasted in articles are about World War II attacks (the Allied bombing of Turin's industrial base, for example). Some are about civilian killings of adults over money or under the influence of drugs or alcohol. Some articles are mere inventions, too. But many more of the depressing stories I read were of teenage and younger children dying by murder, neglect, including freezing to death, starving, contagious disease, fires caused by arson or themselves or untended heaters, abduction, and parental abuse. Scenes with Jack examining the Scrapbook for murderous inspiration were dropped from *The Shining*. However, the last few pages of the Scrapbook are empty, nine or so. They are still waiting for us to fill them in.

WORKS CITED

1408 (2007). *BoxOfficeMojo*. Accessed 1 Nov. 2020.

Barrett, Lisa Feldman, and Daniel J. Barrett. "What Do Ghosts Feel?" *Association for Psychological Science,* 30 September 2016, https://www.psychologicalscience.org/observer/what-do-ghosts-feel. Accessed 5 Nov. 2020.

Doctor Sleep (2019). BoxOfficeMojo. Accessed 1 Nov. 2020.

Duffy, Caitlin. Rev. of *The Philosophy of Horror or Paradoxes of The Heart* (1990), 9 July 2018, https://caitlinduffy.hcommons.org/2018/07/09/the-philosophy-of-horror-or-paradoxes-of-the-heart-1990/. Accessed 2 Nov. 2020.

Edgeworth, Maria. *Harry and Lucy Concluded.* Publishers R. Hunter, Baldwin, Cradock, & Joy, 1825.

James, Bill, and Rachel McCarthy James. *The Man from the Train: The Solving of a Century-Old Serial Killer Mystery*. Scribner, 2017.

Jameson, Fredric. "Historicism in *The Shining*." *The Shining: Studies in the Horror Film*, Deluxe Slipcased Hardbound Edition, edited by Danel Olson, Centipede Press, 2016. 73–90.

King, Stephen. *Three Novels: Carrie, 'Salem's Lot, The Shining*. 1974, 1975, 1977, Penguin, 2011.

Kubrick, Stanley. "11-Minute Interview with Stanley Kubrick Discussing 'Barry Lyndon,' 'The Shining' & 'Full Metal Jacket' with Michel Ciment." *IndieWire*, 1987, https://www.indiewire.com/2013/03/listen-11-minute-interview-with-stanley-kubrick-discussing-barry-lyndon-the-shining-full-metal-jacket-100799/, Accessed 1 Nov. 2020.

———. "An Interview with Stanley Kubrick," by Vicente Molina Foix. *The Stanley Kubrick Archives*, edited by Alison Castle. Taschen, 2019. 460–63.

Luckhurst, Roger. *The Shining: BFI Classics.* Palgrave, 2013.

Magistrale, Tony. "Sutured Time: History and Kubrick's *The Shining*." *The Shining: Studies in the Horror Film*, Deluxe Slipcased Hardbound Edition, edited by Danel Olson. Centipede Press, 2016. 153–166.

Magistrale, Tony, and Michael J. Blouin. *Stephen King and American History.* Routledge, 2020.

NZH Staff, "12-year-old French Triplets Allegedly Flown to Epstein as a 'Birthday Present'." *New Zealand Herald,* 12 Aug. 2019, https://www.nzherald.co.nz/world/12-year-old-french-triplets-allegedly-flown-to-epstein-as-a-birthday-present/S2XRZ4F3KQVVKCGHVCTNDXCXOE/.

Prescott, Nick. Rev. "*1408*, directed by Mikael Hafstrom." Flinders University, 22 Nov. 2007, https://dspace.flinders.edu.au/xmlui/bitstream/handle/2328/8044/Prescott_1408.pdf?sequence=3&isAllowed=y. Acc. 5 Nov. 2020.

Rouse III, Richard. "Match Made in Hell: The Inevitable Success of the Horror Genre in Video Games." *Horror Video Games: Essays on the Fusion of Fear and Play*, edited by Bernard Perron. McFarland, 2009.

Saunders, George. *CivilWarLand in Bad Decline: Stories and a Novella*. Random, 1996.

———. *Lincoln in the Bardo*. Random, 2017.

The Shining. Dir. Stanley Kubrick. Warner Bros., 1980. DVD.

Van den berg, Laura. *The Third Hotel.* FSG, 2018.

Winlow, Simon, and Steve Hall. "Retaliate First: Memory, Humiliation and Male Violence." *Crime, Media, Culture*, 5.3, 2009. 285–304.

Chapter 8

Tempered Violence in Frank Darabont's Adaptations of Stephen King

The Shawshank Redemption *and* The Green Mile

Maura Grady

Two of the most critically successful film adaptations of King's work, *The Shawshank Redemption* (Frank Darabont, 1994) and *The Green Mile* (Frank Darabont, 1999), have been embraced by mainstream audiences often unaware that King is the source or who insist these works are "uncharacteristic" of King because they lack the expected horrific elements. Though writer/director Darabont is himself a creator in the horror genre (Gooden),[1] both films notably diverge from King in how they depict acts of violence onscreen, aligning with early pre-Code (1930–34)[2] horror films which tried to straddle the line between terror and restraint.[3] Adopting a suggestive, more Expressionistic approach[4] allows Darabont to elide some of King's more disturbing and polarizing choices in these prison stories that skirt divisive issues like systemic racial injustice and sexual violence. Darabont attempts to create emotionally satisfying, apolitical crowd-pleasers by smoothing out the grislier edges of King's textual violence to emphasize the stories' humanistic themes—in *Shawshank*, it is that redemption is possible even for a flawed human being and in *Green Mile*, that capital punishment is inhumane no matter how kind the men are who deliver it. King is straightforward in his critique of the practice of execution, describing the actions of the doctor present at an electrocution as hanging back during the event: "Nowadays I guess they just about run such affairs . . . but maybe back then they had a clearer idea of what was right for a doctor to be doing and what was a perversion of the special promise they make . . . to do no harm" (King, *GM* 506). Darabont withholds direct critiques such as this, instead relying on the audience's sympathy with those tasked with execution to suggest the damage of capital punishment without directly condemning it.

Darabont emphasizes violence largely through its visual *absence*, pulling away at the most graphic moments, focusing on individuals operating within an inhumane system in order to emphasize the personal, human drama the violence represents. Some critics have derided Darabont's films as sentimental, but audiences have largely embraced his rejection of cynicism in favor of old-fashioned cinematic comfort food. His beloved King adaptations may have landed well with audiences[5] because, as Tony Magistrale notes, King's "published work is readily suited for presentation on the screen because he writes extremely visual, action-centered narratives" (*HSK* xvi). King uses stomach-churning descriptions of violence, supplying his reader with cinema-like images of torture, suffering, and depravity. In adapting King's work, horror craftsman[6] Darabont omits King's more graphic instances of violence. Commenting on adapting King, Darabont has said: "Stephen is a very old-fashioned storyteller, in the best sense of being old fashioned. Aside from character and absorbing narrative, he has one hell of a knack for suspense, as he's proven time and again. I may be the first person in history that draws a parallel between Stephen King and Frank Capra, but there's a real thread of humanity and humanism in King's work" ("On Adapting Stephen King"). Darabont clearly admires King's work[7] yet the contrast in the depiction of violence is clear, begging the question: why would Darabont "tone down" excessive visceral violence in the adaptations? Is it just to satisfy a mainstream audience? These King adaptations *are* "old-fashioned," brimming with nostalgia for classic film forms, for the periods in which the films are set, and for the kind of slower paced character study that doesn't get made much anymore (Grady and Magistrale 193).[8] It may therefore be productive to think about Darabont's work as a deliberate throwback to these older forms. Pre-Code horror films shocked audiences in the early sound era but appear tame to today's viewers. Though Darabont has not made a direct comparison to *Frankenstein* in talking about these films, there is a strong affinity, especially given that he wrote the screenplay for *Mary Shelley's Frankenstein* (Kenneth Branagh 1994), though he later disavowed the project.[9]

Where King leans into disturbing imagery of and commentary on the violence and sadism of his characters, Darabont leaves more of these details to the imagination, suggesting them through settings used expressionistically. The two prisons used in these films, Ohio State Reformatory (OSR) and Tennessee State Prison (TSP), were built within a few years of each other and boast stunning architecture that evokes early cinematic horror.[10] Mark Kermode describes OSR's imagery "like the lair of some vampiric count" (Kermode 46). TSP is reminiscent of Frankenstein's castle with its central turret, vertical rise and centered location in the frame. The haunting settings work to convey the violence in each story. OSR's gothic architecture has been commented on by numerous scholars as a key element of *Shawshank*, with Mark Kermode calling it "one part cathedral, two parts Castle Frankenstein" (18). Actor Bob Gunton (Warden Norton) felt that OSR "became an unspoken character. It was always looking over our shoulder, standing in our way. Breathing the history of all the lifers that had walked in and never walked out. . . . It just was a place of desolation and it was very daunting . . . I got the heebie-jeebies" (Grady and Magistrale 34). *Green Mile's* TSP also fits the comparison to the gothic imagery of *Frankenstein* and *Bride of Frankenstein*. Crucial scenes in both films feature electrical storms during the dead of night. These underscore the connection to *Frankenstein* but also create a gothic otherworldliness associated with both structures.

Darabont uses melodramatic tropes to gain audiences' emotional investment, directing attention to the affective, rather than the visceral impact of these moments. Much like pre-Code horror, Darabont's films are "strong on atmosphere and minimize overt violence, its implicit presence [is] in the morbid story situations" (Prince loc. 1233). In *Classical Film Violence: Designing and Regulating Brutality in Hollywood Cinema*, Stephen Prince argues that when horror's violence is overt, "it assume[s] blatantly cruel forms, mixed with sadism and torture" (loc. 1239). King explicitly describes violent acts, but Darabont's filmmaking adheres to the edict of early sound horror—relying on subtext and viewers' imaginations over explicit visual depictions of cruelty and violence, with sound used to convey and punctuate violent action: Prince argues the then-new sound technology of the late '20s and early '30s allowed filmmakers to "aesthetically stylize acts of cruelty and violence to make [them] vivid and disturbing at a new and evocative sensory level" (loc. 992), conveying suffering and pain without the use of expressly disturbing images.

Prince asserts pre-Code films were replete with violence, albeit indirect or offscreen. *Frankenstein*'s implied or depicted acts of violence include corpses dug up from the grave and cut from the gallows then stitched together and reanimated, a child being drowned, a man hanged, another man strangled, and characters burned alive (loc. 1234–5). Yet, these very acts of violence and others like them which were featured in early horror films and frightened contemporary audiences are remarkable for their *inability* to move modern audiences. Since the end of the Production Code era in 1968, audiences have become far less adept at reading the subtext that had been necessary when so much had to be expressed indirectly to meet the requirements of the Code. Today, if an act is meant to have happened in the story, audiences usually expect to *see* it. Darabont's omissions indicate he believes modern film audiences are less likely to be deeply terrified or moved by a similarly graphic

Tennessee State Prison. The Green Mile, *Dir. Frank Darabont. Castle Rock Entertainment,*
1999. DVD. Screenshot captured by author.

series of images. In *Shawshank*, horror is being trapped for a lifetime in a
prison filled with violence and injustice. In *The Green Mile*, it's knowing that
human beings who may be innocent, kind, and even Christlike can nonetheless be executed in a gruesome manner by the State.[11]

Modern audiences might expect greater explicit depictions of what is
described in King's novels but, despite existing in a culture that has assimi-
lated increasingly violent forms of entertainment, these two adaptations have
been embraced by mainstream audiences who do not necessarily consider
themselves horror fans and whose motivations in seeking out these films are
likely different than those who hurry to the cineplex for the latest slasher
movie. This division in expectations has long been a part of the critical discussion of King's canon, since "Hollywood producers will often downplay
[King's] connection to a 'mainstream film' in order to avoid typecasting a
movie that does not belong to the 'horror genre'" (Magistrale, *HSK* xiv).
Shawshank Redemption and *The Green Mile* are popular mainstream films,
nominated for multiple awards and starring acclaimed Hollywood actors.
They do not easily fit into the same genre of "scary movie" as *Cujo, IT,* or *The
Mist* and owe more to the indirect and subtle depictions of violence seen in an
earlier era. Darabont pays homage to those horror heroes of the 1930s, creating films that unnerve without jump scares or Rick Baker make-up, relying
on audiences' ability to *imagine* the horrors perpetrated by human monsters
on their fellow human beings, rather than needing to *see* each gruesome act.
As a result, the films' morals are likely felt to carry spiritual and emotional
depth. This is why these films, despite their disturbing scenes of and allusions

The Ohio State Reformatory. The Shawshank Redemption, *Dir. Frank Darabont.*   *Castle Rock Entertainment, 1994. DVD. Screenshot captured by author.*

to violence, are beloved by audiences who are responding to the emotional resonance of human resilience or kindness in the face of injustice, rather than the thrills provided by onscreen violence.

Prince notes that cuts required by censorship bodies in the early 1930s likely made films more disturbing and Darabont can be seen deploying this strategy. In *Shawshank*, the most sustained violent scene is early on in the film. The cold and calculating brutality of the Shawshank power structure is established quickly when, with a nod, Warden Norton orders the head guard, Byron Hadley, to assault a new prisoner who asks a question about mealtimes. This act of violence is squarely in frame. Soon after, the threat of Shawshank Prison is solidified through Hadley's fatal beating of fresh fish "Fat Ass." In this scene, DP Roger Deakins' camera is restrained, shooting the action in a long-shot. The violence and its impact are conveyed through the sound of the blows hitting the body, Hadley grunting with the force of the exertion. The reactions of the seasoned inmates who we might expect to be hardened by now also conveys the horror of the violence: longtime prisoner Heywood's regret at having goaded Fat Ass into crying and Red's silent 1,000-yard stare indicate to the audience the true horror of the situation. The cumulative effect of later beatings (prisoner-to-prisoner and guard-to-prisoner) build on that traumatic moment on Andy's first night.

Prince cites film censors' use of the phrase "unacceptably gruesome" numerous times and notes two genres most "rife with instances of brutality and violence" were horror films and crime films, genres which aptly describe our two films. He argues it is necessary to "disentangle violence, implicit and overt, from . . . other elements" such as references to offscreen violence (loc. 778), giving examples like *Frankenstein*'s monster's scars and sutures, which

Castle from Young Frankenstein. Young Frankenstein, *Dir. Mel Brooks. Gruskoff/ Venture Films, Crossbow Productions, 1974. DVD. Screenshot captured by author.*

allude to grisly work done offscreen that is "saturated with violence" even though we must "infer its presence from the artifacts it has left behind" (loc. 818), such as the marks left on the monster. In a similar way, John Coffey's scars, noticed by Melinda Moores ("who hurt you so badly?") imply the acts of violence he endured offscreen, coaxing the audience to accept that the life-long violence he has experienced leads to his relief at facing death. Coffey's scars and silence about them have left the audience to question the horrors he has suffered. The fact that Coffey does not seem to remember these acts might suggest that he carries no lasting trauma from them, but this is belied by Coffey's actions and words following Del's execution. The pain Del experiences is equally felt by Coffey, as Darabont intercuts scenes of Del's botched execution with shots of Coffey in his little cell crying out in agony with every infliction of pain, calling out with every flip of the switch of the current to the electric chair.

Acts of violence onscreen such as this are more terrifying when audiences see "the delight and pleasure that the tormentor takes in his action" (Prince loc. 846). The sinuous cruelty of Mark Rolston's prison rapist Bogs amplifies the fear the audience has for Andy and intensifies the acts of violence Bogs commits chiefly offscreen. Likewise, sadistic *Mile* guard Percy's deliberate and calculated acts of cruelty against the Mile's inmates are intensified by his smugly vicious attitude. Darabont draws attention to Bogs' physicality in a shower scene added for the film, the camera focused on his muscular upper body, as he confronts a naked Andy. Making Andy look vulnerable onscreen is challenging given Tim Robbins's height of 6'5'" (King describes Andy as diminutive), so when Bogs approaches Andy in the shower, Darabont empha-sizes Andy's lankiness and nakedness. The scene's music is ominous, a minor

Figure 8.4 Frankenstein Castle. Frankenstein, Dir. James Whale. Universal Pictures, 1931. DVD. Screenshot captured by author.

key variation on the musical theme used when Andy first enters Shawshank. The sexual assault is neither shown nor named by any character in the storeroom scene where Andy is first cornered by the "Sisters." The camera tracks away as we *hear* Bogs unbuckle his belt as he stands behind Andy, who continues to be beaten. Red's voiceover narration reinforces what is not being shown: "I wish I could tell you that Andy fought the good fight, and the Sisters let him be. I wish I could tell you that—but prison is no fairy-tale world." In the novella, Red relates to the reader that he too has been likewise victimized and waxes philosophical about gang rape: "It rips you up some, but not bad—am I speaking from personal experience, you ask?—I only wish I weren't. You bleed for a while. If you don't want some clown asking if you started your period, you wad up a bunch of toilet paper and keep it in the back of your underwear until it stops. . . . No physical harm done, but rape is rape and eventually you have to look at your face in the mirror and decide what to make of yourself" (King, *RHSR* 18). King is direct about the multiple sexual assaults Andy and others have endured, as Red's "advice" indicates that this happens often enough to warrant a procedure for dealing with it, but Darabont leaves the exact circumstances vague in the film to avoid a more visceral response by the audience.

Provoking a visceral audience response is frequently the explicit goal of horror, but how to achieve it is not always straightforward. Prince argues "an understanding of violence needs to include both . . . referent and style" since the early horror filmmakers began "exploring the camera set-ups, lens choices, lighting effects, editing choices, and sound designs that could accentuate moments of brutality and grotesquerie and make them more sensual as cinema and more emotional for viewers to experience" (loc. 859). Taking King's written word and embodying it with movement and sound means that Darabont can do more with less. The film does not require King's words be followed to the letter in order to instill the required horror. Pre-Code horror films, tame by today's standard, were easily approved at the script stage because the actual acts of violence *as described* on paper did not alarm censors. But once rendered on screen with moving pictures and sound, the cumulative impact of the scenes was evident.

Shawshank's popularity with mainstream audiences on home video and later cable television[12] illustrates the success of Darabont's strategy, which emphasizes the humanity of its main characters over the brutality of the actions done to them. King describes the murders of Andy's wife Linda and her lover Glenn Quentin in the manner of a court transcript, i.e., rather clinical and detached but explicitly detailed. Darabont presents the crime as a flashback intercut with scenes from the night of the murder with scenes/voiceover of the Prosecutor presenting his closing arguments. Neither the lovers' sex act nor the murder itself is depicted onscreen, just described by the prosecutor. What we do see is the moment the lovers engage each other in Quentin's cabin. It is a highly erotic visual, quite the opposite of the gun violence Blatch will soon bring to them offscreen. Nor are the rapes and murders for which John Coffey is convicted in the *Green Mile* depicted on screen; instead Paul Edgecomb learns of the details of Coffey's alleged crime (actually committed by Wild Bill) from the file that the guards on the Mile are given when the new prisoner arrives. The crimes of the Mile's other inmates are neither described nor depicted. Audiences' ability to absorb violent acts on film vs. on the page was likely a consideration—too many violent scenes might risk alienating or disorienting the audience. Darabont keeps his powder dry for those scenes that illustrate the heartless sadism of his films' villains who delight in cruelty, and even then, these scenes are relatively tame by modern standards of onscreen violence. The violence of Coffey's execution is shown chiefly through the supernatural knock-on effects—the explosion of the lights during the electrocution. Prince notes violence can be depicted in ways other than explicit brutality, torture, or bodily harm. Much of *Shawshank's violence is more subtle—the threat of future violence and the reminder of past violence and in The Green Mile* far more is suggested than explicitly shown. A solo shot of the electric chair in *Green Mile* suggests an unknown number of acts of brutal violence. Darabont never depicts the molestation and murder of the little girls, instead focusing on the physical capture of John Coffey by the armed posse, itself a terrifying spectacle to anyone familiar with America's history of unlawful lynchings. Without synchronized sound, *Green Mile* shows us Coffey, seated on the ground, being slapped and screamed at by a man inches from his face as Coffey looks justifiably terrified.

In both novel and film, we see three executions carried out, starting with Arlen Bitterbuck, the first electrocution that Percy witnesses as a member of the Green Mile staff. This execution, though it goes relatively smoothly, is nonetheless horrific due to the heavy breathing of the prisoner as he is masked and strapped in to "Old Sparky." Prior to this, the top of his head has been shaved and he shares a quiet moment with Paul. The quiet dignity of Graham Greene's performance emphasizes Bitterbuck's humanity, thus rendering his death all the more shocking. What is most disturbing about this sequence is not the death sentence being carried out, but Percy's voyeuristic glee in watching it. In contrast to the other guards and the switch operator who watch solemnly and clearly struggle to maintain their composure, Percy peeks through the barrier separating the switch and the rest of the room with a look of sadistic delight.

Darabont's depiction of the execution of Eduard "Del" Delacroix is far less graphic than King's description of melting flesh and sliding eyeballs, but it is rendered more horrific by the audience's knowledge of Percy's intent to make Del suffer, putting both "sting and spectacle" into the death, the most graphic act of violence in the film. We had seen in the "successful" execution of Bitterbuck that the electrocution victim physically convulses, screams, and is in pain. Percy's cruelty was already evident when he humiliated Bitterbuck's corpse post-execution, slapping his face and saying "Adios, Chief. Drop us a card from Hell and let us know if it's hot enough." Knowing that Percy deliberately plotted to cause additional suffering renders Del's botched execution horrifying, even though it is less graphic than King depicts in writing. King writes that Percy "looked mean," noting "meanness is like an addicting drug and . . . Percy had gotten hooked on it" (King, *GM* 270). Prior to Del's execution in the film, Percy's words are devastatingly cruel, dashing Del's dreams of fame and happiness for his mouse Mr. Jingles. Percy deliberately ignores the protocols which require a wet sponge between the victim's head and the electricity. The switchboard operator, Van Hay, had told Percy that a wet sponge on the head "conducts the electricity directly to the brain—fast like a bullet. You don't ever throw the switch on a man without that." In the novel, Paul narrates "Percy was a good student when he was doing something he cared about . . . Oh yes, Percy knew exactly what he was doing" (King, *GM* 291–2) and Darabont conveys this by showing Percy approach the water bucket and deliberately omit the soaking of the sponge. King describes the disastrous execution in detail and in this one sequence, Darabont comes closer to matching the imagery. An animatronic puppet is used in the film to depict Del's body——itconvulses, smokes, and bursts into flames. Most telling in King's novel and the film is the reaction of the witnesses, who go from celebrating that "Satan's imps are waiting" for Del to rushing the exits in horror at the sights, sounds, and smells of the execution. Darabont clearly depicts the violent nature of Del's death but keeping the black hood on Del spares the audience the grislier details that King includes, like "a large hot section of [Del's] skin simply slid away from the flesh beneath" (King, *GM* 299). Instead, sound amplifies the horror; Darabont wanted the sound of the chair to be terrifying: "I wanted it to sound like a beast that was unleashed . . . like there was a beast in the machine . . . little high-pitched shrieks . . . I wanted it to sound like a beast released from Hell" (Blu-Ray audio commentary 45–46:00).[13]

Throughout the film, the execution routine is repeated multiple times with the same familiar images—the careful polishing and cleaning of Old Sparky, the sweeping and clearing of the execution chamber (essentially a storage shed when not in use), the setting up of the chairs in neat rows for witnesses—looking more like a church service than the state-ordered murder of a human being. During Del's botched electrocution in the novel, King describes Del's eyes as "nothing but misshapen globs of white filmy jelly had been blown out of their sockets and lay on their cheeks" (King, *GM* 296). Darabont focuses attention away from stomach-churning visuals and onto the soul-wrenching tragedy by making a few key decisions—Del's mask stays on his face, preventing us from seeing what the electric current is doing to his flesh and on the horrified looks of the guards (even Percy) and the witnesses (even the woman hoping that Satan's imps were waiting). The horror also comes, as in the pre-Code films, from the *sounds*. We hear a cacophony of Del's screams of pain, electric current, thunder, rain, screams, running feet, and Van Hay shouting over it all: "Should I kill the juice?" Darabont intercuts these sounds from the scene of the execution sounds of exploding lightbulbs on the Mile, Coffey's anguished screams of pain as he feels what is happening to Del, and Wild Bill's shouts of "he's frying now!" as he trashes his own cell. Darabont intercuts images of Del's convulsions with Coffey's in parallel. Positing a raging storm outside as an objective correlative to the horrors inside the building is older than cinema itself, Mary Shelley's novel *Frankenstein* serving as a prominent example. As in *Public Enemy*, "the heavy rain adds an undercurrent of visual energy to the scene with its steady roar on the soundtrack and the reflective light effects of the falling water" (Prince loc. 1415).

Darabont fosters empathy with criminal characters by showing their suffering but also by omitting information about them. When Del is being helped into the chair, Paul thinks to himself, as King's narrator notes: "The fact that [Del] had killed a half-dozen people seemed at that moment the least important thing about him" (King *GM* 287). As with *Shawshank*, in which Darabont withholds the specifics of all the inmates' crimes except Andy's (who is innocent), the film *Green Mile* gives only vague information on the crimes of

Bitterbuck, Delacroix, and even Wild Bill. Darabont as a storyteller is uninterested in those details, seemingly agreeing with King's implication that they are less important than other aspects of these characters. It is the humanity of these flawed men that Darabont emphasizes, depicting despicable characters with some empathy.

The films are very different in tone due to the degrees of violence they depict. The ending of *Shawshank* (both the novella and the film) is exuberant and triumphant, since Red and Andy both escape from Shawshank to end up in a sunny paradise, "a warm place with no memory" with hope for a future of freedom and friendship. *The Green Mile* ends tragically, with the protagonist cursed to continue living an increasingly lonely existence as his loved ones die as his "punishment for letting John Coffey ride the lightning." Red is guilty of one act of violence that could have destroyed his humanity, but finds Redemption through endurance and by emulating Andy's seditious example. He finds a way to survive in prison until he comes in contact with the man that helps him learn to hope again. Paul's living is earned through violence, and though he consistently strives to mitigate that violence through kindness and decency to those around him, he is a cog in a legal but violent machine that brings him in contact with one of God's "true miracles." King and Darabont both avoid an overt condemnation of capital punishment, but some critique of the penal system is vident: human beings are both agents and victims of cruelty. Darabont leaves us in suspense about the guilt of Coffey and Andy for a substantial portion of both films, but he makes sure that we don't need to know these men are innocent to know that the system they find themselves in is violently unjust. We don't need to ignore the guilt of Red, Brooks, Bitterbuck, and Del to know that they are human beings. Darabont's implication is that the American justice system is fully corrupted because there is nothing to ensure humane treatment of inmates other than the choices of individuals to enact or withhold violence. The fate of the men caught up in the system is entirely at the whims of individuals employed by the State. If good men with compassion are in control, executions go smoothly. When evil men are in charge, there is no check on their power. Andy Dufresne uses his intelligence, ingenuity, and persistence to escape and to better the condition of his fellow inmates by building a library, but there is no indication that anything at Shawshank Prison will fundamentally change. Paul's kindness and compassion cannot save John Coffey. As Paul is giving the order to flip the electricity on Coffey, he shakes Coffey's hand and remembers Coffey's words: "they kill them with their love. That's how it is every day. All over the world." The film does not suggest that Coffey's sacrifice will change anything about the cruelty of the world. Although Paul leaves the Mile after Coffey's death, someone else will remain in charge of executions and though

Andy's ledger leads to the death of the Warden and arrest of Hadley, there is no indication that anything will fundamentally change in Shawshank Prison.

Though there have been other artistically successful interpreters of King's work, Darabont perhaps holds the distinction of adapting King's work into films that are not just admired but are adored by general audiences as well as King fans. Arguably, Darabont does such a skillful job with King's work that viewers attribute to King elements that were strictly Darabont touches, and sometimes even King views Darabont's choices as improvements over his own writing.[14] In the case of these two films, Darabont's techniques of scaling back overt acts of violence and humanizing criminal characters perhaps offers a sharper critique of the justice system than King. Darabont gives his audience Frank Capra–style feelings for men victimized by the prison system and by doing so, Darabont amends these King texts in order to salvage and preserve King's humanist architecture which may have otherwise been obscured by the more gluttonous violence of the texts. And yet, Darabont's efforts to fully humanize King's characters by eliminating grisly violence against them ironically erases some of their most definitive suffering—racial violence and trauma—and this gesture by Darabont serves to excuse the audience from the discomfort of acknowledging the significant racism in both narratives. In other words, erasing visual violence in the pre-Code style costs Darabont greatly, because the end result is an apolitical, ahistorical film that dehumanizes those he most wishes to humanize.

A close comparison of the parallels between Whale's monster and John Coffey illustrates the ways *Green Mile* participates in dehumanizing racist tropes even as it attempts to humanize its characters. Coffey's extraordinary height, the torture he has endured, the misunderstanding he faces when his size and gentleness are mistaken for monstrousness all align him thematically with Whale's creation, and though we are meant to sympathize with actor Boris Karloff's creature, comparing a Black man to a monster is at best problematic and could be one trade-off of utilizing older film tropes. The audience is asked to identify with the abuse and torture Coffey has endured in the past so that we accept his wish for death, rather than see it, as Spike Lee does, as "old grateful slave shit" (Kent 119). In his execution scene, Darabont omits more violent aspects of Coffey's execution by focusing on the humane and grief-stricken reactions of the guards surrounding him at his death. Although it may have been Darabont's intention to humanize Coffey by focusing on the emotion instead of the visceral harm, the unintended result is that the audience is left feeling more acutely the pain of the guards than that of Coffey. Instead of feeling the torment of the Black body being murdered, we feel the much lesser torment of guilt by the white guards.

To his credit, Darabont has made efforts to minimize the most egregious articulations of racism from King's book, but cannot fully erase it in this adaptation without dramatically altering the central narrative. Whether this film should have been adapted at all is a question best left to others, but we have to conclude that despite Darabont's efforts to temper King's racialized language, it is impossible to fully subvert "overt and omnipresent racism . . . where John Coffey is a black Christ doomed despite his innocence as a result of being a black man associated with the murders of two white girls in the Deep South" (Grady and Magistrale 138). Darabont omits much of the racialized language King uses throughout his book to refer to Coffey. The word "nigger" is used four times in the film, by three characters in the film, all of them overtly racist (Percy, Wild Bill, and Coffey's prejudiced defense attorney), whereas in King's novel, the word is used ten times by those same characters, but also by Melinda Moores, whose sexualized racism echoes the "exaggerated, delusional, and paranoid racial fantasies" (Williams 17) long prevalent in American culture. Darabont chooses to use Melinda's swearing to illustrate the tragedy of an illness that leads a sweet and lovely woman to call Coffey a "pig fucker" but stops short of the words King puts in her mouth: "Pull down your pants! I've heard about nigger-cocks my whole life but never seen one!" (King, *GM* 405). Contemporary audiences may be more comfortable with words like these in the mouths of villains than characters they are supposed to like. The films may offer critiques of the injustice and cruelty of the judicial and penal systems, but they avoid any meaningful indictment of the systemic racism that is such a feature of the American justice system.[15] As many have discussed in reference to *The Green Mile*, this is a glaring oversight or worse, a revival of racist tropes.

Shawshank avoids being as overtly tone-deaf as *Green Mile*. Nothing in *Shawshank* comes close to being as egregious as the Coffey execution scene where viewers are asked to sympathize more with the white executioners than the Black person being murdered. But even *Shawshank* is not exempt from apolitical, ahistorical errors. By casting a Black man to play Red, the film renders Shawshank Prison as something of a racism-free zone, quite divorced from the realities of majority-white Maine in the time period depicted. Casting Morgan Freeman as Red (who is a white, Irish character in King's novella) allows Darabont to do what he does best: humanize his lead characters. In this case he leverages audiences' perception of Morgan Freeman's soft-spoken soulfulness without acknowledging the racialized trauma that goes along with his Blackness. By casting a Black man to play Red but neglecting to actually *rewrite the character as Black*, Darabont creates another apolitical, ahistorical reality for the viewers.[16] There are few indications of Red's Blackness in the plot, in the character's history, in his standing in prison, nor of racial trauma in Red's background. While Darabont humanizes a Black voice by making it the narrator of the story, it is problematic that the racial aspect of his humanity is largely unacknowledged. *Shawshank* may be more popular precisely because it is "not all about race," delivering minimal racial tension and therefore less guilt over America's violently racist history.

The last decade of Best Picture winners at the Academy Awards may be an indicator of the ways in which audience and critical responses are trending in regards to feel-good movies about race. Best Picture winners typically represent an audience-critic consensus and are the films on which most members of the mostly-male, mostly-white, mostly-older Academy can agree on. A number of the recent winners are revealing of how critical/audience tastes are starting to diverge. For example, *Green Book* (2019 Best Picture) is a sweet, feel-good movie about individuals transcending structural racism to connect on a human level. It was an audience favorite at the Toronto Film Festival and upon limited release it earned an A+ audience score but later faced a substantial backlash from commentators who decried it as yet another "white savior" story in which a white man's awakening about racism is the focus. Critics derided its historical inaccuracies, the exaggeration of the "real-life friendship" at the center of the story and exclusion of black voices in the creative team (Chow). Recent controversies such as this one[17] have begun to reveal the tension between the public appetite for violence-free comfort food and their simultaneous growing disdain for films that ignore racial and political realities that shape even the most humane depictions of great characters in cinema. Pre-Code films are prized today by film historians not just for their more free-wheeling depictions of sexuality, crime, and violence but also for their (admittedly still slight) opportunities for characters of color to express agency onscreen (Scott 61) when compared to the Production Code era. Ultimately pre-Code throwback tropes cost Darabont greatly. *Green Mile* may well end up in the category of other films that resonated with audiences initially but do not have staying power as viewers' tastes change. Racial violence is obviously not the only violence in these films, yet it is the most difficult to ignore. Apolitical crowd-pleasers can be problematic largely because they attempt to skirt real issues of systemic racism and may therefore lose their legacy as classic films.[18] In another decade, films like *The Green Mile* might be dismissed as too tone-deaf to remain so widely circulated and beloved. If tempering violence also means tempering the acknowledgment of racial inequity, American audiences may come to see these films as interesting barometers of cultural attitudes on systemic racism but less compelling stories. As a result, both films may have missed their opportunity to make a truly meaningful comment about the nature of violence.

NOTES

1. Darabont adapted these films, as well as *The Mist* and *The Walking Dead* graphic novel by Kirkman and Moore, which became a successful TV series. Despite not employing a pure translation strategy, Darabont has always claimed in interviews that staying true to King is the most important guiding principle he employed in both of these screenplays, and this ideal features prominently in interview footage promoting the films.

2. In the pre-Code era (1930–34), the formal Hollywood internal censorship machinery (which Joseph Breen would run for decades) was not yet in place. Instead, filmmakers responded to objections by individual regional censorship boards and made cuts accordingly. However, the early era of sound film was entering uncharted waters. It had not been clear what a staggering effect the addition of sound would have on the audiences watching—the impact of each violent action was rendered more terrifying with the addition of sound—and censors could only react after the fact. By 1934, Hollywood began to police itself and to head off potential problems at the script and production stage, as well as after the final cut of a film was completed. The Hollywood Production Code era (1934–1968) is sometimes referred to as Hollywood's "Golden Age," but rules forbidding miscegenation and "sexual perversion" largely excluded overtly non-white, non-heterosexual stories.

3. Stephen Prince describes the terrified reactions to *Frankenstein* by 1931 audiences—describing angry letters to Hollywood from regional officials describing terrified schoolchildren traumatized by the film. Robin Woods notes: "The horror film has consistently been one of the most popular, and at the same time, the most disreputable of Hollywood genres" (Magistrale, *HSK* xiv). Darabont clearly has great reverence for the genre but seems equally to know how to apply its tropes sparingly to reach mainstream audiences. It is not a coincidence that Darabont's adaptation of Stephen King's *The Mist,* though profitable and generally well-received by reviewers and audiences, has not garnered as much highbrow critical recognition—it's too much of a monster movie to get a pass.

4. Darabont felt Kenneth Branagh's rewrites and direction departed significantly from the original concept for the film, noting: "It's kind of like the movie I wrote, but not at all like the movie I wrote. It has no patience for subtlety. It has no patience for the quiet moments. It has no patience period. It's big and loud and blunt and rephrased by the director at every possible turn" (Argent and Bauer).

5. Early Expressionist German film directors illustrated that "perhaps better than any other medium before it, film allows us to visually and existentially explore the dark corners of human psychology." With "stories of despair, betrayal and the occasional sign of hope," the movement is widely credited as the genesis of the horror film genre as we know it today ("German Expressionist Films"). *The Green Mile* even has echoes of the 1920 German film *Der Golem*—like that film's title character, John Coffey is a large figure created seemingly out of the earth who (sometimes) enacts vengeance on evil-doers.

6. *Shawshank,* though generally well-reviewed by critics, tanked at the box office only to find a substantial and loyal audience later, first on home video and then on

cable television. If *Rotten Tomatoes* is anything to go by, both *Shawshank* and *The Green Mile* were even more popular with audiences than with critics (https://www.rottentomatoes.com/m/green_mile).

7. Darabont's first professional work in film was in the horror genre, as screenwriter for *Nightmare on Elm Street 3, The Blob, The Fly 2,* and the *Tales from the Crypt* television series (https://www.imdb.com/name/nm0001104/?ref_=fn_al_nm_1).

8. In an interview on *The Shawshank Redemption*'s 25 anniversary, Darabont interrupted the discussion of the film itself to say: "I would take a moment to shift the focus back to Stephen King for having written this fantastic story in the first place, and how grateful am I that I was able to co-opt his story and turn it into this movie that everybody loves so much" (https://deadline.com/2019/12/shawshank-redemption-25-years-frank-darabont-anniversary-interview-1202759221/).

9. Svetlana Boym's definition of nostalgia as analogous to cinema, a "double exposure, or a superimposition of two images—of home and abroad, past and present, dream and everyday life" (*TSE* 193), could apply equally to both *Shawshank* and *The Green Mile.* The narrative frame of each film grants primacy to the reflective memories of Red and Paul, respectively. Both films are memory plays slowly unspooled from the recollections of the men who relate their fantastic stories to their audiences (Elaine in GM and unnamed in SR).

10. Darabont felt Kenneth Branagh's rewrites and direction departed significantly from the original concept for the film, noting: "It's kind of like the movie I wrote, but not at all like the movie I wrote. It has no patience for subtlety. It has no patience for the quiet moments. It has no patience period. It's big and loud and blunt and rephrased by the director at every possible turn" (Argent and Bauer).

11. Construction at OSR began in 1886, before the first movie in history was made (https://www.bbc.com/news/entertainment-arts-33198686) and many years before filmmakers would solidify the horror genre. Early film drew from art and literature. The gothic imagery of European castles was a major influence on horror filmmakers as well as on OSR's architect Levi Scofield (see Grady and Magistrale 59). TSP opened in 1898 ("State of Tennessee").

12. And powerful individuals like Warden Moores make no effort to stop an unjust execution, even when they have personally witnessed Coffey's miraculous power.

13. *Shawshank* was the number one rented home video title in 1995 (*imdb.com*), in 2010 was still selling tens of thousands of DVDs per week ("The Shawshank Redemption Numbers") and had over 151 hours of cable TV screen time in 2013 alone (Palotta).

Though these sequences are harrowing to watch, Darabont remarked in the Blu-Ray audio commentary that Percy stomping on Del's pet mouse, Mr. Jingles, got by far the biggest reaction from the preview audience—more than any other act of violence in the film. It is striking that Darabont gets more mileage out of violence against a mouse than any of the extreme violence against human beings in the film.

Some examples include King describing *Shawshank*'s Ohio State Reformatory as "like walking into your own head" even though King gives very few details about the look of Shawshank Prison in the text (Grady and Magistrale 34) or the ending of *The*

Mist, which King praised: "When Frank said that he wanted to do the ending that he was going to do, I was totally down with that. I thought that was terrific. And it was so anti-Hollywood—anti-everything, really! It was nihilistic. I liked that. So I said you go ahead and do it" (Reyes).

16. The historic mistreatment of Native Americans by the US government and their disproportionate representation in the prison population throughout US history (Delaney, et al.) is addressed by neither King nor Darabont.

17. For a detailed discussion of race and *Shawshank*, see Grady and Magistrale, *The Shawshank Experience* (135–43).

18. *Crash* (2004), *Slumdog Millionaire* (2009), *The Help* (2011), *La La Land* (2016) are others that proved popular with awards shows and mainstream audiences but were criticized for oversimplifying complex racial histories and dynamics.

WORKS CITED

Argent, Daniel, and Eric Bauer. "Frank Darabont on the Green Mile." *Creative Screenwriting*. 27 July 2016. www.creativescreenwriting.com/frank-darabont-on-the-green-mile/. Accessed December 3, 2020.

Delaney, Ruth, Ram Subramanian, Alison Shames, and Nicholas Turner. "American History, Prison, and Race." *Reimagining Prison Web Report. Vera Institute of Justice*, 2021. https://www.vera.org/reimagining-prison-web-report/american-history-race-and-prison. Accessed January 21, 2021.

"Frank Darabont on Adapting Stephen King." *Diary of a Screenwriter*. 26 November 2018. www.diaryofascreenwriter.blogspot.com/2018/07/frank-darabont-on-adapting-stephen-king.html. Accessed December 5, 2020.

"Frank Darabont on *The Shawshank Redemption*." *Creative Screenwriting*. 22 April, 2016. www.creativescreenwriting.com/frank-darabont-on-the-shawshank-redemption/. Accessed December 3, 2020.

"Frank Darabont." *Internet Movie Database*. www.imdb.com/name/nm0001104/?ref_=fn_al_nm_1. Accessed December 5, 2020.

"German Expressionist Films." *Movements in Film*. www.movementsinfilm.com/blog/german-expressionist-films-1919-1931. Accessed December 5, 2020.

Gooden, Tai. "A Brief History of Frank Darabont's Journey Through Horror." *The Nerdist*. Jan. 28, 2020. www.nerdist.com/article/frank-darabont-horror-history/. Accessed December 7, 2020.

Grady, Maura, and Tony Magistrale. *The Shawshank Experience: Tracking the History of the World's Favorite Movie*. Palgrave/Macmillan, 2016.

"*The Green Mile*" (1999). *Rotten Tomatoes*. www.rottentomatoes.com/m/green_mile. Accessed December 5, 2020.

Kent, Brian. "Christian Martyr or Grateful Slave: The Magical Negro as Uncle Tom in Frank Darabont's *The Green Mile*." *The Films of Stephen King*. Ed. Tony Magistrale. New York, Palgrave/Macmillan, 2008. 117–129.

Kermode, Mark. *The Shawshank Redemption.* BFI Film Classics Series. Palgrave, 2003.

King, Stephen. *The Green Mile.* Kindle ed. Simon and Schuster, 1996.

King, Stephen. *Rita Hayworth and the Shawshank Redemption. Different Seasons.* New York: Viking, 1982.

Magistrale, Tony. *Hollywood's Stephen King.* Palgrave Macmillan, 2003.

"Miracles and Mystery: Creating the Green Mile." *The Green Mile* Blu-Ray *DiamondLuxe* Edition Special Features. Warner Bros, 2014.

"On Adapting Stephen King." Extracted from 'Frank Darabont Interviewed by Daniel Argent & Erik Bauer,' *Creative Screenwriting*, Volume 4, #2 (Summer 1997) & Volume 6, #6 (November/December 1999).

Palotta, Frank. "The Shawshank Redemption Accounted for a Huge Amount of Cable TV Time in 2013." *Business Insider*, May 28, 2014. https://www.businessinsider.com/the-shawshank-redemption-151-hours-of-cable-air-time-in-2013-2014-5. Accessed January 7, 2021

Prince, Stephen. *Classical Film Violence: Designing and Regulating Brutality in Hollywood Cinema 1930-1968.* Kindle ed. Rutgers University Press, 2003.

Reyes, Mike. "The Mist Ending: How it happened and why it differs from the book." *Cinemablend.* October 21, 2017. www.cinemablend.com/news/1716310/the-mist-ending-what-happened-and-how-it-differs-from-the-book. Accessed December 5, 2020.

"The Shawshank Redemption The Numbers: Where Data and The Movie Business Meet." https://www.the-numbers.com/movie/Shawshank-Redemption-The#tab=video-sales. Accessed January 7, 2021

"State of Tennessee Prison Records." 1831–1992. Part 2: Oversized Volumes, Record Group 25. P. 7 https://sos-tn-gov-files.tnsosfiles.com/forms/TENNESSEE_STATE_PRISON_RECORDS_1831-1992.pdf. Accessed January 28, 2021.

Williams, Linda. "Melodrama in Black and White: Uncle Tom and The Green Mile." *Film Quarterly*, 55:2 (2001): 14–21, doi:10.1525/fq.2001.55.2.14.

Chapter 9

Hiding in Plain Sight

Watching and the Unconscious in Stephen King's Mr. Mercedes *Trilogy on Page and Screen*

Brian Kent

In the early spring months of 2020, as the coronavirus landed on American shores, the country faced not only a novel virus but also a novel attempt to keep the biological threat at bay—a complete shut-down of social and economic activities, save those deemed essential to day-to-day survival, both physical and psychological. As most Americans took to their sofas and loungers, they turned instinctually to a primary means for finding comfort and solace in a period of crisis: their screens. As it happened, just at this moment of desperation, of unprecedented demand for content by which Americans might escape the pressure of being locked in, either alone or together, Netflix launched *The Tiger King* into the virtual universe. Infecting viewers with fascination, wonder, and awe, it spread as a cultural phenomenon more rapidly and with more ease than the viral reality that brought its sudden presence at the center of the American psyche into being.

At the end of the introductory sequences prior to the opening episode, during which various "characters" from the series make their initial appearances and offer up tantalizing tidbits of what to expect in the ensuing programs, an Oklahoma TV newscaster appears on screen, recapping the bizarre elements of the showdown between Exotic Joe and Carole Baskin unfolding in her viewers' own backyard, before summing up: "It makes good TV. It's like a train wreck. You can't help but look." A fitting epigraph, indeed, for the role *The Tiger King* would play in the lives of the newly homebound throughout the country. Entering the unknown of a pandemic, in need of comfort and resolve, Americans faced an insidious biological threat to their personal health and economic well-being that called for them to muster whatever reserves of human cooperation and compassion might be at their disposal as they conducted their day-to-day lives. Simultaneously, in their screen lives, a psychic need compelled them to enter en masse into the world of *The Tiger King*, a program whose subtitle makes no bones about the nature of its appeal to viewers: "Murder, Mayhem, and Madness." An appeal, it seems fair to say, that added a perverse sense of irony to the social bromide of the early days of the pandemic, "We're all in this together."

At the time that all this was unfolding I was putting together a draft of this article about Stephen King's trilogy of thriller-detective novels—*Mr. Mercedes*, *Finders Keepers*, and *End of Watch*—which appeared between 2014 and 2016. I wanted to consider how King incorporates unique gothic dimensions of his work into the detective thriller genre in this series of books built around a retired police detective and a serial killer/mass murderer named Brady Hartsfield, dubbed Mr. Mercedes by the Bridgton, Ohio community in which his crimes take place. The detective, Bill Hodges, is haunted by the fact that he was not able, before he retired, to apprehend Brady as the "the Mercedes Killer," responsible for plowing through a crowd of job fair applicants with a stolen Mercedes, killing eight people, including an infant and her mother. As the series of novels begins, Brady remains at large and unknown to the public, but he feels compelled to torment Hodges as a means of taking credit for what he sees as his "masterpiece," both of murder and of getting away with murder. In the process, he hopes to add Hodges to his list of victims. Brady recognizes in Hodges someone driven by dark underlying psychic forces much like his own, first as he sought Brady's capture prior to his retirement and then in his near suicidal depression following his retirement, not having established his own legacy by bringing Brady to justice.

The novel trilogy became the basis for an AT&T Network TV serial drama produced by David E. Kelley, the three seasons of which aired between 2017 and 2019. King's fictional portrayal of Bill Hodges in his pursuit of Mr. Mercedes and the televisual adaptation of that portrayal emphasize the unconscious psychic impulses Brady and Hodges have in common, although the novels and the TV serial reveal opposite outcomes ensuing from the darkness that envelops both men.

In a 1974 essay by Henry Miller concerning a German novel by Jacob Wassermann, Miller assesses the actions of the character Etzel Andergast in Wasserman's story and concludes: "He symbolizes, to an extent, the tragic dilemma of society as a whole, which finds its nemesis in the unconscious. Of what use the noble, exalted ideals inculcated by our culture if we are to be continually betrayed by our ineradicable passion?" (147–48). King's trilogy and the television episodes created from it present readers and viewers with a graphic and compelling representation of what Miller perceives as our society's nemesis, the unconscious. Despite our best efforts to rely on the civilizing dimensions of culture to shape our behavior as human beings, we are too often betrayed by our more primitive impulses. So, as much as we would like to believe that when it comes to society, "We are all in this together," and that this collective wish will help maintain order and social harmony, our baser instincts lead us, ineradicably, in the direction of murder, mayhem, and madness. *Mr. Mercedes*, on both page and screen, suggests that what we watch and how we watch offer insight into the nature of those baser instincts.

In the second novel of King's trilogy, *Finders Keepers*, a scene transpires where prison parolee Morris Bellamy visits the shop of bookseller and collector Andy Halliday, in pursuit of notebooks containing drafts of work by famous and reclusive author John Rothstein, whom Bellamy kills at the start of the book, before making away with Rothstein's writings and a sizable sum of cash from the writer's New Hampshire home. Bellamy ends up killing Halliday, as well, in the back workroom of the shop, before heading into the bookstore itself, where he comes upon a computer with an app for the shop's security cameras. After clicking it open, he finds a view for the back room in which he has just brutally dispatched the shop's owner with a hatchet. When he sees Andy's body, he decides to rewind the camera's recorded images to the point at which he began his grisly work. As King writes: "He watches, engrossed, as he murders his old pal all over again. Fascinating. Not a home movie he wants anyone to see, however, which means the laptop is coming with him" (342).

Bellamy's fascination with his own murderous handiwork is reminiscent of the central act and its aftermath in one of King's more disturbing short stories, simply titled, "Morality." The story turns on an aging and unhealthy pastor named Winston (or Winnie), wanting to experience sin before he dies, but only by proxy. He therefore enlists his personal nurse, Nora, and her husband, Chad, to team up to commit such a sin and videotape the results so that he can view the deed in action. In return, he will pay them a large sum of money, which, given their economic circumstances, makes them vulnerable to Winnie's temptation. Nora's "sin" is to commit a random act of violence against an innocent, unsuspecting child. Once the deed is complete, Nora views her recorded crime repeatedly, first with her husband and then with Winnie. Although not as deadly as Morris Bellamy's horrific carnage at the bookshop, Nora's need to repeatedly witness her actions is born of the same primitive impulse that prompts Bellamy to stare transfixed at the screen that portrays his most pernicious instincts being put into action. Unlike Bellamy, however, her need, in conjunction with the act she witnesses, steadily erodes her basis of self-understanding and morality.

In the scene involving Bellamy, King emphasizes a prominent dimension of his trilogy, conveyed especially through the murderous exploits of Brady Hartsfield, the villain at its center. The act of *watching* plays a crucial role in Brady's cat and mouse game with Hodges. At the start of *End of Watch*, the trilogy's third installment, Hodges' former partner, Pete Huntley is on the verge of retirement, which those on the job refer to as "end of watch." Hodges, himself, despite retirement, "found it impossible to give up watching" (18), an observation that reveals much about the conflicting impulses driving him in his pursuit of Brady.

In attempting to attack Hodges's psyche with the intent of getting him to kill himself, Brady has been tracking his movements and watching his house, often from his job as an ice cream truck driver who regularly parks his Mr. Tastey vehicle in the vicinity of Hodges's home. As Brady himself describes it, his ice cream gig allows him close surveillance of Hodges while also "hiding in plain sight." The control center of Brady's surveillance activities is a computer array he maintains in the basement of a home he shares with his mother. Brady's compulsion to watch is aided by technological gadgetry. In this regard, Brady's basement control room represents primitive unconscious drives. At the top of the stairs heading into the basement Brady's oral command to turn on the fluorescent lights below is CONTROL. Once he descends into his basement domain, the oral cue to fire up his computer command center is, appropriately, CHAOS. Then, to forestall the suicide program that automatically kicks in to scrub his files clean and replace them with gibberish, Brady finishes his sequence of commands with DARKNESS. Hodges's inability to give up watching is more a compulsion of keeping himself at the center of Brady's orbit of evil, and therefore immersed in a world of darkness. King's trilogy and Kelly's production explore through the two men the relationship between the compulsion to *watch* and the impulses of the unconscious, or the relentless demands of the id.

In King's original novel and in Season One of the television serial, Brady exposes how the need to watch, especially when it comes to darkly disturbing and violent images, is an expression of the unconscious, while the watching itself becomes the means of fulfilling unconscious desires while "hiding in plain sight." Brady uses images he has captured from within the Mercedes while plowing through the City Center crowd to haunt and taunt Hodges, whom he knows to be suffering from post-retirement depression brought on by a lack of purpose in his life. What Brady shares with people in general are the primitive chaotic compulsions of the unconscious, a fact demonstrated by how acts of mass killing like Brady's become the loci of fascination for a television audience that feeds on media representations of such hideous crimes. Those crimes become, in effect, the basis for ongoing television *entertainment* for a mass audience that feels compelled to watch and thereby satisfy an inner craving to witness dark and destructive forces at work in their lives and in their culture.

What appears to separate Brady from that mass audience is his willingness to act directly in response to the dictates of his unconscious desires. In a letter to Hodges, he suggests that "a great many people would enjoy doing what I did," referring to his Center City massacre, "and that is why they enjoy books and movies (and even TV shows these days) that feature Torture and Dismemberment." Brady also acknowledges, though, that most people do not act on such impulses, as he has, because they are fitted with Lead Boots when they are just kids, or, in other words, because they develop a conscience, of which, he admits, "I have none, so I can soar above the heads of the Normal Crowd" (*Mr. Mercedes* 28). This reassures readers and viewers that their own attraction to darkness remains within the realm of a healthy psyche, that, ultimately, they exert Control over Chaos and Darkness.

Nevertheless, in Season Two of the AT&T serial, from his basement lair—now representing the deep workings of his subconscious life—Brady commands, "Chaos!," to fire up his screens, and then narrates the nature of the dark fascination his acts elicit from people more generally: "Every act of conquest is a step toward acquiring further knowledge of the ultimate frontier. The collective, atavistic, evolutionary ambition of humanity is, and always has been immortality" (Season 2, Episode 1). Shortly after King presents Brady's taunting letter to Hodges in the novel, he has Brady ruminate on Nietzsche's dictum: "When you gaze into the abyss, the abyss also gazes into you" (53). The implication of Nietzsche's cautionary observation for King's trilogy is that all our watching, or gazing, to feed the chaos of the id may not be as far removed from Brady as we like to assure ourselves it is. The driving force, the unfulfilled urge, behind Brady's initial unconscionable act at City Center is that it will give him celebrity status and, thus, when he is gone, he will nonetheless be remembered, so he achieves a measure of immortality, as perverse and notorious as that immortality might be. Season Two also presents a dream sequence of Brady and Hodges sitting side by side at an open and empty grave, where Brady describes the sad, anonymous, and, ultimately, forgotten future that awaits Hodges, for all the do-good endeavors in his life, including his attempt to find and bring Brady to justice. By contrast, with his one bold and horrific act of mass murder, Brady will be remembered in Bridgton forever (Season 2, Episode 1).

Throughout King's initial *Mr. Mercedes* novel, there are frequent references to real-life incidents of serial or mass killing, like Columbine, 9/11, Son of Sam, the Unabomber, and the Atlanta Olympics bombing. The way in which these dreadful events inevitably turn into media spectacles featuring the horrific impact of violence on the murderers' victims raises the question of whether such gazing, such fascination with watching the ugly achievements of the abyss in human behavior aligns us with Brady in seeking immortality by proxy. By bearing witness to the deranged by-products of those who behave without or beyond conscience, do we somehow share in the immortality Brady tells Hodges of, twisted as that immortality is? In another scene from Season Two, Brady watches from his basement control room as his real-life eyes in the form of a hospital volunteer drives to the City Center spot of Brady's "masterpiece," where Brady can see the shrine that has been placed there to honor his victims. He is disappointed that it is only a large rock with a plaque embedded in it, thinking the degree of depravity his crime represents deserves a more impressive display to mark its remembrance (Season 2, Episode 4). The ironic reversal of intent within the scene from honoring victims to serving Brady's perverse sense of celebrity and immortality forces viewers to consider that when we build monuments to honor the dead and mourn their brutal and senseless loss, we inescapably also memorialize the very events that brought such monuments into being. In this way, the abyss gazes back at us.

Philip L. Simpson echoes such disturbing sentiments in his consideration of Nora's actions in "Morality." "One of the more troubling aspects of King's fiction," he writes, "or any fiction that foregrounds violence as spectacle, is reader complicity in the represented act of violence. . . . King forces his readership to confront their own implication, either through action or inaction in the perpetuation of represented violence as voyeuristic entertainment without any recuperative meaning" (97, 88). One assumes that the same would apply to viewers or consumers of violence as spectacle dressed up in the supposedly more neutral or objective format of "news." Simpson also calls attention to Winnie's remark in "Morality" that "human nature has no bottom. It is as deep and mysterious as the mind of God." Simpson rightly concludes, "Of all the disturbing statements and moments in the story, this philosophical observation stands out, signifying the ultimate unknowability of people's motivations behind their actions" (95).

Season Two is based largely on the third novel in King's trilogy, *End of Watch*, and thereby allows producer David E. Kelly and various screenwriters to enhance the implications of Brady's basement control room as a manifestation of Brady's subconscious. In doing so, the TV serial provides a more thorough exploration of forces in Brady's life that may have driven him beyond conscience or destroyed the nascent sense of conscience within him when he was still a child, especially when it comes to his incestuous relationship with his mother and his culpability in the death of his younger brother. The TV production thus raises troubling inquiries into King's stand on the ultimate source of the evil that Brady represents. In the novel, *Mr. Mercedes*, Hodges says of Brady, "He's broken. And evil. Like an apple that looks okay on the outside, but when you cut it open, it's black and full of worms." Here, King leaves open the possibility that the evil is a consequence of being broken, which is where the forces of personal psychological trauma may come into play in the creation of evil. But as any regular reader of King knows, he often presents characters, or forces, that are simply the unmitigated embodiment of evil, without explanation or excuse. In the penultimate episode of the TV serial's Season One, Brendan Gleeson's Hodges has a conversation with Holly about Brady in which she asks, "What do you think explains him? A person like him?" Hodges responds by stating that for some people, underneath the skin and bones, they are simply black holes (Season 1, Episode 9). At the end of the last episode, Hodges stops at Brady's room in the hospital where he is in a coma, hooked up to a ventilator that is keeping him alive. There is no electrical energy in Brady's brain, suggesting he will never return to consciousness. But before he leaves, Hodges leans over to speak to the unconscious figure before him and tells him, "Hate will bring you back one day. I'll be waiting, and I'll finish it." Hodges' parting words confirm his belief that Brady as a human being is simply a black hole of evil, even as it raises questions about his own desire to "finish it." Still, as a countervailing belief to such pessimistic despair, the same Hodges, in King's novel, concedes that there may be "a fumble-fingered but powerful universal force at work, always trying to put wrong things right" (287).

For much of King's career, readers could, indeed, depend on human acts of goodness and compassion, frequently guided by benevolent spiritual forces, to help fend off and eventually triumph over evil, and restore order, even if only temporarily. But as Mary Findley argues, King's fiction since the mid-1990s often presents us with a "marked increase in sheer brutality, violence, and societal chaos," often accompanied by a monster that wins, thereby reinforcing the belief that "the world is a dangerously cruel and terrible place" (57). And, as with Simpson's claim about "Morality," that it forces readers to confront their own implication in the violence depicted, Findley emphasizes that in the recent past King presents us with a monster that "is nowhere and everywhere," because, ultimately, "It *is* us." (58). King's works after 1995, she concludes, "expose the dark underbelly of humanity and chronicle societal mayhem and cultural fear that are, perhaps, better kept in the closet. This dark underbelly, this monstrosity no longer seeks to 'reaffirm order we crave as human beings,' but seeks, instead, to remind us of a nightmare we might not be able to wake up from" (58). Simpson and Findley together suggest that King's work increasingly reveals forces at work in American society and culture that represent a black hole of brokenness and evil, one which threatens the ability of the countervailing "universal force" for correction to assert itself.

A key dimension of both King's novel, *End of Watch*, and Season Two of the AT&T serial that readers or viewers must contend with is exactly how Brady exerts control over other human beings while lying in a coma in a Bridgton hospital. There is a compelling metaphorical dimension to the conception of neurosurgeon Dr. Babineau, administering an unapproved drug called Cerebellen that eventually kickstarts Brady's sense of interior consciousness, allowing him to slowly reconstruct his identity by mentally descending into his basement control room and using it as a base of operations for the renewal of primal, unconscious urges that constitute the workings of a no longer comatose brain.

The means by which he manifests those urges in the world outside his own mind, however, may stretch a reader's credulity beyond its breaking point. Brady uses his mind to manipulate hospital instruments and machinery or computer game consoles with the commercial name Zappit that have been distributed generously throughout the hospital and surrounding community. By such means he is can "come through the wall from his basement workroom where he had first regained consciousness" (127), get inside the minds of those around him, including Babineau, and compel them to act on his behalf. Of course, such paranormal shenanigans are not new to King's fiction, but here they are handled with a lack of elegance, especially within the context of a detective crime novel. By comparison, the first novel, *Mr. Mercedes*, and the second, *Finders Keepers*, are more circumspect in their homage to the genre.

Despite the contrived element in King's and Kelley's reliance on Brady inhabiting the instrumentation of hospital equipment and gaming consoles, such paranormal dimensions can be viewed in the same light as David Roskies has explained the supernatural dynamics in Isaac Bashevis Singer's fiction, finding in them a "demonic realism," where the devil becomes the storyteller, in this case Brady Hartsfield taking on that role from within his interior consciousness. As Roskies says of Singer, "Where I think the real . . . genius of it is, is that it's narrated by the id. The devil becomes the spokesperson and the driving force of the id, who then proceeds to enter into the consciousness—the minds of each one of his victims—and adopts the voice and sensibility . . . of each one of his victims in turn. He is dramatizing the id, the force of evil, the demonic within each of us" (98). Roskies's purpose in identifying the devil as id was to argue the modernist dimension in Singer's work, but it also aligns with both Simpson's and Findley's contentions that King's more recent work relies less strenuously on the belief in a mysterious malevolent force that continually wreaks havoc on human lives and more on the havoc human beings inflict on themselves due to the promptings of their own urges and desires. In the later stages of the TV serial a more direct echo of Roskies's "devil" appears when John Rothstein extemporizes on Satan's role or absence in contemporary life, which I will get to shortly.

The role of technology in this dynamic, particularly the Zappits, high-lights, again, the significance of watching, especially in the way that the images and messages presented via machine can mesmerize, even hypnotize, to feed the demands of our subconscious urges. Brady, then, becomes the embodiment of such urges. His manipulation of hospital technology and Zappits in King's *End of Watch* and in Kelley's AT&T serial recreation of the novel, provides the mechanism by which he exerts his evil influence over other characters and, ultimately, secures his freedom from the hospital. King's 2006 novel *Cell* offers a similar scenario where technology, this time in the form of cell phones, provides the opening that the Pulse exploits to unleash murderous mayhem within the population at large. Those exposed to the Pulse through their phones, or "phoners," as they come be labeled by those who have escaped their fate by *not* using their phones once the Pulse arrives, are, as Findley describes, "knocked down the evolutionary ladder to their base state, one of aggression and instinct." They are, Findley continues, "Americans laid bare—mindless slaves to their dependence on technology with a kill-or-be-killed mentality that has been honed on the road to capital gain" (59).

King's second installment of the trilogy, *Finders Keepers*, deals with the fallout from the climactic events of *Mr. Mercedes* only tangentially. It is primarily a procedural concerning the murder of famous reclusive author John Rothstein and what becomes of his stolen cash and writing notebooks, which contain a sequel to his 3-volume masterpiece based on the exploits of his iconic character of rebellion, Jimmy Gold. Season Three of the TV serial relies on *Finders Keepers* to tell the story of Rothstein's murder and the sub-sequent fate of his killer and the now posthumous manuscripts. But it does so in a decidedly inferior manner to the other adaptive elements of the series. In *Screening Stephen King*, Simon Brown observes that, at times, screen adapta-tions of King's work, particularly those he has a hand in, provide an uneasy mix of violence and humor, citing *Maximum Overdrive, Creepshow*, and *Cat's Eye* as cases in point. Season Three of David E. Kelley's *Mr. Mercedes* unfortunately falls into that category, especially Kate Mulgrew's campy performance as Alma Lane, the lowlight of which features her singing along to a Liza Minnelli show tune as she saws up the body of one of her victims, before putting the pieces through her backyard woodchipper. Alma has part-nered with Morris Bellamy to retrieve the stolen Rothstein manuscripts. Her wood-chipped victim was Morris's girlfriend until Alma dispatched her with a hatchet blow to the head before stuffing her into the freezer in her backyard shed (using the handy hatchet to cut her legs down to size so that she can fit in the cold storage unit). Bellamy is King's character from *Finders Keepers*, Alma is not. There may be a clue to the tone of this final installment of the series in the opening credits, where one of the shots is the upper torso and head of King himself, laid out at the food prep counter of a restaurant with a bloody knife sticking out of his neck. Season Three is by far the most violent of the TV serial, but Brown notes how such adaptations that go for the mix of humor and violence end up having the humor undermine the seriousness of the horror elements presented. As Brown describes it, the result is what purports to be a serious film, but one that ends up just being silly in places.

The unfortunate aspect of this is that it detracts from how Kelley presents Hodges in Season Three. In contrast to how Brown characterizes adaptations of King that venture off into silliness, Lorna Jowett and Stacey Abbott, in *TV Horror: Investigating the Dark Side of the Small Screen*, explain how long-form TV serial adaptations can sometimes "open up the original story into something entirely new" (181). That appears to be the case with Hodges.

At the end of King's trilogy of novels, the evil that Brady represents has been destroyed. And even though Hodges succumbs to cancer, Jerome and Holly meet at the cemetery eight months after his passing, secure in their love for him, and for each other as friends. Order and tranquility have been restored. The end of the TV Serial is more discomforting. King's original ending may simply be a nod to the tradition of the thriller-detective genre that serves as the foundation for the series of *Mr. Mercedes* novels. The dedications for the three novels lend support to this kind of reading, as *Mr. Mercedes* and *Finders Keepers* begin with "Thinking of James M. Cain" and "Thinking of John D. Macdonald," respectively, while *End of Watch* is "For Thomas Harris."

The more unsettling nature of the TV serial's ending reflects how the long format opens up King's story into something entirely new, although its serious implications are undermined by the campiness of its Morris Bellamy and Alma Lane subplot. Those implications have to do with Hodges's inability to give up watching and how that may link him with the forces of darkness that he ostensibly resists. In the novel, *Mr. Mercedes*, Brady ponders whether he can be blamed for striking out against "the world that made him what he is." He doesn't worry about God or concepts like heaven and hell because "anyone with half a brain knows these things don't exist." He believes "every religion lies" and "every moral precept is a delusion." The truth, for Brady, is darkness (390–391).

Season One of the TV serial conveys this element of Brady's psyche in the video he records for the police before he destroys his house and escapes as the police close in on him. There, as he leads them to believe he is committing suicide with pills, he states that "the truth is blackness" (Season 1, Episode 9). As both King's novels and the seasons of the TV serial progress, the nature of that blackness is more and more associated with the workings of the unconscious in human activity. Near the end of the second novel, *Finders Keepers*, Hodges mulls over information provided by a nurse at the Traumatic

Brain Injury Clinic about rumors and strange occurrences associated with the comatose Brady Hartsfield:

> Hodges's rational mind insists there's nothing to these rumors, and certain strange occurrences have rational explanations, but there's more to his mind than the rational part on top. Deep below that rational part is an underground ocean—there's one inside every head, he believes—where strange creatures swim. (517)

In Season Two of the TV serial, Hodges's ex-wife fears where the strange creatures of that underground ocean will continue to lead him as she urges him to leave his "watching" behind. "Darkness follows you," she pleads with him. "Choose the sun" (Season 2, Episode 3). But he is not ready to do so.

Season Three of the serial presents a Hodges who begins to weigh the costs of his fixation on Brady Hartsfield, which include the estrangement of his family, the death of his girlfriend Janey, and Lou Linklater's traumatization (Freddi Linklater in King's novels). He tells his neighbor and friend, Ida, "Everybody I touch suffers." His own mental deterioration is evidenced in his dreams and hallucinations where he converses with the murdered author, John Rothstein, a hero of his. Rothstein cautions him about pursuing his legacy through pursuits such as finding his killer, just as he had earlier obsessed about Brady Hartsfield. Season Two of the serial presents two scenes where Brady and Hodges appear together in revealing fashion. The first is when they share an ambulance that rushes them to the hospital after Holly has clubbed Brady and Hodges has suffered a heart attack. The second is when they are in adjoining cells at the police station so that Hodges can draw out the old murderous Brady to prove that the new Cerebellen-rejuvenated and morally reformed Brady is a fraud. In provoking Brady's anger, Hodges does indeed draw out the killer inside, but in doing so, Brady says to him, "You're partly to blame. Called me nothing. Accused me of fucking my mother. Would Janey be alive if you hadn't provoked me so? . . . At the end of the day, you're no better than me."

The role of dreams, waking visions, nightmares, and hallucinations in the TV serial emphasizes the degree to which Hodges's subconscious troubles him about the nature of his life and the motivations behind his actions, as well as the actions of human beings more generally. At one point, while at home, Hodges catches portions of a TV interview with Rothstein that is aired after his murder. In it, Rothstein argues, "The worst crime that my generation ever committed is that we murdered Satan. If there is no Satan, then there is no God, and where's there's no God, there's Mr. Mercedes, plowing into a bunch of innocent people looking for jobs" (Season Three, Episode 4). His description bears a striking resemblance to Roskies's argument concerning the role the devil plays in Singer's work as the embodiment of the id's place in human affairs. Later, when Hodges describes for Ida a dream he had of a visit with Rothstein that mirrored the TV interview, he tells her Rothstein was going on about the world needing Satan back because he's better than the alternative. Ida asks, "God?" Hodges responds: "People."

The monster is us. That includes people like Brady Hartsfield, but it also includes those, like Bill Hodges, who become obsessed with the evil Brady represents and surrender their own lives to its influence for reasons they don't fully recognize or understand. As the TV serial nears its completion, while at the Finders Keepers office, Lou offers Hodges a surprising reading of his obsession with Brady that forces him to consider the role darkness may play in giving his life purpose and meaning, although it is not clear whether Lou, at this point, speaks from her own point of view, or from a traumatically induced psychological identification with Brady. In either case, Lou claims that Brady did give something to Hodges, bringing him back to life, providing him purpose and a sense of family. In this scenario, as Lou explains, Hodges is forced to recognize, "I need family to survive." "Now you're a changed man," she continues. "Brady helped effect that change. I know that we all hate Brady here. I'm just saying that maybe we should be a little mindful of what he gave us" (Season 3, Episode 9). This may be the other side of the compulsion to watch, the reliance on darkness to force us to recognize and cultivate our better selves in order to help keep that darkness at bay.

King's trilogy and Kelley's adaptation both emphasize that the monster is us, including we who turn to *watching*, in all its manifestations, to feed the desires and compulsions generated from within—King's readers, viewers of King's works adapted for the screen, and even King himself. In the Introduction to their book, *Stephen King's Contemporary Classics*, co-editors Philip L. Simpson and Patrick McAleer reflect on Simpson's chapter in the book concerning King's story, "Morality," and contend that the husband and wife in it compel a reader's identification with their immoral actions, especially through the need to experience the violent episode recorded on video, and even to *create* that episode, since the video contents are never fully described in the story. "Such conflation between the reader and the protagonists," they argue, "calls into question not only the morality of the protagonists but, by extension, both King as the creator of violent spectacle for mass consumption and King's readership as consumers of violent spectacle" (xvii). In the phony suicide video recording Brady provides for police in Season One of the TV serial, he explains, as a prelude to his later rant about the human need to seek immortality, that a desire to leave his mark on this life drove him to his unspeakable crimes. "Somebody will write a book about me," he boasts, "some horror meister will write a novel" (Season 1, Episode 9).

Surely one must distinguish between feeding the monster of the id through fictional renderings of murder, mayhem, and madness—be they printed word or visual image—and feasting on the real-life tragedies and sufferings of our fellow beings. But Stephen King's works and their subsequent adaptations in the last decade suggest that the line between the two is becoming increasingly and dangerously blurred. Even so, the works also suggest that by confronting the monster directly, by shining the light on our inner darkness, we can discover what strange creatures swim in our underground oceans and come to a genuine understanding that we are, indeed, all in this together.

WORKS CITED

Brown, Simon. *Screening Stephen King: Adaptation and the Horror Genre in Film and Television*. University of Texas Press, 2018.

Findley, Mary. "The World at Large, America in Particular: Cultural Fears and Societal Mayhem in King's Fiction Since 1995." *Stephen King's Modern Macabre: Essays on the Later Works*, edited by Patrick McAleer and Michael A. Perry. McFarland and Company, 2014. 56–63.

Jowett, Lorna, and Stacey Abbott. *TV Horror: Investigating the Dark Side of the Small Screen*. I.B. Tauris, 2013.

King, Stephen. *Cell*. Scribner, 2006.

———. *End of Watch*. Pocket Books, 2017.

———. *Finders Keepers*. Pocket Books, 2016.

———. *Mr. Mercedes*. Pocket Books, 2016.

———. "Morality." *Billy Blockade*. Scribner, 2010. 81–132.

Miller, Henry. "Reflections on *The Maurizius Case*." *Sextet*. New Directions, 2010. 111–149.

Mr. Mercedes. Season One: "Let's Prey," SONY Pictures Home Entertainment, 2018, 3 Discs.

———. Season Two: "Don't Let Him Inside Your Head," SONY Pictures Home Entertainment, 2018, 3 Discs.

———. Season Three: "Finders Keepers," SONY Pictures Home Entertainment, 2019, 3 Discs.

Roskies, David. "The Achievement of Isaac Bashevis Singer: A Roundtable Discussion." *Singer: An Album*. Library of America, 2004. 93–105, 110–119.

Simpson, Philip L. "'Morality': Stephen King's Most Disturbing Story?" *Stephen King's Contemporary Classics: Reflections on the Modern Master of Horror*, edited by Philip L. Simpson and Patrick McAleer. Rowman & Littlefield, 2015. 85–99.

Simpson, Philip L., and Patrick McAleer. "Introduction." *Stephen King's Contemporary Classics: Reflections on the Modern Master of Horror*, edited by Philip L. Simpson and Patrick McAleer. Rowan and Littlefield, 2015. xi–xxi.

Chapter 10

Political Allegory and the Plague of Violence in the Television Adaptation of *The Outsider*

Philip L. Simpson

The representation of violence in media is a contentious and long-standing area of concern among cultural critics, moral crusaders, and all those who seek to find causation or correlation between what is depicted on the page, stage, or the screen and what actually takes place in real time in a real place to real people violently victimized, physically and/or emotionally, by other real people. Sometimes the concern is not so much the relationship between represented and actual violence, but that the act of consuming such violent content desensitizes the individual, stunts moral and emotional growth, degrades the culture, or otherwise accelerates the long, slow dissolution of civilization. Among those creators and producers of violent content to be inflicted upon the masses, surely one name that stands out to many contemporary readers and cinema goers is Stephen King. Indeed, it can be quite plausibly argued that most of his readership expects, if not demands, violent content from him. Under the "Stephen King" brand name, his dozens of multi-genre novels and hundreds of short stories have a kill count that, when one factors in the apocalyptic novels *The Stand* and *Cell*, numbers into the billions of people.

King himself is quite conscious of his reputation as a purveyor of violence in media. At times it seems to trouble him, at times make him defensive. For example, in a column he wrote for *Entertainment Weekly* in 2007, he admits: "Certainly my own lifelong bloodlust puzzles and sometimes disgusts me." That startling confession aside, he goes on to provide a moral defense for violent movies: "I can only hope they serve as a mental gutter through which our worst fears and impulses are channeled safely out of our emotional systems. The Greek word is *catharsis*, and I have used it many times to justify my own violent creations, but I have never entirely trusted it" ("On Violence"). King's invocation of catharsis as first articulated by Aristotle in the *Poetics* as a description of the emotional purgative effect upon the viewer/consumer of tragic drama is long standing and well known by his readers and critics in general, as he has invoked it elsewhere. Take, for example, his reply to his own rhetorical question about the audience appeal of violent representation in horror, as found in his encyclopedic overview of the horror genre, *Danse Macabre*, all the way back in 1981:

> The answer seems to be that we make up horrors to help us cope with the real ones. With the endless inventiveness of humankind, we grasp the very elements which are so divisive and destructive and try to turn them into tools—to dismantle themselves. The term *catharsis* is as old as Greek drama, and it has been used rather too glibly by some practitioners in my field to justify what they do, but it still has its limited uses here. The dream of horror is in itself an out-letting and a lancing . . . and it may well be that the mass-media dream of horror can sometimes become a nation-wide analyst's couch. (13)

So this apologia, as it were, has served King well, at least from a monetary perspective, over the years.

King's cathartic deployment of representations of violence also frequently is linked to American contemporary issues rooted in the past, a point made by Tony Magistrale and Michael Blouin when they say King's "literary and cinematic works reflect a growing cultural unrest regarding History with a capital 'H.' . . . King's corpus echoes a set of ongoing questions concerning the nation's past: whether it is usable or disposable; whether it conveys a sense of indebtedness or release; whether it offers more hope than despair; and the extent to which violence propels events and/or traps individuals in cyclical patterns" (1). The kind of real-life anxieties to which King's fictional horror, as Magistrale and Blouin suggest, gives such eloquent voice certainly have shifted and morphed over the years, even as the legacy of America's violent past (and, of course, King's go-to defense of violent content) remains a constant force or "ghost" which King's characters must confront. The haunted past gives rise to a kind of civic infection or corruption in which trust is destroyed, suspicion falls on anyone and everyone, fear morphs into hatred, the social order falls into disorder and confusion, and violence erupts.

Enter *The Outsider* (2018), King's novel that from its opening pages focuses on a particularly gruesome and sadistic child murder, the latest in a series of such murders that throw communities into spasms of terror, rage, and violence in a pattern all too recognizable in the ugly American social milieu of the late 2010s, capped by an American presidency characterized by antagonistic division and expressed in inflammatory rhetoric all too often resulting in overt acts of politically inspired violence. A ten-episode limited television series of the same name followed, adapted by Richard Price and airing on HBO from January through March 2020. The child's murder goes well beyond the reach of many of King's stories (but certainly not all of them) in its depiction of violence against the innocent. While King is well known for putting child protagonists front and center, children in his literary and cinema *oeuvre* are by no means safe from violent deaths; to give just a few representative examples, Tad Trenton in *Cujo* (novel 1981; film 1983) dies of heat stroke and exhaustion following his protracted ordeal trapped in a car besieged by the titular rabid St. Bernard; Gage Creed is run down by a semi-truck in *Pet Sematary* (novel 1983; adaptations 1989 and 2019, the latter of which switches Gage for older sister Ellie); George Denbrough in *It* (novel 1986; television miniseries adaptation 1990; and two part cinematic adaptation 2017 and 2019) has his arm fatally ripped off; and Bradley Trevor aka "the Baseball Boy" in *Doctor Sleep* (novel 2013; adaptation 2019) is tortured to death by Rose the Hat and the other members of the True Knot. Metaphorically, King equates the death of children such as Gage *et al.* to the death of innocence. Emotionally, King uses these deaths to wallop the reader right in the face as a way of elevating the narrative stakes for the other characters. So for a writer who has so often "gone there" before, in fairly explicit terms of representing what is usually considered one of the "forbidden areas" in fictional representation of violence, the narrative challenge that King takes on in *The Outsider* is depicting a child murder so outrageous that it surpasses anything he has heretofore done, possibly out of a need to outdo himself in terms of shock value. The first episode of the series based on the novel then visualizes the brutal picture painted by King's words.

In both novel and series, 11-year-old Frank Peterson, the child whose death sets the plot in motion, has not just been murdered; he has been savaged in an animalistic way that evokes outrage, horror, and dread in even the most jaded cops and medical examiners. He has been bitten as if by a wild animal and sodomized with a branch nearly two feet long. In the novel, the boy's injuries are described in clinical but graphic detail by Dr. Ackerman, Head of Pathology at the local hospital, thusly:

> Teeth marks were found on the remains of Peterson's face, throat, shoulder, chest, right side, and torso. The injuries . . . suggest the following sequence: Peterson was thrown violently to the ground on his back and bitten at least six times, perhaps as many as a dozen. This was frenzied behavior. He was then turned over and sodomized. By then Peterson was almost certainly unconscious.

> Either during the sodomy or directly after, the perpetrator ejaculated. . . . Parts
> of Peterson's body, most specifically the right earlobe, right nipple, and parts of
> the trachea and esophagus, are missing. The perpetrator may have taken these
> body parts, along with a considerable section of the flesh from the nape of the
> neck, as trophies. . . . The alternative hypothesis is that the perpetrator ate them.
> . . . I am a doctor, I am the county's medical examiner, but I am also a mother. .
> . . I beg you to catch the man who defiled and murdered this child, and soon. If
> you don't, he will almost certainly do it again. (94–5)

What is most striking about this passage, rhetorically speaking, is how, through this experienced medical examiner who has presumably laid eyes upon all manner of unspeakable carnage in her career, the tone moves from clinical detail to a personal and impassioned plea. Another doctor who tested the blood types and DNA from the body concludes his otherwise dispassionate report in like manner: "Although it is outside protocol, I am compelled to add a personal note here. I have dealt with evidence from many murder victims, but this is by far the worst crime I have ever been called upon to examine, and the person who did it needs to be captured ASAP" (79). As these quotes illustrate, King's gambit is to paint a picture of a murder so brutal, and indeed evil, that it moves professional men and women who thought they'd seen it all to engage in uncharacteristically emotional and reactionary behavior. And if such dispassionate professionals let themselves become unhinged, what hope does the larger community have to retain its senses when faced with outrage? Thus does the contagion of violence spread.

The series' depiction of the murder's grisly aftermath is bloody but relatively brief, given the film industry's generally accepted self-imposed limitations of representations of violence against children in visual media where the impact is more visceral and potentially more off-putting to larger numbers of viewers. However, as the camera presents them, the details are certainly graphic enough to convey something of the horror of King's words and thus have substantially the same emotional impact on viewers. The moment of revelation of the child's body is brutal; however, getting to that moment is achieved through a careful escalation of more subtle scenes that generate anticipatory dread. As the first episode ("Fish in a Barrel") opens, a man walking his dog chases his dog into the woods after the dog has been agitated by the scent of a blood spatter at the base of a tree. The scene cuts to a close-up of the panting and whimpering dog stopped up short as it looks at something off-screen. The next cut frames the man's face in close-up profile as he also stares at the same something. The equivalence in framing the faces of man and dog indicates that both have been stricken by the horror of what they have seen, thus engaging and priming the viewer's imagination to picture the worst.

The next scene, set in full dark, continues the build-up to the grisly reveal. As Detective Ralph Anderson and his fellow detective Tamika Collins approach the crime scene, she tells him "it's bad," which further builds a sense of anticipatory dread as to what the viewer might see. A few seconds later, the dead boy is shown from a distance. He is lying on his stomach, encircled by a throng of policemen and criminalists about their work in the harsh illumination of banks of portable lights, as if the boy is on stage set to be revealed to Ralph's (and the audience's) gaze. Through Ralph's eyes, the viewer next sees the boy's blood-streaked face in close-up, his eyes closed and the raw, torn red meat of his throat, shoulders, and back exposed. Rather than reading the medical examiner's actual report as excerpted in the novel, the viewer instead hears the hushed words of Detective Yunis Sablo summarizing such a report to Ralph: "So, the coroner said the tissue tears on the upper torso, there's teeth impressions around the edges." Ralph asks, "Animal?" Yunis replies, "No." As the import of this strikes Ralph, ominous music rises on the soundtrack. In the running time of a few minutes, the episode has thus condensed and dramatized the many instances in the novel that described the condition of the boy's violated body.

In the search for the perpetrator of this monstrous act, the narrative's law enforcement representatives seize upon the wrong, albeit most obvious, suspect. Seemingly ironclad physical evidence ties Terry Maitland—Little League Coach, English teacher, solid family man and citizen, and all-around upstanding guy—to the heinous crime: his fingerprints, numerous irrefutable eyewitness accounts of Terry in the company of the boy near the crime scene as well as Terry covered in blood afterward, and most, damningly, Terry's DNA. At this point, *The Outsider* as narrative still has all the trappings of a mystery thriller: how in the world can a man be in two places at once? The answer to this riddle ultimately presents the skeptical Ralph with a tear in the wall between the natural world and the supernatural. The intrusion of the supernatural into *The Outsider*'s otherwise grounded procedural narrative reality is a border or boundary violation that Barbara Creed argues is central to the horror genre: "[T]he concept of a border is central to the construction of the monstrous in the horror film. . . . Although the specific nature of the border changes from film to film, the function of the monstrous remains the same—to bring about an encounter between the symbolic order and that which threatens its stability" (11). The graphic representation of the atrocious child murder at the center of *The Outsider* is an assault on order in one of the most unimaginable and unbearable ways possible, morphing the narrative slowly but inevitably from mystery/police procedural to horror story, a point also made by Michael Blouin in his analysis of the novel (172).

The real villain of *The Outsider* is an entity that replicates human DNA to become a person's identical double or twin, all the better to carry out horrific murders in that person's form and then subsist on the grief and suffering of the survivors. In some ways, as Kevin Quigley observes, the morphable Outsider is cut from the same cloth as Pennywise, the shape-shifting, child-killing monster of King's *It* (1986). The comparison relies upon the Outsider's identification within the text as *El Cuco*, "a creature of Mexican legend that kills children and wears the faces of innocent people, sort of an inverse It. And as with It, killing children is almost—not quite, but almost—secondary. Where Pennywise thrived on fear, *El Cuco*, the Outsider eats sorrow." The cumulative effect of the Outsider's crime, Quigley concludes, is collective demoralization: "We watch how the Outsider's actions—and the actions of the people who do his work for him—nearly ruin Maitland's family, tear the victim's family apart, and incite the community to unthinking mob violence." Terry's double, or his evil twin or his *doppelganger*, is a creature from some outside realm taking on his face to tear apart and rape an innocent boy. In turn, the double's act of violence against a child begets more violence as the disruption spreads like a virus.[1] The narrative's introduction of the monstrous double bears out Rene Girard's observation, in his interrogation of world myth, that "the double and the monster are one and the same being" (160). In the terms of King's narrative, this kind of doubling is inherently a form of violence committed against the subject, an invasion or violation followed by theft of identity in order to create a self-perpetuating cycle of violence.

The third episode of the series, entitled "Dark Uncle," specifically invokes one of the many names of the *doppelganger* figure in world cultures and introduces a key figure in the shift of the series from the mundane world of the mystery thriller/police procedural to the strange world of supernatural horror. Holly Gibney, an idiosyncratic private investigator recommended to Anderson by Terry's attorney Howie Salomon, consults with Ralph to assist the detective in his quest to somehow explain the inexplicable.[2] She explains what a *doppelganger* is to an initially resistant Anderson:

> I have to say that all these contradicting eyewits, videos, and forensics—sounds like your man has a *doppelganger*. From the German "double goer." The myth is, if it's a myth, everyone in the world has an identical double. . . . Not a twin. . . . A non-biological double. The Egyptians call it a "*ka*," the Norwegians a "*vardoger*," the Finns an "*etainen*," the Swiss a "dark uncle." . . . My particular favorite is "fetch," from the Old Irish. My theory about the *doppelganger* is that it is a primitive construct they used to explain bi-polar disorder, or schizophrenia, or just the everyday struggle between the id and the super-ego.

Holly's mythology lesson, while concluding with a seemingly more fact-based explanation of the *doppelganger* phenomenon, still suggests a certain doubt about that conclusion through her use of the conditional "if it is a myth," a caveat that Ralph notices. He tells her he has "no tolerance for the unexplainable," which Holly turns back on him by saying that he "will have no tolerance for me." She runs through a long litany of the extraordinary savant abilities she possesses: among them, identifying the make and model of cars at a glance, calculating far-off dates and the heights of skyscrapers from moving cars, and quoting lyrics of rock songs from 1984 to the present day. She is, essentially, a human super-computer whose existence defies modern psychiatric attempts to explain how she can do it. Through cataloging her powers in this manner, Holly instructs Ralph, and by extension the viewer, to learn to accept the reality of otherwise inexplicable phenomenon and thus, possibly, solve an unsolvable case only explainable by the existence of a supernatural *doppelganger* that brings with it the socially destabilizing force of violence.

King has written many times before about evil doubles, or *doppelgangers*. One of the most prominent pairings is Thad Beaumont and George Stark in *The Dark Half* (1989), a kind of meta riff on Stephen King and his pen name Richard Bachman, often viewed as (believe it or not) the "darker" side of King.[3] Heidi Strengell calls this kind of twinned character in King's fiction the "Gothic double." Sometimes this Gothic double, Strengell writes, is one part of the character's "split" or "dissociative" personality, very much in the tradition of Dr. Jekyll and Mr. Hyde in Robert Louis Stevenson's 1886 novel of the same name: for example, Odetta Holmes/Detta Walker in *The Dark Tower* series. And sometimes the double is comprised of two distinct entities, more like a traditional Germanic *doppelganger* ("The Monster Never Dies"). Terry Maitland and his "Dark Uncle" in *The Outsider* thus fit squarely within the Gothic Double motif in King's work that Strengell identifies. The split doubles can never reconcile or co-exist, reinforcing the theme of irreparable social violence inflicted by a split double that King invests into the narrative.

Holly's investigation uncovers more evidence of the twisted path Terry's *doppelganger* has traveled, a path that reveals the *doppelganger* has not one particular fixed identity, but rather assumes the form of selected people it encounters and in doing so further spreads violence. In the series' fourth episode, "Que Viene El Cuco" (or, "Here Comes the Boogeyman"), she undertakes a kind of contact tracing in the wake of a supernatural being whose *modus operandi* is to infect selected subjects who have led blameless lives with some kind of communicable disease or figurative "murder virus" (in spite of Holly's insistence that murder is *not* a virus) to pass on to others before the current subject is used up. She discovers that Heath Hofstetter, an orderly at the elder care facility where Terry's father resides and who unknowingly infected the younger Maitland, committed suicide in jail after being arrested for the murder of two girls; Heath's brother subsequently died of an overdose and his mother killed herself in a one-car accident. Heath seems to have contracted the murder virus from a casual contact with a bartender he flirted with in New York named Maria Caneles, who disregarded his advances but whose *doppelganger* later had breakfast followed by sex with him. Maria is in Riker's Island awaiting trial for the murder of a young girl; her father and uncle have been killed by the grandfather of her victim. Finally, the virus has been passed on to Claude Bolton, the ex-con manager of a strip club called the Peach Crease, who is destined to be the Outsider's next form after Terry. An extended circle of personal, violent tragedy surrounds each murder the Outsider commits, which Andy Katcavage, a retired homicide detective who assists Holly in her investigation and becomes her love interest, likens to a plague ("Que Viene"). The viral spread of violence is easy for Holly to track once she is onto what is happening.

Every good villain in fiction needs a motive, so for the Outsider, its violence is a means to an end, which parallels in metatextual fashion the impulse that propels Stephen King to raise the narrative stakes with graphic displays of violence: its psychic consumption of the pain and other negative energy generated by the murderous act.[4] When Holly, interviewing Maria in jail, asks her who killed the child, she refuses to say the murderer's name because "they will send me right from here to a mental hospital." Holly follows up with an interview with a woman who overheard the conversation and passed her a note in the Riker's Island waiting room. Perhaps too conveniently for plot plausibility, the woman is a fount of information about this myth come to life, naming the primary villain for the first time in the series:

> When you were a child, who were you told would come for you if you misbehaved. . .? For me, in Cuba, I was told El Cuco would come. . . . El Cuco, Jumbee, met an old Russian woman once who called hers Baba Yaga [the boogeyman]. . . . All the old cultures, we had the bad habit of turning truth into fairy tales. . . . It can look like a person when it needs to be, but it's not. . . . [It's] the Grief Eater. It takes the child itself. But after, it likes to linger, because it craves the pain of the ones left behind. If the child is its meal, the suffering of the family is its dessert.

Holly's Internet search into these grim fairy tales reveals images of various artistic impressions of El Cuco (alternatively, El Coco), including Goya's etching of *Que viene el Coco* (1797–1798) that gives the episode its title, as well as Goya's gruesome painting of *Saturn Devouring His Son* (1819–1823). Both images focus on a terrifying figure intent on harming children (and in Saturn's case, cannibalizing one). The images also depict a mortal threat to the family; in one, a woman cowers with her two children before a cloaked and hooded figure, and in the other, Saturn's sons face the same grisly fate as the one being consumed. So too are the families consumed by an evil being in *The Outsider*, an act of violence which extends beyond the immediate circle of carnage to destabilize the fragile bonds of citizenship holding communities together.

Again and again, *The Outsider* as a story hammers home its central message: violence is a communicable, and ever-mutating, disease. Through its contagious touch, the Outsider also has the power to not only mimic the human form but control others to do its murderous bidding in an effort to thwart any existential threat when it is at its most vulnerable. To transform, as Holly intuits in the sixth episode "The One About the Yiddish Vampire," the creature must shed the skin of one subject to take another's; during this transitional latency period the Outsider requires human assistance for protection from those who have discovered its true nature. It ensures such assistance through, again, its contaminating touch.

Jack Hoskins, the alcoholic police detective already predisposed to violence of his own who works in the same police department as Ralph Anderson, unwittingly becomes the Outsider's human minion when it touches his neck from behind in the isolated barn where it has previously shed Maitland's blood-stained clothing ("The Dark Uncle"). The mere touch of the Outsider infects Jack's neck, an ugly corruption of the flesh that grows worse when Jack tries to reassert his own agency and abates only when he acquiesces to the Outsider's will. The boils on Jack's neck signify the state of his progressively disintegrating psyche, which alternates between struggles to break free of the Outsider's mental commands and preparations to ambush violently Ralph and Holly's investigation. At one point, Holly in her unfiltered way tells Hoskins he looks like "someone's been trying to rip out your heart": a simile that succinctly sums up Jack's torment ("The One About the Yiddish Vampire"). He may be a hard-nosed cop and an alcoholic loudmouth, but he is not a killer until the Outsider forces him to be one.

Jack's story arc is a cycle of surrender and resistance culminating in his death. He capitulates to the entity, for example, when it appears to him in the form of his deceased mother to beat him as punishment for his failure to derail the investigation ("The One About the Yiddish Vampire"). As a direct result of this attack, he lures Holly into his car to take her to her death, a plot foiled when she tricks him and escapes at a gas station. He then resists the Outsider's will by trying to commit suicide to be relieved of his physical and psychological hell, but either he cannot pull his gun's trigger or the entity won't allow him to ("In the Pines, in the Pines"). Once more fully under the Outsider's malign spell, the broken police officer eludes a surveillance team to remove a weapons cache from his apartment to the bear cave serving as the entity's lair, murders a fisherman to steal his car, and uses his sniper's training and aim to kill three members of Ralph's and Holly's investigative team when they end up at the cave. In the end, however, Jack manages to recover enough of his own identity just long enough to carry through on what he tried to do once before: kill himself with a bullet to the head ("Must/ Can't"). Jack's tragic end, as well as the tragic ends of all those touched by the Outsider throughout its lifespan to become its willing assassins, is one more lethal variant of the disease of violence, originating from the intrusion of the supernatural into the natural world, within each community that has the misfortune to play host to the entity.

Serving as the secondary human antagonist of the narrative, Jack bears more than a passing resemblance to the character of Henry Bowers in the novel and adaptations of King's *It*, a violent bully who also is possessed by an evil outsider to commit acts of violence against the protagonists. Already hostage to lifetimes of anger which lead them to lash out at others, Jack Hoskins and Henry Bowers find themselves all too susceptible to the malign influence of supernatural monsters who use them to commit even greater acts of violence than they would have done on their own. Jack becomes another type of double for the primary antagonist in this regard—not one who has his face and body stolen for violent ends by the Other, but rather his mind consumed to become a violent agent acting on behalf of the Other.

King's use of this Gothic double trope, in combination with his leitmotif of the violence of American history and its impact on the present, can have a powerful impact on a reader who otherwise might not be particularly invested in or knowledgeable of the political issues of the moment but who nevertheless recognizes them at some deeply internalized, maybe even subconscious level. Seen through this lens, the Outsider's presence within the civic order, which both violates and affirms it in the sense that same order has long perpetuated itself through violence, is King's way of providing trenchant commentary on the era of Donald Trump and "fake news," as noted by James Smythe in his review of the novel where he states "the titular Outsider is not the strongest presence of evil in this book. There is an intriguing political undercurrent throughout: from mentions of the Black Lives Matter movement to the shadowy presence of Donald Trump, evoked by a crowd wearing Make America Great Again hats and baying for Terry's blood. . . .You could see *The Outsider* as King's take on fake news, moving it from the political realm to something more personal. Lies being sold as truth: what form could that concept take?" ("An Impossible Alibi"). King's answer to that question is the Outsider, a being as physically mutable and virulent as political lies in the service of violence against persons and the social order. Of course, the term "outsider" is often applied to Trump as an untamable force who was elected by his base to disrupt the political status quo and, as he so often claimed "drain the swamp" of Washington, D.C.: a cultural meme that King, given his well-known antipathy toward the 45th president that resulted in the latter blocking the former's Twitter account, had to have known before settling on the title of his story about the child-killing shapeshifter. Of course, disrupting the status quo is one thing; however, Trump's brand of disruption is typically couched in the language of violence, which often serves to inflame his more volatile followers to commit acts of violence at the behest of their president.[5] It is little wonder, then, that Ryan Vlastelica titled his online review of the novel "Stephen King's *The Outsider* is an *It* for the Trump era." After all, he writes in the body of the review, "don't monstrous times deserve a monster of their own?"

To give one example, King references the Black Lives Matter movement in the fourth paragraph of the book, establishing the political undertone right away. As an unmarked police car pulls up to the baseball field just before Terry's arrest, two young black boys carrying skateboards see the car arrive. One of them says, "That's Five-O," and the two boys promptly skateboard away, thinking of the simple rule their parents have instilled in them: ". . . when Five-O shows up, it's time to go. Black lives matter . . . but not always to Five-O" (3). The rhetorical placement of this scene to open the novel not only sets the novel in a specific time (the year 2018) but primes the reader to look for other references to the discontents of the Trump era scattered throughout the novel. Which there are: a boulder by the roadside outside the city has been defaced with the slogan "TRUMP MAKE AMERICA GREAT AGAIN TRUMP" (234); Ralph thinks disparagingly of a witness he is questioning that the man *"probably voted for Donald Trump"* (343); and in a café Ralph catches sight of a photograph of Trump that has been defaced to give him a Hitlerian dark-colored forelock and moustache (437).

Certainly, these politically charged allusions may serve only to set the story's timeline, a reading King would have his audience believe. In spite of his frequent public (and scathing) criticisms of the 45th President of the United States, King has resisted critical readings of *The Outsider* as some kind of allegory for the Age of Trump. In one interview after *The Outsider* was published, he states, "I'm a storyteller basically, and that's apolitical, and I try to jettison as much of the politics as I can without forgetting that I'm a human being and I have a point of view and people have to deal with that, for better or for worse. . . . What I really don't want to do is to write something that's got an agenda that's anti-Trump or pro–Elizabeth Warren or anything political. I want to tell a good story." Yet in the same interview, King says this of *The Outsider*: "What was important to me was the whole idea of, how do we deal with something that we can't believe but is. Trump's a good example. How do we deal with that on a day-to-day basis? . . . You're in a situation where you say, *I can't believe that this reality guy who once did the WWF, who doesn't have a brain, I can't believe he got elected president. It can't be.* But it is. So you have to try" ("National Nightmare"). He equates his fictional practical realist Ralph Anderson's plight—forced to believe in a *doppelganger* misery-eating monster—with that of the millions of shaken voters having to somehow reconcile themselves with the reality that Donald Trump actually got elected president, which certainly sounds like King is putting forth a political reading of his purportedly non- or apolitical novel. If one grants that *The Outsider* is not a political allegory, as a story it certainly correlates to the Trumpian era as part of King's decades-long agenda to expose the darkness at the heart of supposedly idyllic small-town America, a dark heart that stokes hate and erupts, all too often, into the kind of bloody violence depicted in *The Outsider*.

For the most part, the series eschews more overt references to the political moment, perhaps in the interests of not alienating more conservative viewers. It denies its audience the most obvious signifiers that locate the setting between the years 2015–2020 (spanning the rise of Trump as a viable candidate for the presidency to both the final year of Trump's term and the series' air date). There are no MAGA hats in a crowd, no Trump photo portraits in people's residences, no shout-out to Black Lives Matters (other than perhaps making the main character line-up more diverse than it is in the novel with the casting of African-American Cynthia Erivo as Holly Gibney), and the like. However, the Trumpian subtext as an inextricable link in the chains of the narrative DNA remains. The violent mob that assembles to shout and rage at Maitland when he is brought from the jail to his court appearance, a raw outburst of fury that ends with Ollie Peterson fatally shooting Terry before being gunned down by Ralph ("Roanoke"), is all too recognizable in the context of the Trumpian era of right-wing political rallies where the audience gives vent to wrath stoked by incendiary rhetoric.[6] The mob's violent action, in that it is in response to the horrible murder of a child by an influential citizen, is not that far removed from those QAnon believers who commit violent acts based on a complex, far-reaching conspiracy theory (which rose to prominence during the Trump presidency) that a shadowy global cabal of Satanic pedophiles, including powerful Democrats and Hollywood celebrities, not only molests children but ritually slaughters and eats them in order to gain life extension.[7] The scene where Terry is killed during a riot is probably the one that lingered in Adrian Hennigan's mind as she wrote her review of the series, noting that "HBO's 'The Outsider' . . . is the most unsettling and unnerving thing you can currently see on your screens other than a televised Trump rally" ("Scariest Thing on TV"). Therefore, while many of the novel's more overt references to the Trumpian political era have been excised from the adaptation, the political allegory anchored to the contemporary moment still structures the narrative and explains its impetus to violence.

The Outsider, in conclusion, is both a novel and series that relies in great measure upon the audience's knowledge of the currents (or rapids) of American politics of the last few years for the narrative, already rooted in one of Stephen King's most extreme depictions yet of the corpse of a child who has been raped and murdered, to achieve its maximum impact. One of the most marked characteristics of the years between 2015–2021 has been the overt rhetorical appeals based on enmity toward some politically convenient other, e.g., Black Lives Matter, illegal immigrants, etc., and couched in appeals toward violence based on outrageous lies, with savage denunciations of anyone who dares call out the lies as purveyors of "fake news." Such rhetoric is all too easily manifested in real-world physical violence. Such inflammatory speech, amplified by a receptive media apparatus, is designed to go "viral," the telling metaphor for widespread circulation of a transmitted message. *The Outsider* stands, its author's demurrals aside, as a reflection through a glass darkly of an especially conflicted and partisan time in American history, where neighbors turn against neighbors when passions run high.

NOTES

1. Given this subtext, it is especially ironic that the initial broadcast run of *The Outsider* in January 2020 coincided with the growing public awareness of a novel coronavirus first reported in the Wuhan province of China that by March 11, 2020, just a few days after the last episode of the series aired on March 8, was declared a pandemic by the World Health Organization.

2. Holly Gibney is an obsessive-compulsive private investigator who may, it is implied, be on the autism spectrum. She is a recurring character in King's recent fiction, who first appears in the trilogy of "Bill Hodges" novels—*Mr. Mercedes* (2014), *Finders Keepers* (2015), and *End of Watch* (2016)—working with the titular retired cop. She is also the main character of the novella *If It Bleeds* (2020).

3. George Stark is also an homage to crime fiction writer Donald E. Westlake's *nom de plume* Richard Stark.

4. The Outsider's feeding upon psychic energy connects it to another set of King's villains in his novel *Doctor Sleep* (2013), a sequel to *The Shining* (1977): the cross-country traveling band of psychic vampires known as "the True Knot" who torture children to death to feed on the "steam," or psychic energy, of children gifted with "the shining."

5. A representative sample of such incitement to violence, as catalogued on the *Vox* news website, includes Trump's initial support for two Boston brothers, influenced by Trump's verbal attacks on illegal immigrants, who were arrested for beating and urinating on a homeless man in August 2015; Trump's penchant for targeting, mocking, and having protestors ejected from his rallies; his equation of white supremacists with leftist counterprotestors at the "Unite the Right" march in Charlottesville, Virginia that led to the death of one woman; and most infamously of all, his exhortation on January 6, 2021 (after months of false and incendiary rhetoric about election fraud) to an angry crowd of supporters to march to the Capitol building in Washington, D.C., an act which led to the mob occupying the building for several hours and the deaths of at least five people ("Donald Trump Is the Accelerant").

6. This series of political rallies culminated at the time of this writing in the January 6, 2021 rally turned riot/insurrection at the Capitol Building in Washington, D.C.

7. The Outsider itself, who extends its life through consumption of children, says to Holly in the climactic episode: "[Children] taste the sweetest" ("Must/Can't"). The QAnon belief that the Satanic pedophiles at the heart of the conspiracy eat children is taken to its absurd extreme in the inhuman monster of *The Outsider*.

WORKS CITED

Blouin, Michael. *Stephen King and American Politics*. Cardiff: University of Wales Press, 2021.

Cineas, Fabiola. "Donald Trump Is the Accelerant." *Vox*, 9 January 2021, https://www.vox.com/21506029/trump-violence-tweets-racist-hate-speech.

Creed, Barbara. *The Monstrous-Feminine: Film, Feminism, Psychoanalysis*. New York: Routledge, 1993.

"Dark Uncle." *The Outsider*, written by Richard Price, Season 1, episode 3, HBO, 19 January 2020.

"Fish in a Barrel." *The Outsider*, written by Richard Price, Season 1, episode 1, HBO, 12 January 2020.

Girard, Rene. *Violence and the Sacred*. 1972. Translated by Patrick Gregory. Baltimore: The Johns Hopkins University Press, 1986.

Hennigan, Adrian. "HBO's 'The Outsider' is the Scariest Thing on TV after a Trump Rally." *Haaretz*, 2 November 2020, https://www.haaretz.com/life/television/.premium-hbo-s-the-outsider-is-the-scariest-thing-on-tv-after-a-trump-rally-1.8521786.

"In the Pines, in the Pines." *The Outsider*, written by Richard Price, Season 1, episode 7, HBO, 16 February 2020.

King, Stephen. *Danse Macabre*. 1981. New York: Gallery Books, 2010.

———. *The Outsider*. 2018. New York: Gallery Books, 2019.

———. "Stephen King on Violence at the Movies." *Entertainment Weekly*, 8 October 2007, https://ew.com/article/2007/10/08/stephen-king-violence-movies/.

Magistrale, Tony, and Michael J. Blouin. *Stephen King and American History*. New York: Routledge, 2021.

"Must/Can't." *The Outsider*, written by Richard Price, Season 1, episode 10, HBO, 8 March 2020.

"The One About the Yiddish Vampire." *The Outsider*, written by Richard Price, Season 1, episode 6, HBO, 9 February 2020.

Peitzman, Louis. "National Nightmare." *BuzzFeed News*, 14 June 2018, https://www.buzzfeednews.com/article/louispeitzman/stephen-king-the-outsider-donald-trump-resistance-twitter.

"Que Viene el Coco." *The Outsider*, written by Richard Price, Season 1, episode 4, HBO, 26 January 2020.

Quigley, Kevin. *"The Outsider*: A Novel Critique." *Charnel House*, retrieved 1 February 2020, https://www.charnelhouse.org/theoutsider.

"Roanoke." *The Outsider*, written by Richard Price, Season 1, episode 2, HBO, 12 January 2020.

Smythe, James. *"The Outsider* by Stephen King Review: An Impossible Alibi." *The Guardian*, 18 May 2018, https://www.theguardian.com/books/2018/may/18/the-outsider-by-sephen-king.

Strengell, Heidi. "'The Monster Never Dies': An Analysis of the Gothic Double in Stephen King's Oeuvre." *Americana: The Journal of American Popular Culture 1900 to Present*, Spring 2003, Volume 2, Issue 1, https://www.americanpopularculture.com/journal/articles/spring_2003/strengell.htm.

Vlastelica, Ryan. "Stephen King's The Outsider Is an It for the Trump Era." *AV Club*, 21 May 2018, https://aux.avclub.com/stephen-king-s-the-outsider-is-an-it-for-the-trump-era-1825906254.

Chapter 11

The Invasive Gaze

Surveillance Camera Shots in Flanagan's Doctor Sleep *and Price's* The Outsider

Matthew Muller

Vampire-like creatures, working together in nomadic communes or as solitary predators, have colonized the state in a recent slew of films and television adapted from Stephen King novels, particularly in Mike Flanagan's *Doctor Sleep* (2019) and Richard Price's *The Outsider* (2020). King's new vampires are not just another set of Dracula knock-offs. The True Knot and El Cuco mark a significant departure from his previous archetypal monsters and perpetrators of violence. Further, his new vampires are a striking contrast, perhaps even a subversive response, to the falseness of a decades-long market craze in popular culture that normalized the kind of sexy superhero vampires depicted in *Buffy the Vampire Slayer* (1997–2003), *The Twilight Saga* film series (2008–2012), or HBO's *True Blood* (2008–2014)—a trend, it might be worth noting in its pertinence to this essay, that correlates with the rise of surveillance capitalism out of Silicon Valley. On the contrary, the new vampires are parasitic reavers of civilization, which continuously represses their collusion in a riven planet. And while the children these vampires prey upon to fuel their supernatural lives might seem to be a standard gothic trope in King's oeuvre, the monsters' depersonalized motives and their ability to isolate victims in public space represent a novel form of horror violence. Camera shots in *Doctor Sleep* and *The Outsider* mimic the invasive gaze these vampires represent. It is an inherently violent and violating gaze motivated by the logic of necropolitics: Achille Mbembe's critical observation that sovereignties around the world define themselves with the power to "dictate who may live and who must die" (66). This "necropower" is instrumentalized in many ways throughout history. In the past, "panoptic fortifications" (81) and other war machines, from watchtowers to helicopters, enabled a form of colonial occupation that isolated people in segregated communities (i.e., suburban enclaves, prisons, gated communities, plantations, the inner city). Thus, Foucaultian biopower, Mbembe asserts, is insufficient in describing contemporary forms of sovereignty, which deploy intrusive technology to create "death-worlds" where captive populations "are subjected to living conditions that confer upon them the status of the *living dead"* (92). Likewise, with its power to seduce and feed off the living, the vampire was an invader from without, usually a war-torn frontier of the East. Today though, a sovereign's figurative castle rock could be anywhere in the form of overt and covert surveillance from Earth-observation satellites to the Internet of Things within a private home. For Mbembe, increasingly intrusive surveillance enables sovereigns and quasi-sovereign entities (i.e., nomadic war machines, private firms, terrorist organizations) to disaggregate populations into the death-worthy Other versus brutally secured refugees and civilians. These latter people are segregated demographically, confined to camps, and then left to ulcerate in quiet desperation. This death-dealing oversight is effected by intrusive technology even as it resembles the dreadful panoptic power of Castle Dracula.

Stephen King's new vampires select victims not so much in Manichean terms humans can understand but as a kind of amoral repurposing of people into biocapital. Gothic space in King's canon is no longer confined to the bathroom or the sewers of Derry as in the previous era of Stephen King horror. Elevators of blood, killer clowns, the Randall Flaggs of the King multiverse—these are all monsters King's audience could wrap their heads around in filmic rehearsals to survive and ultimately overcome the fear of death. Life goes on, at least for the viewer—horror film as public health. The True Knot and El Cuco, however, represent a new form of monstrosity in which ghastly sexualized violence is just a means to an end. Flanagan shows this in horrendous detail in *Doctor Sleep* when members of the True Knot hold down a victim in a rape scene that ought to trigger moral outrage in the audience as it does Abra Stone. This, by the way, is a very different affect than traditional Stephen King films are designed to elicit, such as revulsion, horror, or terror. In the case of *The Outsider*, a similar type of sexualized murder happens off-stage; investigators describe its grotesque details in clinical detail. This necropolitical horror of weaponized surveillance is literalized in Flanagan and Price's work, as vampire-like monsters descend from nowhere in a deadly hit and run strike upon the oblivious population in places like Frazier, New Hampshire, or Cherokee City, Georgia. Like Mbembe's war machines, the True Knot and El Cuco leave in their wake collateral damage and torn bodies. Necropower, the power to decide to kill and put to death, subjects a person to an invasive gaze, a gaze that has become ubiquitous and pervasive, and yet treats individuals as an exploitable resource (i.e., metadata, behavioral surplus) at best and at worst, as a potential criminal. This is tolerated in

America, at least by those aware of corporate and governmental surveillance, which ostensibly places a premium on privacy and civil rights. In a sense, contemporary society places faith in fallible necropolitical entities that have histories of violence. Is there something oddly nostalgic about baring one's neck to more powerful creatures whose existence can only be deduced from crime scene clues or the laborious investigation of backstory? Earlier forms of horror violence, the seduction-destruction perpetrated by archetypal monsters, were always personal, especially in earlier Stephen King films where camera shots often focused claustrophobic angles on victims. Before the age of surveillance, the death-worlds that emerged as a consequence of vampiric violence was less intrusive. Victims bore some responsibility in that they trespassed into gothic space or blithely accepted the seductive promises of biocapitalism even while turning a blind eye to resulting genocide or war. Now, vampires, as agents of necropower, are no longer restricted by boundaries real or imagined. Like surveillance capitalists, King's new vampires are outsiders equipped with an unprecedented ability to penetrate society, modify behavior, and extract resources from their victims.

Innovative camera shots in Flanagan's *Doctor Sleep* and Price's *The Outsider* show an invasive point-of-view to defamiliarize and expose the inherent violence of modern-day surveillance. First, I will show how Abra Stone's psychic investigation of the True Knot in Flanagan's *Doctor Sleep* resembles the necropolitics of post-9/11 drone warfare. Then, I will demonstrate how Price uses various camera shots to create a pervasive and paranoiac sense of being watched and perhaps even fed upon by unknown and unseen observers: Is it El Cuco? The police? Ordinary people with camera phones? And finally, in a close analysis of an original scene created by Price for Episode 5 of *The Outsider*, I will show how he uses camera shots to create a victim's sense of being pinned down by an invasive gaze capable of precision killing.

Much has been made of Kubrick's helicopter camera shot in the opening sequence of *The Shining*. Like "birds of prey" (Nelson 201), the spectacular camera swoops over the Going-to-the-Sun Highway to a haunting dirge, "Dies Irae." This iconic shot is "palely echoed" (Browning 201) in the film adaptation for what has been described as King's Vietnam War story, *Dreamcatcher* (Magistrale and Blouin 89–109). Both Nelson and Browning interpret Kubrick's bird-of-prey camera shot as a dark extension of the Overlook Hotel's supernatural grip upon the Torrance family as they drive into a country formerly occupied by Native Americans. Flanagan replicates Kubrick's helicopter shot in *Doctor Sleep* when Abra Stone and Danny Torrance drive to a derelict Overlook Hotel for their showdown with Rose the Hat. Interestingly, Flanagan innovates a new use of eye-in-sky camera work within the canon of Stephen King films by using drone camera shots. This is quite fitting when the primary symbol of the American war machine, once the helicopter during the Vietnam War era (Nguyen), has become the Unmanned Aerial Vehicle, more commonly known as the drone.

Flanagan deploys drone shots when Abra psychically investigates a remote crime scene and retroactively witnesses the True Knot's gruesome murder of Baseball Boy. Interestingly, this complex scene takes place over a school day throughout several locations. Furthermore, an inter-title in the Director's Cut, "Chapter 3 LITTLE SPY," clues the audience to how Abra ought to be perceived. The scene begins with Abra in the school library as she telepathically eavesdrops on students' mental chatter. From Abra's POV, the camera pans around the library from student to student, almost like somebody tuning in to different channels on a radio. Though her peers remain unaware of her psychic surveillance, Abra catches at least one student who is disconcerted by her behavior and thinks to herself, "The freak is staring at me again." The student does not realize that Abra's staring means that she can monitor her thoughts, but Abra uses her power often enough to have been labeled a "freak." Then Abra searches online on the National Bureau of Missing Children for clues about Baseball Boy's identity and his last known location. She scrolls down the webpage until she recognizes the face of the boy she remotely viewed being murdered the night before, Bradley Trevor. With this information, Abra now knows the name of the murder victim and the general location of his abduction by the True Knot. Later, while doing homework on her bed, Abra experimentally touches a printed photograph of Baseball Boy and concentrates. Unexpectedly, Abra's consciousness momentarily projects into the recent past with a tight claustrophobic shot of Baseball Boy on the floor of a van. In a sense, Abra can bilocate or be in two places at once. This psychic phenomenon is similar to the experience of operating a drone, in which the operator, perhaps working from a comfortable space in America, remote controls a drone somewhere in the Middle East. But the horrific vision of the kidnapped boy, and perhaps Abra's newfound ability to control her mental power, shocks her. In crosscut scenes with a corporeal Abra in her bedroom and the out-of-body presence of Abra within Baseball Boy, sound and imagery from the kidnapped victim's POV flash before her. Beneath an overcast sky, cornfields recede into the flatline of the horizon. Barry the Chunk's cruel laughter from the van's passenger seat. A vast expanse of lonely highway. As Abra delves deeper into Baseball Boy's last moments of life, she rapidly learns to control the flow of actionable intelligence. A close-up shot of Abra's face signals this milestone of psychic talent. Her pupils roll back, making her eyes appear white like the eyes of her role-model, Storm, from Marvel's X-Men, signified by a plastic figurine she keeps on her night table. Interestingly, Abra's POV does not fly around like a bird, helicopter, or superhero to view the landscape with a high-angle shot. Instead, the camera shot emerges from Abra-Baseball Boy's POV within the van to hover over the Iowa countryside. This is Abra's psychic eye-in-the-sky, which resembles camera footage shot from a drone. Her consciousness hovers directly over the True Knot convoy as it snakes towards the abandoned ethanol plant where Baseball Boy's "steam" was brutally purified and extracted the night before. Unlike a high-angle shot or wide-angle shot from a helicopter, these shots mimic a drone's top-down camera shot used for military reconnaissance and targeting enemy combatants for termination. Like video footage recorded by a drone, Abra can fast-forward through this imagery to collect pertinent data. Thus, Abra's investigation is an amalgam of cyberspace and the paranormal. Psychic eavesdropping, internet sleuthing, and drone camera shots within the world of this horror film all work in tandem to defamiliarize the new American war machine.

Fortunately, Abra Stone, Stephen King's answer to the superhero genre, uses her psychic talent for a just cause, that is, bringing a nomadic band of evildoers from the Middle East to a justified end. In other words, for various reasons, Abra—in the tradition of American vigilantism[1]—has usurped the sovereign's necropolitical prerogative to conduct espionage and act as judge, jury, and executioner. In essence, Abra's waging of a secret war on the True Knot is not unlike the clandestine use of military drones in the War on Terror. In a trenchant critique of US drone warfare in the Middle East, Allinson describes drone operators' logic within a "kill-chain." Ostensibly, human oversight and strict rules of engagement prevent drone operators from engaging in the sort of vigilantism Abra conducts. First, drone operators are supervised by a screener at a home base, while forward observers on the ground provide human eyes-on details that cannot be verified through drone cameras. Nevertheless, Allinson's close reading of a transcript of a US drone strike on a convoy exposes the war machine's racist necropolitical logic: "drone operators assigned Afghan civilians beneath their gaze to membership of a population worthy of death" (114). After surveilling the convoy in real-time and finding no sign of small arms—a prerequisite for attacking—the drone operator, desirous "to go kinetic" upon Military Aged Males in their "man dresses" (124), decides that even the mere possibility of males disguised as females is a bulletproof case for the convoy's obliteration. Such brutal overkill via drones armed with hellfire missiles is "a horror beyond death" (Debrix 85). In these respects, the actual world under the thanatoptic gaze of the war machine carries over in Abra's drone's eye view of the True Knot's convoy. Unlike military trained and bureaucratically managed drone operators, Abra operates freely to avenge Baseball Boy's murder. Just as real drone operators used a combination of racist and homophobic rationale to pursue dehumanized people deemed worthy of putting to death, Abra's motivation to terminate the True Knot, just as it may be, is tinged with a sense of righteous outrage.

The drone's eye view in *Doctor Sleep* is but one aspect of a set-piece scene in a film about rooting out from America a band of nomadic vampires that traces its parasitic wandering back to the ancient Middle East. But in Richard Price's bleak procedural, *The Outsider*, drone shots—or drone-like shots—are as pervasive as mass surveillance in the real world. Throughout the series, drone cameras are used for traditional overview shots, as in an overview of Cherokee City in the first episode, "Fish in the Barrel." In the second episode, "Roanoke," a drone camera is used for establishing shots of the courthouse besieged by protestors on the verge of a riot. Interestingly, most of the "passionate locals" in front of the courthouse are barely held back by police from lynching Terry Maitland. Like Abra Stone in *Doctor Sleep*, these people have a sense of righteous outrage and are reported as wanting "to see justice against accused killer, Tony Maitland." Perhaps too, they desire "to go kinetic" like the nameless drone operator in Allinson's expose. This set-piece scene captures a threefold use of the camera throughout *The Outsider*. Here, there is a camera as it is traditionally used in film and television. Also, here and throughout the series, characters rely on video footage, ranging from an innocuous recording of a teacher conference to reams of footage made available through ubiquitous mass surveillance—the latter which the shapeshifting-vampiric El Cuco exploits to chute its victims into what Salomon describes as "the justice train, and the train has no brain" (Episode 1: "Fish in a Barrel"). For Salomen, "the justice train" describes the judicial process once an alleged criminal is arrested. "The train has no brain" because the process cannot be stopped, even when new evidence emerges to exonerate the suspect. And so, as soon as El Cuco's framed victim, in this case, Terry, boards the justice train, the vampire begins its own seemingly unstoppable process of regeneration. It does so by psychically harvesting the emotional fallout and ensuing violence in the wake of a child's gruesome murder. In this, El Cuco's vampirism and modus operandi bear some resemblance to the True Knot vampires.

In the last two episodes of *The Outsider*, El Cuco inhales deeply as his telepathically remote-controlled slave, Jack Hoskins, gleefully ambushes Holly's Crew of Light. And, like Abra Stone in *Doctor Sleep*, El Cuco can bilocate. This ability to be in two places at once comes in two forms. First, El Cuco can physically shapeshift into the doppelganger likeness of his chosen victim. And secondly, like a "radio wave" or "hologram," as Holly speculates (Episode 6: "The One About the Yiddish Vampire"), a disembodied projection of El Cuco can surveil and terrorize victims with impunity. Thus, El Cuco's drone's eye view, a more advanced version of Abra's with its ability to inflict pain upon those it brands, is replicated throughout *The Outsider* by a roving voyeuristic gaze. For example, in numerous scenes, camera shots linger on characters seemingly oblivious to the camera/El Cuco's presence. A private conversation in an interior scene unfolds as if being viewed from an invisible spy. Other creepy spy shots let fly from under a table, around the corner, a hospital floor, a ceiling corner, a structure's exit. Such nonhuman camera shots objectify their human subjects, transforming the field of vision into a scavenger's charnel ground ripe for El Cuco. These camera shots also resemble surveillance capitalism's spook's eye view of the world in which people are labeled end-users. Their metadata and online behavior are a profitable resource mined without their knowledge or consent by Big Data firms.[2]

The Petersons' funeral reception in "Roanoke" clearly shows that the camera's gaze is the gaze of El Cuco, which Richard Price uses to defamiliarize the vampiric nature of surveillance capitalism. In this montage of a funeral reception, low-angle shots of people grieving, accompanied by a soundtrack of eerie, menacing music and inaudible voices, show the roving invasive gaze of El Cuco. After surveying three sets of funeral-goers, El Cuco's gaze, like an invisible mini drone, moves into the dining room and settles upon a close-up shot of corncobs glistening with butter. The shot's soft-focus blurs the human subjects in the background. These camera shots signify El Cuco's POV and its perception of dehumanized subjects as an energy resource. After the reception, the scene plays out from a stationary low-angle shot centered on the table as El Cuco watches the Petersons clean up. This camera shot remains immobile for most of the scene as if a secret panel conceals a spy camera within the fourth wall. While the father washes dishes in the kitchen, the mother and son clear the dining room table of dishes. As the oldest son stalks between the kitchen and dining room, the grief-stricken mother moves in slow motion, hesitating before a photograph of her youngest son in a baseball uniform. It is a picture of El Cuco's latest victim. Even as the scene's pace quickens, character action unfolds in slow motion. This cinematic effect suggests that El Cuco is savoring every moment of the family's suffering. Then the mother grabs her son's baseball bat. As grief turns into fury, the mother goes berserk. She bashes her way into the kitchen, forcing her husband and son to flee her path. Finally, the camera's shot tracks leftwards, the better for El Cuco to follow in her grievous wake and sight in on her collapse. Violin strings menacingly accompany this scene's fade to black, as El Cuco psychically projects itself into the next scene to terrorize the Maitland household. All this subsequently leads to Mrs. Peterson's oldest son's decision to shoot Terry Maitland, and ultimately, his father's attempted suicide, which results in him going into a vegetative coma. To harvest their grief and suffering, El Cuco must spy on and monitor the Petersons and everybody else in their social network. But is there not something like El Cuco in the real world? In a sense, by using smart devices and other internet connected devices equipped with cameras and microphones (i.e. the Internet of Things), ordinary people like the Maitlands and Petersons of Cherokee City, GA, have invited into their homes something that is inherently invasive and potentially violent in how it dehumanizes people (end-users) as a resource. Or so Richard Price suggests in *The Outsider* by defamiliarizing the surveillance capitalism and showing how El Cuco preys upon an oblivious population ideologically predisposed to disbelieve in its existence.

What else can we make of Richard Price's camera shots throughout *The Outsider*? In addition to the spy camera shots mentioned above, after a wide-angle shot of Cherokee City at the beginning of the first episode, the shots shuffle through a seemingly random montage of drone's eye top-down shots. When Ralph Anderson arrests Terry Maitland, the scene opens with a top-down shot of the baseball diamond. Uncanny shadows cast by the morning sun dwarf the baseball players. Again, this camera shot dehumanizes its human subjects. In a sense, the baseball diamond—which is under the gaze of what appears to be a Google Earth–style satellite—is ground zero for Cherokee City. Here, bleacher democracy, as the city's citizens know it, is about to be tricked into believing the Peterson murder was an inside job. Like a dirty bomb, the emotional fallout from Terry's arrest—precipitated by El Cuco—will have long-term consequences on community health: everybody in Cherokee City will now be harried by the fear that somebody else, even a pillar of the community, could be a BTK Strangler.

After Holly collects enough evidence to deduce El Cuco, she begins her road trip from Dayton, OH, to Cherokee City, GA. Her progress is stalled by gridlocked traffic, unbeknownst to Holly, due to a directly related and active crime scene elsewhere in Dayton. Thus, Price's original subplot scene begins with a close-up shot of a car's steaming tailpipe. The vehicle belongs to Heath Hofstadter's cousin Tracey, an African American former soldier, whom Holly ran into during her investigations. Having been painfully enslaved by El Cuco, Tracey has decided to decolonize himself the hard way. After grabbing a gun, Tracey emerges from his car to leave it idling beneath a highway underpass, setting his sights on a nearby white man going about his business.

Tracey seemingly takes him hostage. The scene crosscuts with other scenes, mostly with Holly stuck in traffic as police sirens wail in the distance. The next beat shows Tracey besieged: police cars block egress, police officers aim pistols from behind their vehicles, and SWAT snipers train their scoped-rifles down upon him—all this to a soundtrack of helicopter blades whirring in the distance and tense music. Police shout "Put down the gun," as a freight train—Salomon's proverbial "justice train"—screeches by in the background, airhorn wailing like a banshee. Note, unlike the civilian traffic distal to this active crime scene, the death-train stops for nothing. As Tracey examines the closing space around him and ignores the orders of the police and pleas of his hostage, a low-angle shot with Tracey's head eclipsed by the afternoon sun helps the audience see a claustrophobic, breathless world as seen through the eyes of a young black man in postmodern America. Moreover, it only becomes more stifling as the police continue shouting, "Tracey, give it up!" even as a SWAT armored truck inches closer. The camera pans quickly from police car to truck to the sky, where the camera sights the dark underbelly of an Apache attack helicopter: Tracey is literally cordoned off by an entangled alliance between the police, the military-industrial complex, and commerce. When Tracey releases the hostage and points his revolver at the police, three snipers immediately gun him down with a burst of automatic fire. Interestingly, the camera shot goes from a long shot of Tracey kneeling with soldierly precision and then aiming his revolver at the snipers to two modified cowboy shots of the snipers themselves. As in Sergio Leone Westerns, a traditional cowboy shot shows the character in a medium shot from the waistline to head. This allows the audience to see the character's eyes and facial expression, and holstered weaponry. But Richard Price's cowboy shot of the snipers, Tracey's last conscious vision, subtly casts the snipers as monstrous cyborgs: the sniper's most vulnerable body parts are shielded by concrete, their rifles on target, and their faces devoid of emotion. The aimed rifle obscures half the face so that each sniper appears to have one human eye. In a sense, these snipers from above on the overpass are cyclopean extensions of an invasive surveillance complex that pervades America in *The Outsider* from East Harlem and Rikers Island to the impoverished countryside of the Tennessee Valley Authority. While eyes in the sky surveil the populace from satellites, security cameras, drones, and helicopters, these snipers represent the kind of eyes-in-the-sky that have necropower. Their gunfire echoes into the next scene with Holly still stuck in traffic. She, too, is locked up in a different kind of claustrophobic-breathless space, surrounded by motorized vehicles, pollution from tailpipe exhaust, the angry sounds of honking car horns. The keystone that links these two seemingly disparate scenes together—one that is slow and boring and the other tense and spectacular—is built upon synchronicity: when Tracey dies, so does Holly's Honda Civic. Her car's engine sputters out, and the camera zooms away to show her vehicle, adding to the soul-deadening chaos of the sprawling rustbelt city of Dayton. Once again, the sound of whirring blades from an offscreen helicopter drives home the point that Holly and Tracey are figurative twins. By keeping the camera focused tightly on Tracey's POV, the audience identifies and empathizes with a person who is as much a victim of police brutality as he is of El Cuco.

In a 2002 interview with Tony Magistrale, Stephen King talked about the as yet to be released film *Dreamcatcher* (2003) directed by Lawrence

Kasden (*Hollywood's* 6–9). As previously noted in this essay, Magistrale and Blouin posit that King's novel problematically transposes the horror of the Vietnam War upon the wintry backcountry of Maine (Magistrale and Blouin 89–109). Kasden's adaptation too exposes a logic of necropolitics in the figure of Colonel Curtis. In the film, Curtis decides to exterminate American citizens. As Curtis deems, exposure to the alien infection warrants their death, even as there is some indication that not all infected humans become aliens. He tells this to his protege in the calm voice of military managerial reasoning. Interestingly, the infected dead, humans and animals alike, are bagged up for transport to an unspecified location in the south, perhaps Fort Detrick, Maryland (the headquarters of USAMRIID). Like the drone operator Allinson refers to in his essay, like Abra Stone in *Doctor Sleep*, like the El Cuco and the snipers in *The Outsider*, Curtis embodies a single-minded vision of justified and self-seeking violence. As King tellingly reveals in that 2002 interview with Magistrale, "There is a terrifying fear of the government that runs throughout *Dreamcatcher*, and that's something that runs through many of the films—*Firestarter, The Stand*—the idea that they would rather kill all of us than tell the truth. This is something we should all remain afraid of." Perhaps King is right, especially in light of myriad events since the beginning of the War on Terror and the rise of an Orwellian surveillance state. And yet, King's paranoia, suffused as it is throughout his fiction and films, reifies the fears many people use to justify usurping a sovereign's necropower. But by showing how an invasive and violent gaze works through the lens of horror in *Doctor Sleep* and *The Outsider*, Flanagan and Price draw attention to the range and depth of necropower and how, with what is almost a psychopomp's unerring precision, the predator uses weaponized surveillance to gauge individuals as prey. In a sense, their innovative camera work helps the audience grasp the full power of surveillance capitalism to imagine the unimaginable—just as Holly Gibney guides Detective Ralph Anderson in overcoming his disbelief in El Cuco. This raises the specter of a new kind of bleak impersonal horror. What was essentially researched, designed, and perfected for the necropolitical domination of the Middle East during the War on Terror, has now come back to roost in America with all of its seductive promises of civic, commercial, and security uses—a bona fide cure-all for everything the evening news presents as an unraveling of the social fabric.

NOTES

1. Mortensen in "Vigilant Citizens and Horrific Heroes" defines the vigilante "as an individual (or group of individuals) who takes 'the law' into his or her own hands

but often vigilantes are not only concerned about pursuing what is or is perceived to be legally right, but are ultimately more concerned with *pursuing what is just from their own perspective*" (142, emphasis mine).

2. In *The Age of Surveillance Capitalism,* Shoshana Zubof describes Silicon Valley surveillance capitalists such as Amazon, Facebook, Google, and Twitter in gothic terms. Collectively termed Big Other, their ability to spy on users and profitably exploit their metadata to predict behavior and influence online behavior and even shape their perception of the world bears remarkable semblance to vampiric creatures like El Cuco: "At its core, surveillance capitalism is parasitic and self-referential. It revives Karl Marx's old image of capitalism as a vampire that feeds on labor, but with an unexpected turn. Instead of labor, surveillance capitalism feeds on every aspect of every human's experience" (9).

WORKS CITED

Allinson, Jamie. "The Necropolitics of Drones." *International Political Sociology*. 9:2 (June 2015): 113–27. Print.

Browning, Mark. *Stephen King on the Big Screen*. Chicago, IL: Intellect Books, 2009. Print.

Debrix, François. "Horror Beyond Death: Geopolitics and the Pulverisation of the Human." *New Formations: A Journal of Culture/Theory/Politics*. 89: 89 (2017): 85–100.

Doctor Sleep. Dir. Mike Flanagan. Screenplay by Mike Flanagan. Warner Brothers, 2019.

Dreamcatcher. Dir. Lawrence Kasden. Screenplay by William Goldman. Castle Rock Entertainment, 2003.

Magistrale, Tony. *Hollywood's Stephen King*. NY: Palgrave, 2003. Print.

Magistrale, Tony and Michael J. Blouin. "The Vietnamization of Stephen King" in *Stephen King and American History*. NY: Routledge, 2020. Kindle.

Mbembe, Achille. *Necropolitics*. Trans. Steven Corcoran. Durham, NC: Duke University Press, 2019. Print.

Mortensen, Erik. "Vigilant Citizens and Horrorific Heroes: Perpetuating the Positive Portrayal of Vigilantes," in *Violence in American Popular Culture*. Ed. by David Schmid. Santa Barbara, CA: Praeger, 2016: 142–164. Print.

Nelson, Thomas Allen. *Kubrick: Inside a Film Artist's Maze*. Bloomington, IN: Indiana University Press, 2000. Print.

Nguyen, Viet Thanh. *Nothing Ever Dies: Vietnam and the Memory of War*. Cambridge, MA: Harvard University Press, 2016. Kindle.

The Outsider. Showrunner Richard Price. Dir. Jason Bateman, Andrew Bernstein, et al. Screenplay by Richard Price. HBO, 2020.

The Shining. Dir. Stanley Kubrick. Screenplay by Stanley Kubrick and Diane Johnson. Warner Brothers, 1980.

Zubof, Shoshana. *The Age of Surveillance Capitalism: The Fight for a Human Future at the New Frontier of Power*. NY: Public Affairs, 2019.

Chapter 12

"Murder Is Damnation, But Murder Is Also Work"

Violence, Patriarchy, and the Work Ethic in 1922

Jason Clemence

Ideological conflicts between rural and urban settings have played a massively influential role in American politics and popular culture, perpetuating the idea that "the country" and "the city" are inhabited by fundamentally different kinds of people and values, and in turn produce fundamentally different cultural institutions. Rahsaan Maxwell put it as plainly and reductively as possible in a recent argument piece in *The Washington Post*: "In both North America and Western Europe, the political divide is increasingly a geographic divide. Urban areas are more liberal, and rural areas are more conservative" (Par.1).[1] This simple dynamic has played a fundamental, if somewhat misleading, role in the political crises of the current American moment. It has also formed the backbone for a vast variety of films that cut across genre and filmmaking trends, with the German silent masterpiece *Sunrise* (Murnau 1927) and the high-concept allegory of *The Wizard of Oz* (Fleming 1939) representing early and accessible examples. Hollywood, as well as independent and global cinema, has persistently portrayed the city as a hub of excitement, spectacle, opportunity, hedonistic enjoyment, and progressive sociopolitical visions, and the rural as a locus of simplicity and (depending on the genre) either traditional and wholesome values or a perverse inversion of such values.[2]

This contrast directly shapes the representations of violence in *1922* (Hilditch 2017; based on the 2010 novella by Stephen King). The story begins essentially *in media res* with a festering disagreement between Wilfred James (Thomas Jane) and his wife Arlette (Molly Parker) concerning each character's uncompromising adherence to their own fantasy of an unfettered rural life (in Wilfred's case) or an unfettered urban life (in Arlette's). Wilfred (from here on referred to as "Wilf") owns 80 acres of land in Hemingford,

Nebraska. He is neither affluent nor poor. He establishes his personal values in one of his very first lines of voiceover: "In 1922, a man's pride was a man's land. And so was his son." Arlette, however, having inherited an additional adjacent 100 acres from her father,[3] wishes to sell *both* pieces of property to the Farrington company, which wants to build an industrial pig farm and slaughterhouse. She dreams of using the proceeds from this sale to move to the "big city" of Omaha and open a dress shop.[4]

Wilf sees this as a situation in which compromise is not possible. He remarks that "cities are for fools," as though it is less an opinion than a matter of common knowledge, and fixates instead on his desire to "pass [the farm] on to my boy, Henry Freeman James (Dylan Schmid), and to his thereafter." Wilf's attachment to the land and the farm, and his fantasies of a patriarchal/patrilineal transmission of property to his son and grandson and so on, makes the idea of leaving unthinkable. It also has the effect, in a manner similar to *The Shining* (Kubrick 1980) of aligning the viewer with Wilf's desires. As Elizabeth Jean Hornbeck argues, "In an economy of shifting audience identification, viewers' initial identification with Jack makes them uncomfortably aware of the abuser's perspective" (691). Hilditch performs a similar maneuver by framing Wilf's desires as modest, normative, and reasonable, before showing the monstrous lengths he is willing to go in order to fulfill them. Like a variety of King protagonists—not just Jack Torrance, but Louis Creed in *Pet Sematary*, Bob Anderson in *A Good Marriage*, Nora in "Morality," and others—it is difficult to view Wilf as fully villainous, despite his clearly malevolent behavior, because the desires established for him at the outset of the narrative are framed as relatable, and rooted in typical, traditional, all-American aspiration. The motif of viewer complicity and Wilf's conflation of pastoralism and desire is also touched upon in Eric Kohn's review of the film: "[The] premise takes shape against the startlingly beautiful backdrop of vivid green cornfields and sunny open country. . . . There's a deep yearning to these early scenes indicative of the unreliable narrator's utopian ideals" (Par.4). Arlette, however, "never took to the farming life" and insists that "life is rarely fair—*especially out here*." In other words, the fundamental conflict that initiates the film's narrative is a disagreement about the merits of country life versus those of city life. The outcome of this conflict in *1922*, at the end of the film's first act, is Wilf's brutal murder of Arlette with help from Hank, whom he "cozens" into participating after Arlette drunkenly insults his girlfriend Shannon Cotterie (Kaitlyn Bernard).[5] In the second half of the film, Hank gets Shannon pregnant, and the two of them run away together, gradually turning into a Bonnie and Clyde archetype as they rob banks throughout Nebraska and Colorado to stay alive. Wilf, meanwhile, goes gradually insane from a fever caused by a rat bite. In the film's clearest gesture toward traditional horror, he hallucinates Arlette's reanimated corpse, surrounded by a coterie of rats, accosting him in the farmhouse and torturing him by recounting how Shannon, Hank, and their baby are all killed in the midst of a robbery.[6]

Wilf's obsession with farm life, or at least with his fantasy of farm life, thinly conceals that his violent acts are truly motivated by the allure of reaffirming patriarchal social structures (represented by the rural) in the face of burgeoning social progress (represented by the urban), in particular the threat of cultural movement toward feminine independence—the ability to function as a person, mother, and business owner—that Arlette robustly symbolizes. Furthermore, this motivation is bound up in Wilf's understanding of the work ethic, not as an ancillary necessity of Protestant piety and an indicator of being in God's favor (as Wilf's ancestors likely understood it) but as a *personal* means of solidifying his role and identity in the world, and of repressing cultural, as well as visceral, fears and anxieties.

We encounter in *1922*, then, a critique of highly familiar and intractable 21st-century conflicts, played out in the domestic sphere of the farm, between values coded as old-fashioned and those coded as progressive. Hilditch evocatively captures the grim potential for violence when ideology is tied to inflexible perspectives on work and cultural identity.[7] Its contemporary relevance, when one considers the social, economic, and political crises of 2020 (to fixate as insistently as Wilf does upon a particular year as a point of reference), as well as the willingness of Trump and his supporters and unofficial militias to unleash violence in response to progressive impulses, is unmistakable. The film's ideological concerns resonate today in an economy that relies increasingly on gig employment—a mechanism that by design alienates workers from their work—and further stratifies those who can work from home and those who can't. Recently on National Public Radio affiliate WBUR, Michael Sandel identifies a major driver of the "populist backlash" in 2016: "What made it so combustible, I think, was the sense of demoralization, even humiliation, by those who were left behind not only by the economy, but also, in many ways, by the culture; the *work they did* was no longer respected, accorded the social esteem that it once was" (4:27-4:48, my emphasis). Though Sandel is discussing a political moment nearly a century removed from the setting of *1922,* obsessive humiliation attached to one's sense of geographical identity and relation to labor is also at the root of Wilf's violent resistance to progress.

Wilf's protectiveness of his bucolic world, and the extremes he indulges to maintain it, invites parallel readings of two horror subgenres, both of which are rooted in dialectics of progress and tradition. The "backwoods horror" genre has done much to undermine the fantasy of the rural setting as pastoral and immune to the supposed toxicity of urban values. Identifying *The Texas Chainsaw Massacre* (Hooper 1974) as the first true entry of the genre,

Andrew Welsh points out that such films are thematically structured around the "demarcation of rural people and spaces as 'deviant' or 'other' . . . the worst nightmare for [the genre's] liberal and progressive middle-class audience—they are socially backwards [and] an impediment to human progress" ("The Rural Other in Backwoods Horror"). In other words, in a large body of horror cinema, rural settings present inexplicable violence not just *alongside,* but bound up in and motivated by, cultural regression. The violence can and should be read, almost without exception, as a lashing out at representatives of modernity and affluence that the rural Other understands to be an affront to the tattered remnants of their own culture that mass industrialization and the subsequent creation of mass culture has left behind.

This is a crucial facet of *1922.* Wilf's desire to hold onto or expand his property is not motivated by pragmatic business concerns. One could imagine an alternative plot conflict in which, for instance, Wilf is in financial trouble and believes that only the acquisition of Arlette's 100 acres can save him. But that land is never discussed as an economic necessity. Rather, it symbolizes the fantasy that Wilf projects onto the identity of farming and the rural landscape: the fantasy of an unchanging patriarchal society over which he can exert minute control, a society whose resistance to change is not organic, but maintained by threat of violence.[8]

Wilf's opening narration that, in one sentence, privileges the land and the son, encapsulates his desire to take his place in the male-dominated social economy by passing along the family farm. But he also perceives the fulfillment of this desire as blocked by the idea of progress, the encroachment of technology, and its attendant changing of norms, upon his fantasy. These changing norms are largely linked to gender and sexuality, and Arlette is depicted from the outset as inimical to two of the most crucial aspects of Wilf's fantasy. But she is also a woman who speaks up, who makes her own desires known, who arranges visits to attorneys' offices in the city when she needs to defend what's hers, who wishes to be a businesswoman, and who is apparently unafraid to be a single mother. In effect, she embodies a variety of traits that we would now likely describe as liberated, progressive, and feminist; all of these traits are channeled through and reinforced by her desire to move to the city.

One of the darkest moments in the story comes not during a scene of gruesome violence, but during one of rumination. Shortly after murdering Arlette and dumping her body down an old well, interring her within the land that she wished to escape, Wilf narrates about the not-too-distant past:

> In those days, all sorts of things happened on farms out in what we called the middle. Things that went unremarked, let alone reported. In those days, a man's

wife was considered a man's business, and if she disappeared, well . . . there was an end to it. (25)

Here, Wilf looks nostalgically to the past for violent inspiration. Especially when we consider the extended version of his speech in the book,[9] we see that Wilf paradoxically conflates normative values—wholesome communities, civic participation, and, in Wilf's case, farming—with the socially-sanctioned ability to commit unchecked and unpunished acts of violence. The domestic sphere, which provides succor to the patriarchal power that poses as a benevolent defender of social decency, is also a site of sinister abuse, of women who are annihilated when they do not fulfill their husbands' expectations: the dark side of the American pastoral. By longing for this socio-familial model, Wilf expresses resentment toward a marginally more progressive world in which women—or wives, at any rate—are protected by the law and the social contract, and even granted the autonomy to, say, broker a real estate deal and open a dress shop in Omaha with the proceeds. This resentment, coupled with nostalgia, is especially pronounced when Wilf recounts his envy toward his more prosperous neighbor, Shannon's father Harlan Cotterie (Neal McDonough). Wilf mentions Harlan's "shiny blue Cadillac" and his "indoor plumbing," but fixates most emphatically on his "plain-faced, biddable wife whose sweetly given reply to any problem would be 'whatever you think is best, dear.'" In other words, what he truly envies of Harlan is not his ability to accumulate the latest technologies of the time (which would gesture toward a fetishization of the modern, the *future*), but his ability to have a wife who conforms to expectations consonant with the *past*.[10]

In the larger context of horror cinema history, Wilf's murder weapon becomes especially significant. Hank, persuaded to assist with the killing but wary of the brutality of this method, suggests smothering, which Wilf dubiously dismisses as more painful and drawn-out. Despite using guns in several other scenes, he does not simply shoot her point-blank either. Rather, he opts for the perverse intimacy of throat-cutting and, when that fails, frantic stabbing. Whether he truly believes it will be the fastest and most merciful—despite his clear monstrosity, he seems genuinely concerned with sparing Arlette from suffering physically and (especially) Hank from suffering emotionally—the actual act is messy, gruesome, and anguished. In its clear representation of phallic failure and the frantic rage that results, the scene also suggests the impotency of patriarchal authority, underscoring for the audience that the very system Wilf attempts to revivify through violence is beyond being saved.

Whatever its motivation, Wilf's method of killing aligns him with yet another horror genre, the iconic "slasher" films of the 1970s and 80s. And when we consider his *reason* for killing in the first place, his desire to rein in social forces that challenge his patriarchal ambitions, the similarities crystallize even further. Of the many subgenres of horror cinema, the slasher is arguably the most critically-linked with reactionary suppressions of women's ascensions to positions of power and independence, and of social progress in general. A wide body of work, especially by Carol J. Clover, has made such readings of films like *Halloween* (Carpenter 1978) and *Friday the 13th* (Cunningham 1980) into essentially conventional wisdom.[11] Tony Magistrale summarizes this position when he writes that slasher antagonists kill "as a reaction against the emerging independent female of a fledgling women's liberation movement and the corresponding erosion of power and gender identity associated with the traditional patriarchy" and that they "embody the rage and frustration that attended the challenges occurring in the patriarchal hegemony" (149). And in Wilf's choice of the unabashedly phallic butcher knife, as well as his anxiety concerning both cultural progress and the technological progress within which it is intimately ensnared, we might recall Clover's observation that "in some basic sense, the emotional terrain of the slasher is *pretechnological*. The preferred weapons of the killer are knives, hammers, axes, icepicks, hypodermic needles, red-hot pokers, pitchforks, and the like" (81, my emphasis). The impetus for murder and its method, in Wilf's case, are distinctly intertwined.

In addition to embracing social freedoms and the possibility of independence, while still adhering to the expectation that her primary duty is maternal, Arlette is also presented as a sexually open and expressive woman, though it is important to note that, from Wilf's perspective, her sexuality is marked as transgressive and "vulgar." The scene prior to Arlette's murder carefully conflates the erotic with the violent. On the front porch, Wilf lies to Arlette, telling her that he and Hank are both prepared to move to Omaha after all. Arlette believes he is sincere and immediately becomes affectionate—the first time we see anything other than hostility in their marriage. As Arlette begins (excessively) drinking wine to celebrate that "the boy talks sense and the man listens, at long last!," she becomes crudely flirtatious. Spilling some wine on her dress, she says, "If you're good, Wilf, you can suck it out of the cloth later."[12] In the meantime, he continues to fill her glass, as his plan involves getting her drunk and immobilized enough on their bed that she will be unable to fight back when the murder begins. In other words, his role in her intoxication seems on the surface like a stereotypical attempt to get her "in the mood," what we would now, of course, rightly consider sexual assault, but in the 1920s was more likely to be characterized as "seduction." That the murder is preceded by flirtation, and that it takes place in their shared marital bed, further cements a reading in which gendered violence inflicted upon the sexually liberated woman is a means of reaffirming the patriarchal power and normativity of "country life."

Even more significantly, Arlette's sexual banter is not limited to Wilf. When Hank grimaces at her lack of inhibition, she tells him:

> Oh, no need to be so prissy, I've seen you with Shannon Cotterie. Pretty face and a nice little figure. Mmm. If you're not getting a touch of that, you're a fool. Just be careful. Fourteen's not too young to marry out here in the middle . . . here's to Shannon Cotterie and her new bubbies, and if my son don't know the color of her nipples, he's a slowpoke. Just make sure when you're laying down with her in the corn or behind the barn, that you're a *no-poke*. Explore all you like, and, you know, rub it with your Johnny Mac until he feels good and spits up. Just stay out of the home place, lest you get locked in like your mummer and daddy!

This is a crucial moment, both in terms of plot and subtext. It is the last straw that convinces Hank to help Wilf kill her. As Wilf puts it in the book, "Very young men cannot help but put their first loves on pedestals, and should someone come along and spit on the paragon . . . even if it happens to be one's mother" (13). But even more importantly, it establishes Arlette as not merely strong-willed and prepared to live independently, outside the immediate strictures of rural patriarchy, but also as what Barbara Creed termed "the monstrous feminine"—a woman whose monstrosity lies in transgressing conventional perceptions of femininity and, especially, *motherhood*. Indeed, it is jarring, even by 21st century standards, to hear a mother drunkenly encourage her son in this way. Her only reservation is emphatically pragmatic: she wants to prevent Hank from being "locked in for life" with the literal girl next door, and from perpetuating the norms of cultural reproduction that, we can reasonably infer, she and Wilf enacted when she became pregnant with Hank.[13] She does not object to her fourteen-year-old son engaging in sexual activity on the sort of moral or religious grounds that we might typically associate with motherhood, especially in this time and place; she objects only to the idea of it reproducing a lifestyle that she herself is prepared to abandon.

Arlette's performance in this scene is, at least insofar as Wilf and Hank react to it, a queering of sexual and familial discourse. Even after Arlette's murder; even after Shannon's father tells Wilf that she has "a bun in the oven, and I guess you know who did the damn cooking" (69); even, somehow, after Hank and Shannon turn to an ill-fated life of crime to sustain themselves—their relationship is presented as pure and wholesome, as precisely the sort of coupling that will perpetuate the patriarchal structure that Wilf values and Arlette rejects. It is not surprising, then, that Wilf acts tenderly toward the young couple (though, admittedly, he does leverage Hank's lovesickness into matricide), while Arlette not only seems to cheapen and demean their relationship, but actively discourages it from being anything *more* than an erotic thrill, from flowering into marriage and children, precisely what the normative culture of family demands. In his reformulation of queer theory, *No Future,* Lee Edelman advances "a simple provocation: that *queerness* names the side of those *not* 'fighting for the children,' the side outside the consensus by which all politics confirms the absolute value of *reproductive futurism*" (3), an ideology in which Wilf and Hank alike are deeply invested.[14] It is certainly not unreasonable for a mother, even in 1922, to not want her 14-year-old son to impregnate someone; what is transgressively, *queerly* shocking is her couching of this preference in the language of *enjoyment*, rather than prohibition.[15] It would be typical to dissuade a teenage boy from impregnating his girlfriend. However, it is deeply anti-normative to, at the same time, crudely encourage him, like "a smelly whorehouse madam instructing a green young customer" (13), as Wilf puts it, displacing the figure of maternal purity with one of obscenity and shameless sexual exploration. Just as the slasher victim's desire for enjoyment and sexual fulfillment is inextricably linked to her death at the hands of Michael Meyers or Jason Voorhees, Arlette's queered relation to sexuality and futurity, in Wilf's regressive ideology, marks her for death.[16]

While the slasher film performs a fantasy of violence against the fruits of second-wave feminism in the 1970s, Wilf and Arlette, as the film's title constantly reminds us, exist in an historical era in which patriarchal authority is also firmly challenged. It is not merely Arlette's personal embrace of freedom and autonomy, or her lack of sexual inhibition; it is also a time in which women's suffrage has just barely come into existence, in which a burgeoning sexual revolution will produce the Flapper, in which the post–World War "lost generation" will challenge the basic tenets of civilization. With its Dionysian signifiers of jazz, prohibition and the speakeasy, the automobile, and, of course, the cities and their promise of nightlife and revelry, the decade of the 1920s represents the first insistent 20th-century undoing of traditional values. Wilf's desire to keep the status quo of his life and surroundings intact is made plain in the novella when he is visited by one of Farrington's attorneys. As soon as he sees the car approaching, he acknowledges: "We were about to have a visit from the world that Arlette wanted so badly to be a part of" (29). The film's sound design also contributes to this link between Arlette and that "world." *1922*'s score is composed primarily of ominous, ambient instrumental music, but Hilditch also includes a diegetic allusion to the kind of music that will become the soundtrack of youthful revelry and liberation in the 1920s, a culture in which Wilf likely fears Arlette will immerse herself. During the scene on the porch, as Arlette flaunts her unrestrained willingness to speak about sex, a jazz record plays in the background. The same song eerily plays the first time that we see Arlette return as a desiccated corpse. The soundtrack to Arlette's two most prominent moments in the film, in other words, are accompanied by what was, in the 1920s, generally regarded as music that signaled licentiousness and posed a threat to the racial and gender norms that are intrinsic to patriarchal structures. This is especially relevant in contrast to the kind of music that is presumably more often played on the farm; in the novella, Henry asks Wilf if he can "start the generator and play *Hayride Party* on the radio" (53). Whatever kind of music is played on that program, one can assume it is a world away from the syncopated beats and sensual horns emerging from New Orleans and New York in the 1920s. Arlette's affiliation with the cultural markers of the Roaring 20s, and her family's fate within the narrative, are also interestingly aligned: Hank becomes a bandit in the style of a variety of Jimmy Cagney–type gangster characters—it's also notable that a variety of burgeoning cities serve as the site of his criminality—while Arlette embodies the style and cultural iconoclasm of the Flapper. Both characters meet abrupt and grim deaths, as surely as the progressive ideologies of the Roaring 20s will be soundly put down at the outset of the Great Depression.

But if Wilf's violence was committed to keep his home—as he puts it himself—and to preserve the patrilineal transmission of property, one of the final shots of the film demonstrates how self-defeating his plan actually was. After losing his farm altogether, Wilf finds himself in Omaha, of all places, living in a hotel, writing the confession that forms the filmic narrative, and going slowly mad. As he finishes his confession, he looks up to see Shannon, Arlette, and Henry—all of them gruesomely disfigured from the harm that Wilf either inflicted or indirectly caused—staring reproachfully. It is a stark reminder that the elements necessary for Wilf's fantasy of passing along the farm to his son, "and to his thereafter," hinges upon not *only* his son, but also the presence and vitality and labor (in every sense of the word) of the very women whom his patriarchal violence has obliterated.

From a superficial standpoint, it would be logical to assume that Wilf is a product of the Protestant Work Ethic, the set of ascetic values outlined by Max Weber in which productivity and humility mark the individual as chosen by God. In the Puritan calculus of predestination, as Karl Thompson puts it, "the harder you worked, and the less time you spent idling and/or engaged in unproductive, frivolous activities, then the more likely it was that you were one of those pre-chosen for a life in heaven" (Par.9). As a multigenerational farmer in the early 20th century rural Midwest, with a name that is an Anglicization of the German *Wilfried*,[17] the character loudly signals a heritage traceable back to the German Puritan and Lutheran immigrants whose descendants largely settled in Nebraska and its surrounding areas, and who promoted the work ethic as an expression of ascetic piety. Indeed, throughout the film, we see Wilf fully devoted to the upkeep and productivity of the farm as a personal, not merely pragmatic, necessity. After Henry runs away with Shannon, Wilf accepts the local banker's offer of a $750 mortgage to finance a variety of repairs and improvements on the farm. While the banker suggests this in the spirit of financial reward and investment, concerns that square with the Protestant Work Ethic as well as plain capitalistic self-interest, Wilf sees it as a psychological necessity. After his first vision of Arlette returning to him, his solution is situated within ambitions of work. As he puts it in the novella:

> Fixing a leak would take only a day or two. I needed work that would keep me through the winter. Hard labor would drive out thoughts of Arlette on her dirt throne, Arlette in her burlap snood. I needed home improvement projects that would send me to bed so tired that I'd sleep right through, and not lie there listening to the rain and wondering if Henry was out in it, maybe coughing from the grippe. Sometimes work is the only thing, the only answer. (89)

Despite Wilf's multifaceted embrace of the farming life that is definitive of his rural world, his clearly assiduous relationship to his own labor, it would be a mistake to characterize it as a *Protestant* Work Ethic. The most telling statement made by Wilf concerning religion occurs when Hank asks if they'll go to hell for murdering Arlette. Wilf, gesturing to the corn fields, responds: "How can you say so, when heaven is all around us?" Wilf entirely avoids answering the question by responding with his *own* question, and, of course, conflates the literal hell of the Books of Matthew and Mark and Revelation with the quite metaphorical (and arguable) heaven of a Nebraskan cornfield, as opposed to the potential hell of land despoiled by the Farrington plant. The point is clear: for Wilf, that cornfield, and his ownership and stewardship of what it produces, is the only "heaven" that matters. Wilf's sense of identity and place in the world entirely eclipses any need for spiritual or religious fulfillment. He embraces work as performed by and for *himself,* as well as for the son and the land he sees as extensions of himself. His adherence to the work ethic is genuine, but he has no interest in the religious strictures and rewards that theoretically make that work ethical and pious.[18] When the work ethic is decoupled from Protestant ideology, the film argues, there is no hell to be afraid of, and no moral authority but the violent whim of the dominant normative culture.

James Kendrick observes that "in most film genres, violence has no *inherent* ideological meaning because said meaning will develop only in relation to how the violence is structured within the film's syntax" (71, my emphasis). *1922* is a complexly violent genre film that borrows iconography and themes from suburban gothic thrillers, backwoods horror, and the classic slasher— and that is before we even begin to address the intertextual connections with supernatural horror that consume the film's final act. Its violence, within the film's syntax, is pressed forcefully into the ideological service of maintaining a fantasy of patriarchy, land, power, work, and normativity in the face of what our protagonist views as cultural atrophy. For Wilf, this violence is parallel to and motivated by idealized notions of place—and, most significantly, of the work that he performs in that place, work that is formative to his entire identity. Violence, location, and labor are explicitly entwined: murder, as he observes, *is* work. The violence that he uses to maintain his idealized notions, in this phrasing, becomes in turn a *facet* of those idealized notions. If work is an innate feature of Wilf's ideology, and murder is work, then murder must also be a feature of that ideology. Such is the fundamental gesture of the repressive social order that Wilf works to sustain throughout the film: It disavows violence while simultaneously keeping it ready to hand to restrict and punish those who transgress. And, as in our fractured politics of 2021, we might argue that it is a mistake to demarcate such impulses as primarily geographic or economic. For Wilf, and often for us, 99 years later, the over-blown illusion of rural-urban difference merely feeds the larger machinery of American violence.

NOTES

1. Because it represents something of a compromise between rural and urban, the small town or suburb, of course, is a more complex entity, at least in popular discourse. Its very existence, in fact, became a flashpoint in the summer of 2020 when Donald Trump promised, as Annie Karni put it, "to protect suburbanites from low-income housing being built in their neighborhoods, making an appeal to white suburban voters by trying to stir up racist fears about affordable housing and the people who live there" (Par.1). Cinematically, the small town has been the subject of a wide variety of subversive films, especially throughout the 1990s and early 2000s. In his wide-ranging book *The Architecture of David Lynch,* Richard Martin foregrounds his analysis of Lynch's *Blue Velvet* (1986) by discussing the "array of cozy images" in Ronald Reagan's infamously saccharine 1984 "Morning Again in America" re-election ad. Martin points to the ad's fetishization of small-town America as evidence that that particular form of community, at least within mainstream textual representation, "remains the nation's most reliable site of neighborly goodwill and harmonious relations" (33). Of course, *Blue Velvet* and other films like it have repeatedly interrogated this representation, and instead portray the small town as a site of duality in which civilized society is little more than a hypocritical front for chaos and criminality. Hitchcock's *Shadow of a Doubt* (1943), featuring Joseph Cotten's iconic line "Do you know that if you ripped the fronts off of houses, you'd find swine?" is perhaps the most historically-obvious example, but countless other American films, particularly in the 1990s and early 2000s, have explored this dynamic, including *Edward Scissorhands* (Burton 1993), *Serial Mom* (Waters 1994), *Happiness* (Solondz 1998), *Apt Pupil* (Singer 1998; also based on a King novella), *The Ice Storm* (Lee 1999), *American Beauty* (Mendes 1999), *Donnie Darko* (Kelly 2001), and *Little Children* (Fields 2006). The plots and characters and approaches to

verisimilitude and realism differ drastically, but each film, at its core, poses a cynical argument: that the boundary between wholesomeness and malevolence, if one exists at all, is dangerously porous. The American suburb or small town's deployment as a blank slate for collisions between normative banality and violent derangement is so effective because the small town, as a geographical entity, would seem to represent a compromise between the two ideologically fraught modes of living, the urban and the rural, that are integral to the cultural ethics of *1922*, a narrative in which compromise is regarded as impossible (see n4).

2. For instance, we might compare a backwoods horror film (more on this genre later) like *The Hills Have Eyes* (Craven 1977) with a stereotypical Hallmark Christmas movie, the plot of which frequently revolves around an overworked urban young adult returning to the restorative simplicity of their small hometown for the holidays. Similarly, for an urban setting, we might compare the representation of New York City in both *Manhattan* (Allen 1979) and *Taxi Driver* (Scorsese 1976). In each case, the two examples obviously have very little in common, yet they each rely on shared intertextual assumptions of what the city and the country must signify.

3. As later sections of this essay will note, *1922* signifies Wilf's sense of cultural impotence in a variety of ways, and the very fact that Arlette's 100 acres surpasses Wilf's 80, both in terms of size and market value, contributes to this motif as well.

4. Though Wilf and Arlette both seem willing to separate from one another—Arlette mentions divorce and Wilf does not reject the idea—there is nonetheless no room for compromise on either side. The various potential outcomes of the conflict are as follows:

Arlette moves to Omaha with Hank—Wilf is unwilling to have his son taken from him, and fears that his land will be ruined by the Farrington plant

Arlette moves to Omaha by herself (which is the cover story Wilf eventually fabricates)—Arlette is unwilling to leave without her son, plus Wilf would still have to contend with Farrington's impact on his land

The whole family moves—Wilf is unwilling because of his attachment to the farm and rural landscape

The whole family stays and maintains the status quo, incorporating Arlette's acres into the existing farm—Arlette is unwilling. The land is legally hers, and she intends to capitalize on it regardless of Wilf's approval (hence her embodiment of progressive and cosmopolitan values)

Wilf buys the land from Arlette, allowing her to go to Omaha and Wilf to remain without the intrusion of the Farrington plant—Wilf pitches this idea, but Arlette recognizes that he will not be able to pay as much as Farrington; plus, the issue of who Hank lives with would remain in question.

The irreconcilability of these various options is essentially what drives Wilf to decide that murder is the only plausible option.

5. It is unfortunately outside the purview of this article, but the violence of *1922*, which turns out to be one of King's most overtly Freudian works, is continually suffused with inverted Oedipal tropes.

6. Of course, this being a Stephen King story, the actual nature of Arlette's reanimation is epistemologically complex. Whether it is actually supposed to be happening—as in the reanimations of Church, Gage, and Rachel in *Pet Sematary* (1983)—or

is a figment of Wilf's feverish imagination, is never clarified. However, given that the entire primary story set in 1922 is meant to be a visual representation of Wilf's confession in 1930 (rather similar to how Neff's confession in *Double Indemnity* [Wilder 1946] dictates and shapes almost everything we viewers see), I would argue that Arlette's reappearance should be understood as a hallucination, an unreliable manifestation of Wilf's psychosis, just as the primary narrative itself is an unreliable manifestation of Wilf's guilt. In other words, the 1922-set events may not be what occurred, but a *version* of what occurred, a recasting of events that allows him to live with the horrors he has caused.

7. In Wilf's case, this ideology is primarily situated within geographical location and, of course, time. However, it is interesting to note that, in 2021, while the electoral map still suggests reductively rigid boundaries between blue and red states, ideology actually tends to override such reductive divisions. The January 6 storming of the Capitol, which occurred as this article was in its final stages, for instance, turned out to be committed by people from a notably wide variety of occupations, locations, and socioeconomic strata.

8. Another notable cinematic example of this comes from *Calibre* (Walsh 2017), a horror-ish indie Scottish film released the same year as *1922*. Beginning with two men from Edinburgh taking a hunting trip to a remote village, it contains many of the superficial signposts of backwoods horror, though most of these tropes are ultimately complicated or subverted. What is kept intact from the genre, however, is that the two most prominent villagers, Logan and Brian, represent opposing ideas about progress and tradition. Logan recognizes that the village must modernize, and seeks investment from outsiders that would allow them to compete with the "massive country club" that is harming their tourist industry. Brian, however, looks directly to the past, calling the very idea of investments "shite," and argues that the village should redouble its closed-off provincialism and sense of self-reliance, by doing "whatever's necessary to look out for ourselves. Whatever's necessary. Like folk used to." Inevitably, Brian is the one to react violently to the film's central conflict, while Logan calls for a measured reaction within the boundaries of the social order. In this category of horror cinema, hostility toward the possibility of progress is always attended by a capacity for violence.

9. In the novella, Wilf expounds further on this point: "especially if he happens to be a respected farmer: a fellow who paid his taxes, went to church on Sundays, supported the Hemingford Stars baseball team, and voted the straight Republican ticket" (25).

10. As with so many aspects of the novella and film, this centering of *resentment* as a motivating emotional force also connects the story with the political and cultural shape of 2020. Legions of commentators have postulated that resentment is a central driver of the near-fanatical devotion and loyalty that Donald Trump seems to command. His signature campaign slogan—"Make America Great Again"—would seem to align Trumpism with Wilf's wistful sense of nostalgia—a sense of nostalgia that, crucially, is preoccupied with obsessive thinking about what *other* people have and are able to enjoy. As Thomas Edsall puts it in a December 2020 New York Times piece:

"Hierarchal ranking, the status classification of different groups . . . has the effect of consolidating and seeming to legitimize existing inequalities in resources and power. Diminished status has become a source of rage on both the left and right, sharpened by divisions over economic security and insecurity, geography and, ultimately, values."

The film makes clear, in this scene, that geography and values are far more important to Wilf than economic security. Throughout the film, this aspect of his life is continually de-emphasized in favor of his attachment to the farm and the principles that it embodies.

11. It is, however, important to note prominent readings that go against the grain of this position. For instance, in *The Stereotypical Portrayal of Women in Slasher Films: Then Versus Now,* Chad Brewer, citing the work of Adam Rockoff, points out that:

"(The slasher antagonist) often witnesses a devastating event or he is the victim of a humiliating prank or tragic event. Often it is the anniversary of such an event that triggers the killer's desire to kill those who directly caused his pain or those who might symbolically represent them. He often returns to the place of the event, or one similar to it, to seek his revenge. Holidays and special occasions, such as Christmas or a high school prom, are also times when killers often seek revenge for past atrocities" (7).

This analysis suggests that the pathology of the slasher should be read less as a systemic representation of patriarchal prejudices and impulses, and more as a behavioral reaction to *personal* torment and trauma. To what extent the personal should be read, in this instance, as an allegory for larger social forces, is a matter of debate. It is clear, however, that Wilf, insofar as he embodies some of the slasher's methods and motivations, does so as a reaction toward the external world, rather than as a result of internalized trauma.

12. In the book, this theme of Arlette becoming increasingly vulgar (again, according to Wilf's perspective) is amplified. She also tells Wilf "You needn't get me drunk to get what you want. I want it, too. I've got an itch." And later, with "sour grapes on her breath," she says, "You may get that thing you like tonight, Wilf. That *nasty* thing (10, author's emphasis)."

13. I am indebted to Tianna Tagami for this insight.

14. Hank very much takes after his father in this way. In both the film and novella, he is not particularly upset about having impregnated Shannon. In fact, he wants to marry her and raise the baby. His sense of anguish comes not in reaction to the pregnancy, but to Shannon's father Harlan's decision to send her away to a Catholic boarding school and give the baby up for adoption. In his own way, Harlan signals his allegiance to patriarchal authority over the feminine when he says in the film "(Shannon) doesn't know it yet, but it's gonna happen."

15. For the language used to convey this insight, I am indebted to the early theoretical work of Todd McGowan, in particular *The End of Dissatisfaction: Jacques Lacan and the Emerging Society of Enjoyment* (2004).

16. For in-depth insight on queerness in the fiction of Stephen King, Cf. Magistrale and Blouin, *Stephen King and American History.*

17. The German name Wilfried is derived from "Wille Frieden," which roughly translates to *will to peace*. In the context of *1922*, the name is at once ironic and not. Ironic, of course, because of the traumatic violence that Wilf commits throughout the

story. Unironic because that violence is motivated by his desire to live peacefully and quietly, undisturbed by outsiders and the encroachment of modernity.

18. Indeed, piety, or some distorted version of it, is a crucial feature of the backwoods horror genre as well. More often than not, the horrific elements of such films are filtered through the iconography of religious fundamentalism and its attendant Old Testament approach to violence.

WORKS CITED

1922. Dir. Zak Hilditch. Screenplay by Zak Hilditch. Perf. Thomas Jane, Neal McDonough, Molly Parker. Campfire Productions, 2017. Netflix.

Agathocleous, Tanya, and Jason R. Rudy. "VICTORIAN COSMOPOLITANISMS: INTRODUCTION." *Victorian Literature and Culture*, vol. 38, no. 2, 2010, pp. 389–397. *JSTOR*, www.jstor.org/stable/25733481.

Brewer, Chad. *The Stereotypical Portrayal of Women in Slasher Films: Then Versus Now*. Thesis. Louisiana State University, 2009.

Clover, Carol J. "Her Body, Himself: Gender in the Slasher Film." *The Dread of Difference: Gender and the Horror Film,* edited by Barry Keith Grant. Austin, TX: University of Texas Press, 2015, pp. 37–67.

Creed, Barbara. *The Monstrous-Feminine: Film, Feminism, Psychoanalysis*. UK: Routledge, 1993.

Edelman, Lee. *No Future: Queer Theory and the Death Drive.* Durham, NC: Duke University Press, 2004.

Edsall, Thomas. "The Resentment that Never Sleeps." *The New York Times*, 10 Dec. 2020, https://www.nytimes.com/2020/12/09/opinion/trump-social-status-resentment.html.

Hornbeck, Elizabeth Jean. "Who's Afraid of the Big Bad Wolf?: Domestic Violence in The Shining." *Feminist Studies*, vol. 42, no. 3, Jan. 2016, pp. 689–719. EBSCOhost, doi:10.15767/feministstudies.42.3.0689.

Karni, Annie, et al. "Trump Plays on Racist Fears of Terrorized Suburbs to Court White Voters." *The New York Times,* 29 Jul. 2020. https://www.nytimes.com/2020/07/29/us/politics/trump-suburbs-housing-white-voters.html?auth=login-email&login=email.

Kendrick, James. *Film Violence: History, Ideology, Genre*. New York, NY: Wallflower Press, 2009.

King, Stephen, *1922.* New York, NY: Scribner Books, 2010. Print.

Kohn, Eric. "*1922* Review: *The Shining* Meets 'The Tell-Tale Heart' in the Year's Most Impressive Stephen King Adaptation." *IndieWire,* 23 Sep. 2017. https://www.indiewire.com/2017/09/1922-review-thomas-jane-stephen-king-netflix-1201879528/.

Lopez, German. "Bernie Sanders and Guns, Explained." *Vox Magazine.* January 17, 2016. https://www.vox.com/2015/10/13/9514933/bernie-sanders-gun-control-democratic-debate.

Magistrale, Tony. *Abject Terrors: Surveying the Modern and Postmodern Horror Film.* New York, NY: Peter Lang Publishing, 2005.

Martin, Richard. *The Architecture of David Lynch.* London, UK: Bloomsbury Press, 2014.

Maxwell, Rahsaan. "Why are urban and rural areas so politically divided?" *The Washington Post,* 5 Mar. 2019. https://www.washingtonpost.com/politics/2019/03/05/why-are-urban-rural-areas-so-politically-divided/.

McGowan, Todd. *The End of Dissatisfaction: Jacques Lacan and the Emerging Society of Enjoyment.* Albany, NY: State University of New York Press, 2004.

Sandel, Michael, guest. "The Trap of Meritocracy." *On Point,* WBUR, 31 Dec. 2020. Apple Podcasts.

Thompson, Karl. *Max Weber: The Protestant Ethic and the Spirit of Capitalism.* ReviseSociology.com, 2018. https://revisesociology.com/2018/08/17/max-weber-religion-society-change/.

Valera, Sergei, and Joan Guardia. "Perceived Insecurity and Fear of Crime in a City with Low Crime Rates." *Journal of Environmental Psychology,* vol. 38, 2014, Abstract. https://www.sciencedirect.com/science/article/abs/pii/S0272494414000140.

Welsh, Andrew. "The Rural Other in Backwoods Horror." The Abominable Dr. Welsh, Jun. 2018. https://theabominabledrwelsh.blog/2018/06/01/the-rural-other-in-backwoods-horror/.

Chapter 13

Lost in the Supermarket

When "The Mist" Fogs Our Mind . . . When Basic Emotions Transform into Monstrous Acts

Alexandra Reuber

INTRODUCTION

"We are living in very challenging times. But we are not powerless," states Deputy Communications Director at the City of Philadelphia, in her editorial "Stand Up Against Violence During COVID 19" published on the city's website on March 31, 2020 (Cofrancisco). Since the virus took hold of our daily lives, we have been facing challenges on many fronts: societal, economic, communal, professional, personal, etc. Whereas many citizens follow governmental recommendations or restrictions without further questioning, others oppose them violently. Imposed stay-at-home orders and the unknown of how the virus affects our future often lead to peoples' immediate appraisal of the situation, based on their internal states triggering emotions like sadness, fear, anger, and contempt. This emotional response creates a high potential for aggression and violence directed at others.

Frank Darabont's film *The Mist* (2007), based on Stephen King's novella (1980) of the same title, also focuses on man's fear of the unknown, aggression towards the other, and its implicit threat to mankind. More precisely, the story observes the transformation of man's basic emotions (happiness, sadness, surprise, fear, anger, disgust) into violent outbursts, a change caused by the sudden presence of the mist and the resulting humanitarian hardship on the people of Bridgton, Maine.

Despite the fact that the novella and film appeared well before COVID-19, *The Mist* serves as an allegory for our present time, because fictional works and current events highlight society's deep flaws: consumer-driven identity, social and political marginalization, existential despair, strong ideological beliefs, ethnocentrism, populism, and most of all, our violent behavior when engaging with one another at a time of crisis.

Based on the study of Paul Ekman's basic emotions, Nathan C. DeWall's General Aggression Model (GAM), and Eric Slotter's I³ Theory, this chapter focuses on the relationship between basic emotions, intergroup conflict, and violence. Special interest is given to Darabont's visualization of the three basic moral emotions (contempt, anger, and disgust) (CAD)—also known as the hostility triad—and their infringement on moral codes (community, autonomy, divinity) as they relate to aggressive intergroup behavior; a behavior that according to DeWall depends "on how an individual perceives and interprets his or her environment and the people therein, expectations regarding the likelihood of various outcomes, knowledge and beliefs about how people typically respond in certain situations, and how much people believe they have the abilities to respond to a variety of events" (18–19). Differently put, behavioral transgressions result from an interplay between person and situation input, one's internal states, and respective appraisal of the situation. As such, they are the product of Slotter's identified instigating trigger, impelling forces, and inhibiting processes, and can easily result in aggressive and violent behavior as illustrated in *The Mist* and by current events in our country.

SETTING THE STAGE: NATURAL VIOLENCE AS PRELUDE

The movie opens with David Drayton, main character, his wife Stephanie and son Billy standing by the window observing and hearing a summer storm closing in: rain, lightning, and rolling thunder. This first scene could not have been more symbolic. The family standing at the window alludes to the future customers pressing against the windowpane of the supermarket observing the outside forces. The individual flashes of lightning hint at man's poignant strikes of violence to come, and the constant rumbling of thunder in the background insinuates the intra- and interpersonal conflict every character of the film will face while in Bridgton's supermarket. The resulting "transgression of natural and moral laws, aesthetic rules and social taboos" (Botting 1), all to be illustrated when fighting for survival in the store, find reference in a brief glimpse at David's artwork foreshadowing the arrival of man's dark half: an entity personifying man's repressed past, instincts, emotions, and conceptions, as well as his latent aggressive and violent traits of character, which surpass any moral or social code when pushed to the limit under extraordinary circumstances.

After the passing of the storm, fallen trees and live electric wires on the ground illustrate nature's violent force. The combination of wires—a visual that later finds replication in the massive tentacles on the ground of the supermarket—and uprooted trees symbolize threat to one's physical safety as well as the uprooting of traditions and values. Furthermore, it insinuates the approaching death to strike the family and community. Notions of destruction and death are further stressed when a high-angle camera shot shows David and his family standing in front of their ravaged boathouse; an image which foreshadows peoples' unstable and destructive mindset fueled by an existential fear resulting from the external threat as much as from harbored feelings of "loss of validation," social marginalization, ethnocentrism, and the latent but "addictive lust for revenge" (Edsall).

Similar to the strong wind causing destruction, peoples' intensifying emotional storm will overturn their reasoning and eradicate socially acceptable behavior the longer they feel threatened by the mist. Like the mechanical force of the chainsaw used to clear the debris, peoples' emotions will divide the group of customers confined in Bridgton's "Food House" into in- and outgroups, an action resulting from threat, prejudice, and "a self-righteous belief [to be] on the correct side of history" (Edsall). It is an action that fuels aggression and violence directed at one another.

OFF TO THE SUPERMARKET

Looking at the lake, Billy asks his father: "What's that, Dad?" David responds: "Fogbank . . . a little left over from the storm . . . Two fronts meeting" (King 25). Although these words seem to be of meteorological importance, Darabont's careful choice of images and camera angles at the beginning of the film leads the viewer quickly to the true meaning of the fogbank. Like the current pandemic, the mist is an aerosol-borne threat closing in on the town and people of Bridgton, causing extraordinary circumstances for and triggering strong reactions from its residents, partitioning them into believers and non-believers.

Still unsettled by the past storm and the destruction left behind, residents flock to the local store to stock up in case they should face another natural disturbance. Entering the supermarket, alternating long and medium shots reveal aisles densely populated by brands and people, products arranged according to "modern marketing techniques" requiring costumers "to walk past all the impulse items known to modern man" (King 45), long checkout lines, overly friendly cashiers, and superficial chit-chat between customers. Though consumers seem to enjoy the here and now and exemplify their best behaviors, Bridgton's supermarket hints at America's modern "values and knowledge in [a] 'post-traditional society'" (Trentmann 373). It illustrates a collectively adopted consumer-driven identity promoting a false notion of freedom, happiness, "self-actualization and belonging" through material possessions (Corey). This profusion of and identification with goods and objects, which is so characteristic of our modern times, easily leads to a decrease of traditional values: neglect of family and community, deprivation of reciprocity, and loss of compassion and respect for one another. Moreover, it fosters a "search for 'authentic sociality'" by promoting a constant fight for self-promotion and self-identification (Trentmann 377).

Yet people do not reflect upon the consequences of exchanging traditional with modern consumer-driven values until in crisis. Only when confined in the store, they start to see the commercial place for what it truly is: a location of social categorization and differentiation, as well as of geographical and psychological "restriction and constraint" (Sears 157), where anguish, anger, and fear replace once purchased happiness. These emotions result from a long-suppressed individualism, on the one hand, and from the sudden threat, on the other. While confined in the store, these notions slowly transform the apparent place of choice and freedom into a battlefield where suppressed basic emotions run high, making everybody fight for his/her own survival.

"WELCOME TO THE DARK AGES"

Basic emotions can be defined as "short-lived psychological-physiological phenomena that represent efficient modes of adaptation to changing environmental demands" (Levenson 481). They are physical and instinctive agents "prompting bodily reactions to threat, reward, and anything in between" (Farnsworth). In *The Mist*, the following four are of particular importance: Fear, Anger, Contempt, and Disgust.

Fear is man's "vital response to physical and emotional danger" ("Fear"), prompting "behavior with a high survival value" in a time of heightened uncertainty (Burton). Set free by the mist's and COVID's sudden appearance, inexplicable origin, and imposition on peoples' daily lives, fear affects peoples' behavior, transforming a place that once appeased everybody's desires—a store, one's home, or one's country—into a location where "the development and regulation of interpersonal relationships" determines bodily safety or harm (Ekman 47).

"Welcome to the dark ages" (00:08:08). Those are the words of Darabont's young cashier greeting David upon entering the store. Whereas she jokingly refers to the non-functioning of the electronic checkouts due to the previous storm, her words have broader implications. They remind viewers of superstitious beliefs as well as "images of war, destruction and death" that characterized the early medieval period ("Dark Ages"). Although referring to the past, her words hold a bleak warning for the future: the dark ages will descend on Bridgton—and on the US as a whole—unmasking a society built on conspiracy theories, social framing, ethnocentrism, and dehumanization: a society where fear is the governing force, and whose survival or death rate are determined by "a field of social relationships between" aggressors and victims, between believers and non-believers, between you and me (Ray 19). Fueled by people's "strong moral convictions" (Skitka 99), opposing ideological beliefs, and respective fears, a geography of crime unfolds according to the three main foci of the GAM and Slotter's process-oriented I^3 theory.

GAM

Ruled by fear, peoples' reading of the challenge at hand defines the model's first focal point: Person and situation inputs, which provide "the most direct guiding force behind aggression behavior" (DeWall 20). This focal point presents itself early in the film when Dan Miller comes running to the store screaming: "Something in the mist took John Lee!" (00:12:07). The situation input, the presence of the mist, in combination with the man's bloody nose and pronounced affective behavior, underscore the mist's implied existential threat and stresses the already unsettled mindset of the people inside. Medium shots of individual consumers reveal their facial expressions indicating emotional stress: raising eyebrows, widened eyes, tightened lids, and dropping jaws.

Situation and person input are further highlighted when a young mother expresses the necessity to return to her children left playing at home. While seeking a volunteer to accompany her, everyone she addresses rationalizes disengaging his moral obligations to helping her (Ray 13). The social significance of family and solidarity once substituted for consumer values are further replaced by disengagement. This "indifference to the feelings of others" (Eller 20) highlights two things: First, it exemplifies the superficiality of an egocentric and narcissistic society, in which self-perpetuation and self-advancement take precedence over the well-being of the community. Second, it indicates the importance of situation and person input as contributing factors for future aggressive and violent behavior, thus pointing to GAM's second and third focus point: internal states, which "serve as mechanisms underlying the relationship between person and situation variables and outcomes of appraisal and decision-making processes. Affect, arousal, and cognition represent the three most significant internal states" (DeWall 21).

Peoples' fear of the ever-thickening mist or the fast-propagating COVID-19 virus joined with the cognition that institutional pillars of modern society—governmental agencies, military, police, etc.—have failed, heightens their affective arousal. This deprivation of "resources necessary to meet basic needs—physical, emotional, psychological, and social" accounts for another situation input (DeWall 26), which "facilitates the spread of a 'pandemic of violence and fuels an enveloping climate of fear'" in the store and our country (Ray 83).

David Drayton underscores this assumption when stating that people only behave in a civilized way as long as they "can dial 9-1-1" (01:12:37). However, when thrown "in the dark" and ruled by emotion, one can "see how primitive they get" (01:12:25). His words unconsciously refer to Mrs. Carmody's exclamation "It's death" as much as they allude to the current threat of COVID-19, President Trump's "campaign about re-centering Whiteness as what it actually means to be American" (Richeson), and his repeated falsehoods about election fraud. Each of these factors puts people "in the dark," allowing for GMA's third focus, namely "outcomes of appraisal and decision-making processes," to manifest (DeWall 20).

DeWall distinguishes between immediate appraisal and reappraisal processes. Whereas immediate appraisal refers to an automatic and emotional response to the situation, which "may include fear and anger-related affect," reappraisal points to "more controlled processes" (21). While David's statement above is an example of the latter, Mrs. Carmody's exclamation—"It's death"—and facial expression—jawline dropped, her eyes wide open and focused on the outside (00:13:20)—are examples of the former. Yet, when stating, "It's death out there. . . . It's judgement day and it's come 'round at last" (00:14:39; 00:20:36), she underscores her initial two-word reaction, thus reappraising the situation. Her apocalyptic proclamation plays into person and situation input and foreshadows future interpersonal conflict.

I³ MODEL AND SOCIAL CATEGORIZATION

At this point, Darabont introduces the three main effects of Slotter's I³ Aggression Theory: instigating trigger, impelling, and inhibiting forces. With no rescue in sight, the instigating trigger, namely the situation input, and the impelling forces, namely people's processing of the situation, are high. The longer the confinement and uncertainty about the external threat last, the more does fear of the unknown and anger due to the deprivation of resources drive people's "behavioral and cognitive responses" (Kowalska 2). Interpersonal conflict based on group consciousness and categorization as well as the violation of social norms are the result. When instigating trigger and impelling forces supersede inhibitory processes, "the threshold above which aggressive impulses . . . manifest themselves in aggressive behavior" is high (Slotter 40), leading to violent outbursts and destruction of property in the film and in our country.

Whereas in *The Mist*, residents oppose out-of-towners (Biker and Brent Norton), blue collar workers (Jim and Myron) question white collar workers (Brent Norton, David Trayton, Amanda Dunfrey, Irene Reppler), and creationists (Mrs Carmody and her circle of followers) fight evolutionists (Amanda, David, Private Jessup), in our current climate, "true Americans" oppose African Americans and immigrants, media outlets and administration officials politicize COVID mitigation measures, and citizens believing in conspiracy theory such as QAnon question scientists and healthcare officials. As the resulting social circles include some but exclude others, they violate basic social concepts like community, inclusion, cooperation, collective efficacy, etc.

Jim's behavior towards David in the storage area exemplifies this violation. Whether he ridicules the "big shot artist with connections in New York and Hollywood" (00:23:45) for having heard noises in the back, arrogantly reminds him that *his* connections "don't make [him] better than anybody else" (00:23:49), or menaces him when stating the "next time you have something to say, you count your teeth, because I'm sick to death of your bullshit" (00:24:21), Jim's verbal aggression exposes David to his profound anger. Moreover, Jim's behavior showcases identification with *his* group of people (uneducated, hard-working yet marginalized), but excludes others, those "who went to college" (00:23:54). His lack of self-esteem and "resentment toward successful white elites" (Edsall) establish "differentiation and conflict" (Williams), which function together as dyadic impelling factors for his response to the instigating trigger, the situation at hand.

Another example illustrating social disintegration within the store's microcosm is the differentiation between in and out-of-towners, one of whom is Brent Norton, an African American attorney from New York. Instead of listening to the in-towners' explanation of Norm's death, Brent accuses *them* of a "pathetic attempt at a joke" (00:34:32) at his cost, thus projecting his latent anger for never having been fully accepted by the community outward. His anger also manifests itself in his "alterations in voice tone" and intonation (Levenson 485), choice of contemptuous vocabulary when calling Jim and Myron "hicks" (00:34:50), "postural adjustments" directed at Jim (Levenson 485), purposeful aggression aimed at David when pushing him into the shelves, and in his threat, "I'll sue your ass again!" (00:35:46). While hiding behind his powerful legal role, Brent's anger, displayed in the form of verbal and physical violence, is a reaction to the instigating trigger of the current situation and to harbored personal and dyadic impelling factors like feelings of powerlessness, "of vulnerability, or insecurity in [his] relationship" with the white in-towners (Slotter 40).

In both examples, social marginalization and subsequent intergroup conflict result from fear and anger, on the one hand, and from "a fracturing of information," on the other (Falzone)—a well-known phenomenon of our current times. Yet, violent behavior can also be tied to the two moral emotions of contempt and disgust. Whereas contempt "is often linked to hierarchy and a vertical dimension of social evaluation," sociomoral disgust is associated with "situations in which people behave without dignity or in which people strip others of their dignity" (Rozin 575). Despite difference in their nuances, both emotions "involve a negative evaluation of others and their actions" (Rozin 575). As protests against COVID-19 lockdowns in Michigan in May 2020, the subsequent kidnapping attempt of Michigan Governor Whitmer in October 2020, and the Capitol riots on January 6, 2021 have shown, they can lead to violent behavior.

In *The Mist*, Darabont visualizes the importance of contempt and disgust in relation to conflict and violence through Amanda Dufrey's encounter with Mrs. Carmody in the restroom. Secluded in the dark stall of the restroom, Mrs. Carmody's seemingly religious monologue reveals her distress. While first appearing good-hearted, one discovers soon that she is only willing to "save a few" in order to "have earned [her] place at [God's] side" (00:40:22). Despite her pretense to be interested in the common good of the people, her action is self-oriented. She wishes to establish *her* superiority among those of whom most *she* perceives as deficient, inferior, and salient to her "own standard" (Miceli 207). Her contempt for her fellow citizens shows when stating: "Let me shine your light, 'cause they're not all bad. . . . They can't all be bad." (00:40:01). The negative evaluation of "they" is based on *her* moral values and moral convictions, which stand in stark contrast to scientific advances and her long-felt shame, rejection, and humiliation by Bridgton's community. Her facial expression—tightening eyelids, squinting then closing eyes, stretching and sucking her lips—and behavioral cues—staring and pointing the finger at the teacher—when addressing Amanda underscore her contempt towards "these people" (00:39:32), of whom the young schoolteacher is one.

Accompanied by "heightened agitation and distress" (Shaver 74), Mrs. Carmody's behavior also exemplifies the basic emotion of disgust, "a rejection response to distasteful stimuli" (Miceli 215). With tightened eyelids and raised upper lips, she states: "A day I need a friend like you, I'll just have myself a little squat and shit one out" (00:41:31). Her degradation of Amanda illustrates her "dangerously inflated self-esteem" (Eller 21). Moreover, it illustrates the necessity to free herself from the danger that could corrupt *her* integrity and moral standards. Hence, instead of accepting the young woman's emotional support, Mrs. Carmody reminds Amanda of her inferiority and

indignity by equalizing her existence to one of human's basic bodily function: defecation. This devaluation and rejection of the young woman is later
projected onto other customers, triggering a "concern for the integrity of the
social order" within the store (Rozin 575); an order that due to the instigating
situation input and respective impelling person factors at play will soon be
overthrown. When social order crumbles and people in the store behave like
"uncultured barbarians, evil tyrants or superstitious peasants" ("Dark Ages"),
one recalls the cashier's words: "Welcome to the dark ages."

NORMS, TRADITIONS, AND VALUES UNDER ATTACK

The fact that people's situation-specific behavior (expressions of judgement, anger, contempt, and disgust) quickly turns violent suggests that
social categorization has been a long-established characteristic of the town.
In addition, Darabont's identification of man's social identity (ranging from
bag boy, retired schoolteacher, famous artist, to important lawyer, etc.) and
affective state at the beginning of the film insinuate that the solemn pledge
of allegiance under which Americans should stand as "one nation, indivis-
ible, with liberty and justice for all" neither applies to Bridgton, nor to our
country (Pledge of Allegiance). Group consciousness, latent ethnocentrism,
and respective social categorization and defamation are intricately woven into
social and communal fabrics.

Darabont's film, our life under COVID-19, as well as the insurrection
attempt of the Capitol show that, when in crisis, emotions associated with
group consciousness become "the main motivating force[s] in human affairs"
(Lazarus 234), leading to subjective and often aggressive reactions based
on an individual's or a group's long-lasting enforced categorization and
processing of the situation at hand.These impelling forces generate first the
expression of CAD, then of infra-humanization and dehumanization,[1] before
ending in violence. When partitioning one's citizens into "the human and
the non-human, the more- and the less-human, the properly human (those
whose inalienable dignity demands respect) and the spectrally human (those
who may justifiably be dispossessed, disenfranchised or reduced to chattel)"
(Feola 134), the store, alias for the US, turns against itself and allows the
monsters to come out.

WHEN THE MONSTERS COME OUT

Derived from Latin *monstrum*, the noun monster holds the meaning of "divine
omen (especially one indicating misfortune), portent, sign" ("Monster").

Figuratively, it points to a "repulsive character, object of dread, awful deed, abomination" and should always be understood within "the intricate matrix of relations" whether social, cultural, socio-economical, sexual, etc. (Cohen 5). This implies that the monster's body and meaning change depending on the cultural and or social significance of the moment, the feeling, and the place of its manifestation. Hence, the monster is difficult to identify and define.

When Dan Miller refers to an outside force that "took John Lee" he is unable to articulate who or what it was that took the man's life, triggering "fear, desire, anxiety, and fantasy" in him and others in the store (Cohen 4). While pressing themselves against the store's front window in order to detect the aggressor outside, people unfortunately do not realize that the monster is actually growing within America's "Food House," a place where it finds its nutrition in every single aisle. Its unidentifiable body manifests itself in the form of people's group consciousness as well as voyeuristic and aggressive tendencies; tendencies that are closely linked to the basic emotions of fear, contempt, and disgust and, as the fog thickens, increasingly replace human outreach and support. Examples are: Jim and Myron staring at the monstrous tentacles cutting into Norm's leg before pulling him out into the mist (00:25:43ff), customers watching the young mother, Brent Norton, and the anonymous biker being swallowed by the mist, or onlookers eyeing the bloody rope attached to the biker's torso being pulled back into the supermarket (00:53:52).

The biker's bloody body parts trigger two form of disgust: animal and contamination disgust. Whereas the former implies a "revulsion at the thought of one's death and the fragility of one's corporeal form" (White 440), which is closely linked to people's existential fear, the latter refers to "anything that indicates pollution or that may cause disease" (White 440). Pulling the lower body parts towards the slightly open door of the supermarket could be viewed as an invitation to whatever is outside to come inside and to contaminate America's body and soul. However, as already stated, the monster has long been inside America's "Food House," embodied by "those who witness, or who are victims of, certain acts, rather than of those who perform them" (Riches 3). Hence, the blood-stained cord reminds all onlookers that despite not having actively committed the violent act against their fellow citizens, they watched it unfold. Here, the blood stains also speak to *us,* viewers of *our* civil duty, unable to intervene when injustice is done, instead participating in "a culture of voyeuristic violence" by watching the violent act unfold or recording and posting it on social media, as was the case on January 6, 2021 and days thereafter (Ray 63).

Nourished and strengthened after the biker's death, the monster takes on various supernatural forms, attacks the market and its people, and fuels the cycle of violence. The viewer identifies the following: super-size insects crawling up and down the store's glass front, a gigantic flying reptile resembling a pterodactyl breaking the glass, flying scorpions with extensive stingers, as well as several dog-size and thousands of baby-size grey spiders in the neighboring pharmacy. Although similarities between these "supernatural" abominations and nature's insects and arachnids exist, King's monsters remain transgressive. Nevertheless, they all have two things in common: First, while free in form and manifestation, they themselves prevent mobility, something Mrs. Carmody expresses on multiple occasions throughout the film: "You can't go out!" (01:38:04). Second, they somehow contaminate and selectively kill those who come in contact with them, just like conspiracy theorists, COVID-19 disbelievers, insurrectionists, etc. Hence, they represent everything that is outside of the realm of what is known and familiar and transform Bridgton's "Food House" into the US, into a "contested cultural space" (Cohen 7).

Symbolically associated with "greed and sensual pleasure" (Jaffe), plague, sickness, and destruction, it is of no surprise that King chose insects to flock towards a commercial place that feeds human senses and a constant longing for more. Nonetheless, despite its opulence, the store reminds those inside of their socio-economic status and spending ability, thus establishing and revealing difference, which easily leads to social conflict, violence, and destruction. Via the insects' rather larger size, Darabont underscores people's immoral desires and behaviors—consumerism, envy, marginalization, defamation, etc.—which are based on harbored feelings of contempt, anger, and disgust directed at the other. Like insects, these feelings attack Bridgton's, alias for the country's, already weakened social/communal infrastructure, which finds symbolic representation in the store's cracked window that neither duct tape nor bags of dog food will prevent from breaking.

Representative of the growing basic emotions within the store, the number and size of insects increases as well, until they conflate into one flying reptile resembling a pterodactyl. When the dinosaur-like creature attacks those inside, people try to fight back by torching the aggressive intruder. Despite the fact that a torch is often understood as a symbol of intelligence and spirituality, those attempting to light the torch need multiple attempts to do so. This observation is significant as it illustrates people's difficulty fighting the monstrous invader, an alias for the long-harbored hostile emotions towards their fellow men. With people's inhibiting mechanisms like self-regulatory strength and community commitment weakened, America's "Food House" lives up to its name and feeds its monsters.

It is then that Mrs. Carmody takes the floor, reappraises the situation and perception of her fellow men, most of whom she judges as less virtuous, even "less than human, and [thus] as deserving of a violent fate" (Eller 18). Darabont emphasizes this difference in virtue when showing an oversized scorpion landing on Mrs. Carmody's abdomen. According to the *Book of Revelation*, the scorpion signifies transformation, death, and rebirth through great suffering. Yet, the insect crawls over her chest, lifts up its monstrous stinger, and flies off. The fact that the scorpion does not torment her (see Revelation 9:5 ESV) suggests her seemingly moral and religious superiority. Furthermore, it underscores her falsely inflated self-esteem and contributes to her apocalyptic narrative, according to which "the end time has come, not in flames, but in mist" (00:43:55). Perceiving the mist and its monsters as a sign from God who "now demands retribution in blood" (00:45:45), her understanding of the situation justifies violence and death. It points to the (re) birth of its *true* monster: man's dark half, foreshadowed by David's paintings, now embodied by Mrs. Carmody.

Moving slowly around while eyeing her listeners, she weaves her web like a spider. Similar to President Trump's expressed falsehoods about the virus or a stolen election, Mrs. Carmody carefully spins her story, reminding her listeners of peoples' unlawful desire "for going against [the] forbidden rules of old" (01:32:26). Like the mother spider who captured and used the MP and Bobby Eagleton as womb for the breeding of thousands of baby spiders, President Trump and Mrs. Carmody cocoon those willing to listen, widen their web, and give birth to the enactment of man's most basic instincts, drives, and monstrous behaviors. At the moment that anger directed at those violating their conservative belief system is secured, they encourage their audience to take sides between those who "are endowed with all goodness and rightness and [those] with all badness and evil" (Eller 150). This "encouragement" for irrevocable group formation, practiced in film and reality, illustrates contempt and moral disgust for the other—scientists, educators, progressives, out-of-towners (immigrants)—leading to the division of the people.

In *The Mist*, this group formation allows Mrs. Carmody to make all those pay who violate *her* established "ethics of autonomy, community, and divinity" (see Rozin 576), and, by doing so, belittle *her* morally and socially. She now takes the opportunity to go after those who have been attacking her self-concept and belief system. While the constantly turning camera alludes to her unstable mind, her always audible voice highlights the omnipresence of her thoughts. Her words, just like the President's innumerable tweets, sow division. Two groups form: those who blindly follow the radical views expressed and those opposing them. Controlled by anger—"the most powerful emotional determinant of aggressive behavior" (Halperin 316)—followers enact Ollie's remark that when in crisis "people turn to whoever promises a solution" (01:13:03), even if it comes in form of human sacrifice.

Identified and accused by Mrs. Carmody as *the one* being responsible for the occurrence of the mist and its abominations, her followers subject Private

Jessup to verbal violence in form of accusations and name-calling, psychological and emotional violence as a result of framing, infra-humanization, and deindividuation, and to physical violence when stabbing him multiple times with a knife. Rattled by fear and anger and mislead by Mrs. Carmody's defamation and call for "expiation," her "baby spiders" agree to and engage in the collective persecution of the young soldier despite his repetitive statement: "It ain't my fault" (01:31:46). Perceiving Jessup's opposition "as an extreme deviation from moral norms," his words become "an adequate trigger of violence" ultimately leading to his killing (Halperin 321).

While engaging in the murderous act and screaming "feed him to the beast" (01:33:45), Mrs. Carmody and her followers take on the shape of the monstrous Other. As they carry the heavily injured man through the aisles of the supermarket, their hands and arms remind the viewer first of the wires on the ground, then of the Lovecraftian tentacles pulling the bag boy Norm out of the storage area into the mist. Despite Norm's and Private Jessup's screams for help, bystanders watch and follow the murderous act, transforming every single customer into "the outsider, the antithesis of order, peace, and stability" (Eller 7), and allowing the monster to shape-shift between voyeurism, Mrs. Carmody, and her followers.

To remind Bridgton's customers and the viewers of the film of the consumption and practice of voyeuristic violence, Darabont uses tilted high-angle camera shots following Jessup's procession out of the store, insinuating further the eyeing of the bloody deed. His subsequent focus on Jessup's bloody handprint on the store's door underscores *everybody's* guilt of having succumbed to and not fought against the hostility triad and its triggered *angerworld*. It is Darabont's visual call for action: to fight for our democracy and to protest anyone who proposes the implementation of a cult-like following and a division of the people by extreme force; a realization that draws our attention again to events in our country.

BRIDGTON'S SUPERMARKET ALIAS AMERICA 2020/21

As previously stated, Bridgton's town and "Food House" serve as an allegorical representation of America's "failure of social fabrics" and of the "monstrosities of violence and anomie that lurk within them" (Sears 156): economic and educational inequality, social and racial disparity, social and political divisions, bigotry and populism, disinformation and lies pertaining to the severity of COVID-19 as well as to election results, etc. Similar to King's fictional town, the US exemplifies a deeply divided society in which binary perceptions of us versus them seem the new norm: "true white" Americans oppose African Americans and immigrants, polarized media outlets and administration officials politicize COVID-19 severity and mitigation measures, and citizens believing in conspiracy theories question scientists, healthcare officials, and 2020 election results. Moreover, as the "microcosm of our culture" (Moore), Bridgton's supermarket exemplifies America's flaws and violent outbursts in time of crisis. In 2020, these find, for example, expression in irresponsible accusations of who to blame for COVID-19, unjustified executive actions, and lies about election fraud. President Trump's language calling COVID-19 a hoax, "Chinese Virus," "Wuhan" or "Kung Flu" (Nigam), followed by his use of "the pandemic as pretext to implement dramatic immigration restrictions" (Zak), and his unfounded allegations of voter fraud have solidified the country's divisions, stirred people's basic emotions, and resulted in violent intergroup conflicts.

Yet, while he "rejects political correctness," he always appeals to the basic instincts of freedom and choice and promulgates his "doctrine of 'America First'" (Edsall). This manifests itself in his peddling to anti-science proponents turning "vaccines and masks" into symbolic references of "anti-freedom, anti-American" (Caulfield), to immigration opponents implementing a ban on asylum seekers, the suspension of refugees and legal immigrants, the termination of visa appointments, etc., and to his base to question presidential election results. One could say that similar to Bridgton's monstruous formations, President Trump allowed America's longtime suppressed monsters to come out: science-skepticism, xenophobia, jingoism, ethnocentrism, populism, etc.

However, what "incorporates fear, desire, anxiety, and fantasy" is neither linked to scientific advances, nor to be found outside of the American border (Cohen 4). It is masked and stored in our society—our own "Food House"—and manifests itself in peoples' acts of social framing, aggression towards others, and the proliferation of opposing ideologies such as: "a distrust of traditional sources of scientific knowledge" and "an emphasis on freedom and choice" (Caulfield), a violent opposition to anyone being other (race, culture, political affiliation, belief system), and a refusal to accept anything that threatens one's world view, freedom, and individualism.

This said, the mist and Mrs. Carmody may be fictional, but the threat they represent to Bridgton's community is symbolic for the current state of our country. As Mrs. Carmody's propagation of falsehoods and wrongful accusations of Private Jessup lead to group formation between believers and non-believers, so do President Trump's initial belittling of the severity of the virus, his repudiation of science, his mockery of those who oppose his science-free approach, and his lies about election results. His divisive language serves as "an effective strategy to draw people into [his] community and to facilitate the uncritical acceptance of contentious scientific [and political] perspectives," causing significant harm to the American people, of whom many belittle the severity of COVID-19 (Caulfied), exemplify a "declining faith in social institutions" (Bradshaw), show an increased interest in conspiracy theories, and even storm the capitol. In film and reality, "the spread of bunk" by group leaders—Mrs. Carmody, The President, opposition leaders, administration officials—and constant reference to one's constitutional rights of choice and freedom are ultimately responsible for "increased stigma and discrimination" (Caulfied) and the loss of American life.

Bridgton's "Food House" as well as the US, formerly associated with choice, freedom, and prosperity, have become places of limitation, violent opposition, and death. Both places have fallen victim to interpersonal and intergroup conflict resulting from fear, anger, and contempt, on the one hand, and the belief in and pursuit of conflicting ideologies, on the other. Whether in film or in our times, the monster is born "at times of crisis" and has to be understood as "an embodiment of a certain cultural moment" that draws attention to and fuels conflict (Cohen 6; 4). As every cultural moment is different, so is its monster. Whether in the form of tentacles, oversized insects, aggressive spiders, virus, publicized falsehoods, cult-like behavior, or defamatory language, the monster "refuses easy categorization," yet "threatens to destroy" what is known (Cohen 6; 12): our culture, society, and beliefs.

CONCLUSION

No matter how unbelievable text and film may appear, the story's "examination of fear" and the consequential transformation of "human nature and human behaviors" makes its content timeless and applicable to our time (Darabont). Similar to the mist, COVID-19 is an existential threat causing fear and physical and emotional suffering. In combination with other basic emotions, this fear eventually triggers man's irresponsible, aggressive, and violent behavior. As Stephen King points out in his conversation with Frank Darabont, even though "things happen to [the people in the supermarket] that are inexplicable or not normal, . . . sooner or later every one of us faces those things in our own life" (King, interview). Unfortunately, that time has come.

The inability to come together and to work towards a common good reflects the current state of the US, which has transformed into a country where ideological differences and individual advances dominate the sense of community, where name-calling and infra-humanization stir intergroup conflict, where our leaders promote fear, anger, and contempt through continuous false statements blaming other countries for the outbreak of COVID, as well as accuse political opponents of using the pandemic to promote their own political agenda and rig an election. As the store is divided, so is our country in which defamation, violence, and death seem to have become the norm.

As *The Mist* paints a bleak picture of Bridgton and its citizens, most of whom lose their lives in the spider webs of their own doing, the story makes us reflect upon the "journey of the human condition" and the implicit dangers to our society (Darabont): eradication of traditional values, consumerism, group consciousness, ethnocentrism, and a fear-driven environment that generates disrespectful and aggressive behaviors towards others often ending in violence and destruction. Hence, *The Mist* should be understood as a warning *and* wake-up call to what truly matters in life: family, community, outreach, love and respect for one another. David Drayton personifies these characteristics. Not only does he engage in an unselfish fight for the survival of the community, he does everything in his power to protect his son from the monsters, even if that means killing him in the end and leaving himself behind in an unrecognizable world of emotional suffering and solitude. Darabont's message is clear: We *all* need to make sacrifices for the greater good of society and humanity as a whole, and no matter the hardship, we need to remain hopeful while fighting against the dark forces.

NOTE

1. Whereas infra-humanization is a social "process by which people consider their ingroup as fully human and outgroups as less human and more animal-like," dehumanization "of an outgroup implies that its members are no longer humans at all" (Leyens 140; 143).

WORKS CITED

Botting, Fred. *Gothic*. New York: Routledge, 1996.

Bradshaw, James. "Why Has America Become Such a Fractured Society?" *Mercatornet. Navigating Modern Complexities*, 28 Jan. 2020, https://mercatornet. com/why-has-america-become-such-a-fractured-society/46509/. Accessed 20 Dec. 2020.

Burton, Neel M.D. "What are Basic Emotions? Emotions Such As Fear And Anger Are Hardwired." *Psychology Today*, 7 Jan. 2016, www.psychologytoday.com/us/ blog/hide-and-seek/201601/what-are-basic-emotions. Accessed 24 July 2020.

Caulfield, Timothy. "Covid Vaccine and Mask Conspiracies Succeed When They Appeal to Identity and Ideology." *Think, Opinion, Analysis, Essays* https://www. nbcnews.com/think/opinion/covid-vaccine-mask-conspiracies-succeed-when-they-appeal-identity-ideology-ncna1251761. *Accessed 21 Dec. 2020.*

Cofrancisco, Kelly. "Stand Up Against Violence During COVID-19." *City of Philadelphia*, 31 Mar. 2020, www.phila.gov/2020-03-31-stopping-the-violence-during-covid-19/. Accessed 7 May 2020.

Cohen, Jeffrey Jerome. *Monster Theory*. Minneapolis, MN: University of Minnesota Press, 1996.

Corey, Sam. "How Coronavirus Changed the Symbolism of Supermarkets." *Sam Corey*, 27 Apr. 2020, https://medium.com/@RelatableBrand/were-all-lost-in-the-supermarket-f854a02f7df9._Accessed 16 May 2020.

"Dark Ages." *Medievalist. Net*. www.medievalists.net/2014/02/why-the-middle-ages-are-called-the-dark-ages/. Accessed 24 June 2020.

DeWall, Nathan C., and Craig A. Anderson. "The General Aggression Model." *Human Aggression and Violence. Causes, Manifestations, and Consequences*, edited by Phillip R. Shaver and Mario Mikulincer. American Psychological Association, 2014, pp. 15–33.

Edsall, Thomas B. "Opinion: White Riot. How Racism, Grievance, Resentment and the Fear of Diminished Status Came Together to Fuel Violence and Mayhem on Jan. 6." *The New York Times*, 13 Jan. 2021, www.nytimes.com/2021/01/13/opinion/capitol-riot-white-grievance.html. Accessed 15 Jan. 2021.

Ekman, Paul. "Basic Emotions." *Handbook of Cognition and Emotion*, edited by Tim Dalgleish and Mick Power. John Wiley & Sons, Ltd., 1999, pp. 45–60.

Eller, Jack David. *Violence and Culture. A Cross-Cultural and Interdisciplinary Approach*. Cengage Learning, 2006.

Falzone, Diana. "'It's the Trump Bubble': The Right Has Created a Wave of COVID Patients Who Don't Believe It's Real." *Vanity Fair*, 19 Nov. 2020, www.vanityfair.com/news/2020/11/a-wave-of-covid-patients-who-dont-believe-its-real. Accessed 21 Dec. 2020.

Farnsworth, Bryn. "How to Measure Emotions and Feelings (And the Difference Between Them)." *Imotions*, 14 Apr. 2020, https://imotions.com/blog/difference-feelings-emotions/. Accessed 18 May 2019.

"Fear." *Psychology Today*. www.psychologytoday.com/us/basics/fear. Accessed 24 June 2020.

Feola, Michael. "Norms, Vision And Violence: Judith Butler on The Politics of Legibility." *Contemporary Political Theory,* vol. 13, no. 2, 2014, pp. 130–148.

Halperin, Eran. "The Emotional Roots of Intergroup Aggression: The Distinct Roles of Anger and Hatred." *Human Aggression and Violence. Causes, Manifestations, and Consequences*, edited by Phillip R. Shaver and Mario Mikulincer. American Psychological Association, 2014, pp. 315–331.

Jaffe, Eric. "Insect." *Dictionary of Symbolism*, 2001, *Fantasy and Science Fiction*. www.umich.edu/~umfandsf/symbolismproject/symbolism.html/I/insects.html. Accessed 10 July 2020.

King, Stephen. *The Mist*. New York: Signet, 2007.

King, Stephen and Frank Darabont. "Stephen King and Director Frank Darabont Talk *The Mist*." Interview by Movieweb Contributor. *Movieweb*, 13 Nov. 2007, https://movieweb.com/stephen-king-and-director-frank-darabont-talk-the-mist/. Accessed 30 July 2020.

Kowalska, Magda, and Monika Wróbel. "Basic Emotions." *ResearchGate*, July 2017, pp. 1–6, www.researchgate.net/publication/318447136. Accessed 30 May 2020.

Lazarus, Richard S. *Emotion and Adaptation*. Oxford, UK: Oxford UP, 1991.

Levenson, R.W. "The Intrapersonal Functions of Emotion." *Cognition and Emotion*, vol. 13, no. 5, 1999, pp. 481–504.

Leyens, Jacques-Philippe et al. "Infra-humanization: The Wall of Group Differences." *Social Issues and Policy Review*, vol. 1, no. 1, 2007, pp. 139–172.

Miceli, Maria, and Cristiano Castelfranchi. "Contempt and Disgust: The Emotions of Disrespect." *Journal for the Theory of Social Behavior*, vol. 48, 2017, pp. 205–229.

The Mist. Dir. Frank Darabont. Screenplay by Frank Darabont. Darkwoods Productions, 2007. DVD.

"Monster." *Online Etymology Dictionary*, www.etymonline.com/word/monster. Accessed 26 June 2020.

Moore, Nolan. "The Ending of *The Mist* Finally Explained." *Looper*, 13 May 2019, www.looper.com/152716/the-ending-of-the-mist-finally-explained/. Accessed 28 Sept. 2020.

Nigam, Aanchal. "Donald Trump Calls COVID-19 An 'Odd Name', Asks 'What Is 19?'" *Republicworld.com*, 25 June 2020, www.republicworld.com/world-news/us-news/donald-trump-expresses-confusion-over-the-name-of-covid-19.html. Accessed 27 July 2020.

"Pledge of Allegiance." www.ushistory.org/documents/pledge.htm. Accessed 25 Sept. 2020.

Ray, Larry. *Violence & Society: Second Edition*. Newbury Park, CA: Sage Publishing, 2018.

Riches, David, editor. *The Anthropology of Violence*. Oxford, UK: Basil Blackwell, 1986.

Richeson, Jennifer. "Email." Received by Thomas B. Edsall. https://www.nytimes.com/2021/01/13/opinion/capitol-riot-white-grievance.html. Accessed 15 Jan. 2021.

Rozin, Paul et al. "The CAD Triad Hypothesis: A Mapping between Three Moral Emotions (Contempt, Anger, Disgust) and Three Moral Codes (Community, Autonomy, Divinity)." *Journal of Personality and Social Psychology*, vol. 76, no. 4, 1999, pp. 574–586.

"Scorpion." *Revelation* 9:5. www.bibleref.com/Revelation/9/Revelation-9-5.html. Accessed 12 July 2020.

Sears, John. *Stephen King's Gothic. Gothic Literary Studies*. Oxford, UK: Oxford University Press, 2011.

Shaver, Phillip R. et al. "A Behavioral System's Perspective on Power and Aggression." *Human Aggression and Violence. Causes, Manifestations, and Consequences*, edited by Phillip R. Shaver and Mario Mikulincer. American Psychological Association, 2014, pp. 71–87.

Skitka, Linda J., and G. Scott Morgan. "The Social and Political implications of Moral Conviction." *Advances in Political Psychology*, vol. 35, no. 1, 2014, pp. 95–110.

Slotter, Erica B., and Eli J. Finkel. "I³ Theory: Instigating, Impelling, and Inhibiting Factors in Aggression." *Human Aggression and Violence. Causes, Manifestations, and Consequences*, edited by Phillip R. Shaver and Mario Mikulincer. American Psychological Association, 2014, pp. 35–52.

Trentmann, Frank. "Beyond Consumerism: New Historical Perspectives on Consumption." *Journal of Contemporary History*, vol. 39, no. 3, 2004, pp. 373–401.

White, Theresa L. et al. "Individual Differences and the 'Selfish' Connection between Empathy and Disgust." *American Journal of Psychology*, vol. 131, no. 4, 2018, pp. 439–450.

Williams, Ricardo. "Anger as a Basic Emotion and Its Role in Personality Building and Pathological Growth: The Neuroscientific, Developmental and Clinical Perspectives." *Frontiers in Psychology*, vol. 8, 2017, www.ncbi.nlm.nih.gov/pmc/articles/PMC5681963/. Accessed 5 July 2020.

Zak, Danilo. "Immigration-related Executive Actions during the COVID-19 Pandemic." National Immigration Forum, Nov. 18, 2020, https://immigrationforum.org/article/immigration-related-executive-actions-during-the-covid-19-pandemic/. Accessed 21 Dec. 2020.

Chapter 14

Stephen King's *Big Driver*
A Utopian Road to Justice

Patrick McAleer

Perhaps the most oft-quoted line from Stephen King's *Danse Macabre* is his delineation of how he approaches his craft: "I recognize terror as the finest emotion . . ., and so I will try to terrorize the reader. But if I find I cannot terrify him/her, I will try to horrify; and if I cannot horrify, I'll go for the gross-out. I'm not proud" (25–6). Yet what happens when one is unable to neatly and cleanly classify a King tale, or film, into one of these demarcated categories? Quite possibly a text, then, opens up to more fruitful discussion as, at times, the constraints of classification and generic labeling are extremely limited and limiting. To that end, with respect to Stephen King's 2010 collection *Full Dark, No Stars*, the Constant Reader encounters four novellas in which all of the included tales involve characters taking life and/or law into their own hands, which certainly carries, on the surface, a nod towards terror and horror because of the brutality (and even grossness) involved in carrying out "justice" as defined by the primary characters. Further, and perhaps uncoincidentally, three of these stories—*1922*, *Big Driver*, and *A Good Marriage*— have all been adapted to film, leaving the "tame" *A Fair Extension* as solely a written story, which suggests that the violence and questions about in/justice, vigilantism, and righteousness within the more violent stories (as the "deal with the devil" in "Fair Extension" is fairly indirect in its violence) carry a particular, and possibly revealing, appeal to the Constant Viewer. As such, with a focus on the cinematic adaptation of *Big Driver*, this essay considers King's take on violence, violation, and if/when it just may be appropriate to take the law into one's own hands.

Admittedly, giving credence to self-governed executions of justice seems rather dangerous, the stuff of comic book heroes, or even just overly simplistic if not delusional; yet, for better or worse, throughout the Stephen King Universe, sometimes the simple solution with respect to attaining justice is, arguably, the most appropriate one. There are, of course, instances of exceptionally dubious acts of "justice" within the King canon, especially in *Full*

197

Dark, No Stars as Wilfred James of *1922* kills his wife to stop the sale of their land, most of which she owns, as this transaction would necessitate a move into the city that conflicts with James' simple desire to remain in the rural lands of Nebraska, and the gross imbalance on display—a life for a house and land—brings many questions to the forefront regarding violence and its legitimacy in King's fiction and films. Moreover, *Fair Extension* finds one Dave Streeter making a literal deal with the devil (with perhaps one of the least creative *nom de plume* in King's oeuvre: George Elvid) to magically transfer Streeter's terminal cancer to a "friend" of whom Streeter is rather envious. Both James and Streeter reflect a dangerous sense of entitlement behind their devious actions, and while one could easily trace the thoughts behind each action, each instance of violence (whether direct [murder] or indirect [cancer]), an *understanding* of each character hardly leads to *condoning* their actions. And King has certainly "been here before," suggesting a keen interest in acts and actions on a spectrum that finds selfishness on one end and finds meritorious courage on the other. James and Streeter are clearly on the selfish end of the spectrum, while, arguably, characters like Johnny Smith of *The Dead Zone* and Dolores Claiborne of the novel of the same name or even Darcy Anderson of *A Good Marriage* can all be found on the other side as these characters are almost universally seen as heroes. Indeed, accepting the acts of murderers, or would-be murderers, seems to be an exercise in some rather dangerous thinking, yet the lionization of individuals like Smith, Claiborne, and Anderson indicates that there are times when violence is acceptable. In *The Dead Zone*, *Dolores Claiborne*, and *A Good Marriage*, each of the protagonists make the decision to end the life of an individual who has shown clear patterns of evil, almost as if they are following a critical axiom of the novella *Big Driver*: "'When a person does a bad thing and another person knows but doesn't stop it, they're equally guilty'" (234). In this sense, there is more than a strong resistance to potential guilt among King's vigilantes—there is an imperative to bring about a greater good by ending the real and reasoned likelihood of continual pain and destruction brought about by agents of evil. Johnny Smith, after exhaustive homework and consideration of numerous pathways leading towards the same goal, ultimately decides that murdering Greg Stillson is justified because of the suffering that will be eliminated; similarly, Dolores Claiborne and Darcy Anderson create deadly "accidents" for their husbands, Joe St. George and Bob Anderson, so as to prevent future death, pain, and predation. Perhaps most importantly, these "accidents," like Johnny Smith's assassination attempt, are direct, if not banal, scenes of violence—there is no joy in these schemes, and each individual acts for the greater good, with, for example, Claiborne willingly giving up any semblance of a relationship with her daughter just so that she, Selena, will not ever have to endure the disgustingly lecherous acts of her own father. And just as Johnny Smith, Dolores Claiborne, and Darcy Anderson (among others) ultimately act for the benefit of many, for *others*, and in a way that limits spectacle or reward, so too does Tess Thorne of *Big Driver* seek to accomplish more than mere revenge: she acts upon her own pain as a rape survivor while also serving as the only knowing party of the many deaths for which Big Driver is responsible, and future deaths of which there is little reason to believe there is an end in sight, thus legitimizing another (reasonable) murderer in King's canon.

While *Big Driver* is hardly a blockbuster film, or even one of King's more original and innovative stories, he, like many authors, is proud of his creation. King even blurbs the film as "the movie Stephen King fans and suspense lovers have been waiting for," highlighting his turn from terror and horror to suspense, something that he has experimented with fairly consistently from *The Colorado Kid* to the Bill Hodges trilogy. But even considering *Big Driver* as merely a suspense film misses the mark as the suspense here is a pathway towards more than resolution/revelation; the suspense ultimately leads towards questions of legitimate violence, and the paced time of the suspense, complete with false leads and diligent sleuthing, allows both Tess and the viewer to think critically as to the rationality of her plotting. Another concern regarding the film comes with the network on which it originally aired as the move from page to screen via the Lifetime Network creates a sense of triviality. The stigma associated with this network, particularly from the popular culture television show *Family Guy* in which Lifetime is dubbed "Television for Idiots," suggests that most any production put forth by this network is hardly serious ("When you Wish"). While it may be difficult for some to set aside some of the common threads among repetitive films on this channel that depict wronged females seeking to find a sense of safety, closure, or justice, or even the plentiful holiday films that air on this network that promote a repetitive theme of purity being rewarded with romance and apparently rare chivalry with a series of hunky men, there is certainly something frightening about the consistency of such plotlines and how they work against the serious nature of *Big Driver*. Yet, when one compartmentalizes the suspense genre as well as separates King's story from any similar stories on Lifetime, including those within the rape-revenge genre (such as *I Spit on Your Grave* or *The Last House on the Left*), the story that is sifted out reveals a noteworthy examination of the boundaries of justice, especially among the restraints of violence and the limits of self-administered retribution.

Assuredly, such a view may be naïve, or Utopian, perhaps revealing the larger concerns behind *Big Driver*—that an arguably childish desire to embrace violence as a reasonable response that may be handled responsibly by those seeking justice regardless of how one may *subjectively* define the notion of justice. In order to, in essence, justify Tess's murder of her rapist (or, rather, justified killing . . . definition and degree matters), a few pieces of groundwork must be considered. On the basic note of definition, consider that "justice" is "the administration of what is just ['morally or legally right']," which is not wholly helpful as establishing what is right, just as definitions of "moral" ("of or relating to principles of right and wrong") leave much to be desired, particularly when issues of righteousness and legality are, at times, quite arbitrary. Indeed, it is akin to the comedian George Carlin's take on "the sanctity of life": "We made the whole fucking thing up!" (*Back in Town*). While Carlin's glibness here may be taken as a rather sharp turn from the serious conversation at hand, it serves as a reminder of how difficult and delicate it is to find ways of explaining and even championing Tess's actions and emerging beliefs as they, too, are made-up and not necessarily grounded within an established or universal system of justice. Attempting to provide a reasonable foundation for Tess's revenge plot based upon ideas and ideals that are as varied as the humans themselves who make up these self-formed guidelines is a bit of a dead-end as seeking a perfect/Utopian rationale for Tess's form of justice has little chance for success. So, while a perfect foundation of "right" may be ephemeral and non-existent here, a slight shift in attention may yield something a bit more tangible and reasonable. For that matter, to understand, if not embrace, Tess's desire for "revenge," "an act or insistence of retaliation to get even," and then considering that she does so not necessarily to attain justice as defined by her surrounding community, but, instead, seeks "retribution," or "something administered or exacted in recompense," perhaps a new definition/understanding of justice, and a common-sensical one at that, emerges alongside an understanding, if not advocacy, for such.

On the surface, *Big Driver* does appear to be fairly basic in its construction and purported theme of *just* revenge, particularly as the tagline for the film simply reads "Murder is a Two-Way Street." Indeed, to reduce the film to solely a matter of revenge (after the main character, Tess Thorne, is brutally raped) sidesteps the trail of literary/cinematic breadcrumbs for the Constant Reader/Viewer to follow; in this case, the end of the road is a delicate question as to whether or not self-executed justice can ever be indeed just. Such a question is much, much older than King himself—if (vigilante) justice can be considered actual justice—but, unsurprisingly, King does not flinch at the opportunity to assess this question and offer up his particular take, ultimately confirming his belief that "Every day, in real life, the good guys win" ("On the Importance" viii). To be sure, King may make it easy for the "good guys" to win throughout his works, yet evil does triumph from time to time, even though many of these antagonists are neutered in one way or the other (consider, for example, Randall Flagg's arrogance and how the resulting blindness disrupts his plans in both *The Stand* and *The Dark Tower* series). Still, the generally consistent depiction of evil as, at the least, fragile is certainly heart-warming, and perhaps echoes a sense of optimism that King has and which some may see as the core of *Big Driver* as, in this case, the good girl wins. Then again, Tony Magistrale and Michael Blouin argue that "at the heart of King's fictional universe is a profound awareness of the most deep-seated American anxieties regarding their latent linkage to a national H/history. . . . King serves as a moralist for our era, concerned with telling cautionary tales about a nation on the verge of destroying itself from within" (19). On the one hand, with *Big Driver*, there is a sense of concern for and despair towards the fractured American landscape, among which a rapist has not only been able to escape capture but also has been, essentially, coached and supported by his family to enact his form of evil (similar to Frank Dodd [*The Dead Zone*] and Brady Hartsfield [*Mr. Mercedes*]). This growth and nurturing of a truly detestable person is clearly concerning, and easily gives credence to any pauses one may have regarding the arguably misguided belief in the benevolent socialscape of America. On the other hand, *Full Dark, No Stars* is comprised of novellas that promote the notion "in the long run Karma will prevail and evil will pay its price," suggesting that evil is both punished and that evil can be viewed as a subsequent blip on the radar, so to speak (Anderson 191). One only needs to look back at Wilfred James of *1922* to see that his descent into madness for a heinous crime as just one example of this "karma" that arguably finds favor in King's fictions, just as one could consider Annie Wilkes' demise at the hands of Paul Sheldon to be just deserts. That said, it is certainly difficult to refute the idea that King is a bit saccharine with many of his endings (as King himself amusingly recognizes in his cameo appearance in *IT: Chapter 2* when he tells Bill Denbrough that he does not care for the way the latter ends his novels), and that these endings may temper otherwise serious concerns within his stories. And with *Big Driver*, as Tess triumphs in her plan of revenge, indicating that those who have transgressed the boundaries of decency that is expected or desired for normal, kind, every-day citizens are punished, what remains is a sense of balance, or "fairness," that may likely appeal to most any reader. But as Tess is indeed able to kill her rapist (and his complicit family members), therefore finding a sense of relief and ease regarding her violation, there is a competing sense that questions if balance, peace, or even justice has genuinely or legitimately prevailed. And herein lies the critical concern of *Big Driver*: is the justice that Tess finds actually reasonable, justifiable, or legitimate?

To King's credit, he, at the very least, engages the viewer with the primary concern that propels all of his creations: beginning with the question of "what if . . .?" In the case of *Big Driver*, viewers are ultimately asked to consider *what if* vigilante justice is not wholly bad, which may be the height of idealism, but King nonetheless encourages consideration of such a proposition, especially as the perpetrators of evil in *Big Driver* are not all that nuanced and are nearly immediately reviled. The primary antagonist who Tess dubs as the titular Big Driver has had, the view learns, a consistent appetite for rape and violating females since his late teens, and his mother, Ramona Norville, refuses to believe that her son's monstrous, disgusting acts are indeed reprehensible while the brother becomes an accomplice so as to cover the tracks of his sibling because it is, after all, what (a twisted) family does; consequently, this triumvirate becomes rather easily, and rather unsurprisingly, hated within the film. This suggests that any sort of violence or retribution aimed at wholly evil people is acceptable in terms of its simplicity, both in terms of bringing about some form of justice to those who have willingly violated the law and their fellow humans, as well as propelling the notion that, sometimes, justice need not be dragged through the morass of the legal system. Perhaps it is as if King channels Thomas More's 1518 text *Utopia* where the latter describes law in a way that appears to be rather appealing to King and his characters (and maybe even King's readers/viewers):

> They [the Utopians] have very few laws . . . Indeed, one of their primary charges against other nations is that endless volumes of law and interpretations are not sufficient. But they consider it quite unjust to bind people by laws which are so numerous no one can read through all of them or so obscure that no one can understand them. Moreover, they ban absolutely all lawyers as clever practitioners and sly interpreters of the law. For they think it is practical that everyone should handle his [or her] own case and present the facts to the judge as he [or she] would to a lawyer; in this way there will be less confusion and the truth will be easier to determine. (101-2)

More is not necessarily advocating for vigilante justice but, instead, argues for a simplicity in law and language so as to promote expediency and common sense: "as for interpretations [of law], they [the Utopians] consider the most obvious the most correct" (102). In *Big Driver*, King, at the least, meets More (and his philosophical predecessors) at the center of the argument, which is that matters typically reserved for the courts can be, apparently, understood if not sorted out without the burdens and baggage of various legal loopholes and technicalities, that "common sense," or even an understandable desire for "an eye for an eye," need not be tainted or delayed by flawed and feeble court systems. Ultimately, King reduces the larger theme of "justice" in *Big Driver* to an exceptionally simple sentiment via the words of Doreen Marquis, an imaginary character from the fiction penned by the protagonist of *Big Driver*: "We can't always be polite and logical, can we? Sometimes it's just about friggin' payback." Yet, just like other creations of King's mind (think "Dolan's Cadillac" among others already mentioned), this simplistic "payback" is not necessarily so simple . . . and neither is it to be wholly condemned.

The looming distrust of the legal courts, much less the court of public opinion, within *Big Driver* certainly brings about a reasonable concern for the practices and procedures of the American judicial system. The distance that Tess desires from typical legal channels is not necessarily a new approach for a King protagonist, and yet it resonates loudly with recent events like the Black Lives Matters movement and the calls for more than basic protest. In some respects, protest and raising awareness has been met with deaf ears, and, arguably, louder voices (or, rather, louder actions) have necessarily resulted. By the same token, Tess feels the need to "speak loudly" as "The literary rape–revenge narratives, while not bringing about social change, at least present readers with women who have retaliated to violence and disrupted the idea of the silent rape victim. They are protagonists who have gone beyond 'awareness raising' and enacted justice" (Pâquet 396). Moreover, as one of Tess's concerns regarding police involvement is that her violation would become exceedingly public (not to mention the 6th Amendment right to "face your accuser" that would likely bring Tess into the same frightful room as her violator is an implied fear), there are certainly some causes for trepidation, particularly as following the letter of the law may yield few satisfactory results. In Tess's case, if Tess were to fully follow the letter of the law—to make her accusation against Big Driver, to go on record with her accusations, to be made available as a witness, etc.—she would, undoubtedly, be coerced into reliving the atrocities that she has survived, especially as "In rape investigations, a woman's body is the scene of the crime and thus becomes the subject of scrutiny" (Pâquet 386). Still, while there is certainly functional rationale behind making criminal accusations and charges public so as to avoid frivolous or outright fabricated declarations of criminal activity, perhaps certain exceptions or adjustments are necessary. But, until such a day comes when a rape victim can navigate the legal system without undue stress and trauma, there may be reason to believe that Tess's actions carry some merit. In Tess's case, while the bulk of her payback is to protect herself from victim blaming and the prying eye of the public (as she is a popular author and, thus, a very visible figure), she does not hunt down the man who rapes her and leaves her for dead for mere pleasure; Tess is motivated with her plans for vengeance because of the faces and unknown memories of others who, she has discovered, have been subjected to what she has endured but who cannot enact justice as they are all dead. In this way, Tess would appear to share something else in common with Darcy Anderson from *A Good Marriage* who also kills in part to revenge the women her husband has killed and therefore cannot obtain proper justice themselves. Tess also understands that there is an unnerving pattern to Big Driver's despicable transgressions, and while patterns are not necessarily proof of continued or future actions, patterns do nonetheless carry weight, whether in legal terms or more general ones. Yet Tess's successful execution of what she considers to be justice comes with much debate as to its validity and whether or not it should be embraced and celebrated, and such tension is compelling and something that King has included in numerous other fictions, including *The Running Man* as Ben Richards can be seen as both a hero and a terrorist, as well as *The Gunslinger* as Roland Deschain is established as the protagonist (or, rather, the main character) only to murder an entire town a mere fifty pages into the *Dark Tower* series. At the least, this violence and these tensions afford the Constant Viewer a critical chance to reflect upon a subtler horror within Stephen King's tale, which is to say that sometimes the short road to justice is not necessarily absent the needed context and cogitation to ensure a form of viable justice that even the most hardened realist might be willing to admit is reasonable, if not legitimate.

Like many protagonists in King's oeuvre, Tess is a writer, and her attunement to the human condition that is necessary for creating realistic characters (in theory) is revealing, and admittedly useful for the development of her revenge/retribution plot. Most directly, within the opening scenes of the film, Tess speaks to an eager audience of fans and would-be/wanna-be writers about her craft and opines "The most important thing about writing is an author knows about human nature, the contradictions we all have, the lies we pretend are truths, the fears we pretend are strengths, the greed and revenge that we have that we won't admit to ourselves." In this sense, Tess offers up an argument that humans have predilections towards divided loyalties, and with respect to the law and the discussion at hand, there is a sense that the law is all that separates humans from animals, to be a bit cliché, and that in a civilized society, such a system is a beacon of hope, of structure, of order, of, well, justice for if/when any given citizen has been "wronged." On the other side of this divide is the more emotional consideration of justice, that there are conceivably limits to the law, and that different pathways towards justice, or at least retribution and balance, may warrant consideration. As Tess herself also recognizes, "Logic will only get us so far in solving a crime" and, as such, that "Given that emotion, and not logic, is the key to our human behavior and to crime itself, I propose we fully change our investigative focus from forensic to psychological, from the crime to the perpetrator." As Tess decides to forgo established legal procedures and, instead, decides to lean towards the raw, emotional approach to justice, she ultimately seems to simply be looking for a way to justify a plan of revenge, to advocate for a plan that will bring her a sense of satisfaction and pleasure by focusing her efforts, her anger, towards a fulfilling, brutal plan of "balance" aimed at simply killing an individual who has clearly wronged her and did so with malice aforethought and no remorse to be found anywhere in his heart. Understandably, Tess ultimately makes her vendetta personal, and in her own words, "I won't make excuses for what I've done, nor can I say I did it while of unsound mind. I wanted an eye for an eye. I got my justice." But even with this declaration suggesting that Tess simply kills Big Driver (and his mother and brother) for "friggin' payback," one cannot wholly reduce her actions to basic vengeance as there is much more thought involved despite the earlier suggestions otherwise. To wit, within Tess's writings, she creates the fictional Willow Grove Society, a group of elderly women who are constantly pulled into various scenes of murder and mayhem, and, as extensions of Tess's mind/persona, it is important to *also* consider that "In the Willow Grove Knitting Society, we never reacted violently, but we don't disparage vindictive musings when the circumstances are sufficiently heinous." Although this may be a thin means of mitigating Tess's own non-fictional statement relating to payback, the notion cannot be discounted as it can be argued that the genesis of Tess's desire for payback stems from a place of understanding that she is not blindly flailing about with her machinations. Instead, she recognizes that she has experienced something "sufficiently heinous," and that violent thoughts, or "vindictive musings," have a reasonable foundation particularly as humans have different needs (and desires) relating to law, justice, resolution, and peace of mind. But to consider Tess's actions as reasonable still prompts debate as, again, what is common sense to her may be vilified by others.

As the *ends* of Tess's musings and machinations are generally understandable and condonable, the *means*—murder—to achieving her justice are likely to be met with resistance and dissonance. To that end, perhaps one would do well to consider murder as legitimate if the primary goal is *resolution*, but only if that resolution escapes "reasonable doubt" and escapes a *wholly* personal focus (e.g. Tess murdering Big Driver *only* for her own satisfaction). Further, if the resolution sought may prevent future agony and torment because it stands to reason that a pattern of such pain will indeed occur otherwise, and that there is reason to believe the normal legal process will be more damaging to the victims, then seeking such a resolution, even if violent, could be argued as legitimate. In this vein, viewers must negotiate with their own conceptions of what is "right" and what is "wrong"; however, sympathy for Tess tilts the scales towards a sense of righteousness. In this sense, it is posited that "The power of the rape-revenge scenario is in the calculable intensity that sexual violence (or the threat of sexual violence) holds over the film as a whole" (Heller-Nicholas 4). And this is where *Big Driver* creates some ambivalence for the viewer as the film does exhibit some cheekiness and cheer with bright images and bountiful smiles within the early scenes, not to mention the presence of a talking GPS ("Tom") with which Tess converses both before and after she is assaulted. Also working against the possibility of compassion is that Tess does appear to have a mocking smirk on her face before she pulls the trigger and kills her violator. But the lapses in tone and the dissonance created as Tess exhibits apparent pleasure in exacting her revenge do not necessarily eliminate sympathy. Just as Carrie White from *Carrie* comes to enjoy her rampage in both the book and film(s), "her actions are understandable. In fact, in some way, the reader is with her, rooting for her as she destroys her tormenters." (Anderson 15). Similarly, Heidi Strengell argues that King "is able to adapt them [his fictions] to the emotional needs of the audience," and in the case of *Big Driver*, there is clearly a need for empowerment, self-actualization, or the ability to enact justice when despair becomes the first thought when considering whether or not to leave justice to the American justice system (262). Still, a "need" for "justice" may not necessarily lead to actual justice. In fact, as Tess herself notes about her writing "I sell peace of mind," she has become her best customer as she walks herself through the maze of reasons and justifications for her murderous plans and comes to the conclusion that her decision to kill is the best course of action. But a closer look at Tess's words, and deeds, provides a crucial and mitigating insight: she settles on her plan not necessarily out of a sense of revenge, or pleasure, but, rather, to simply put her mind at ease *and* to ensure that no one else will endure what she has endured as Big Driver clearly has an appetite for rape and murder as evidenced by numerous photographs and mementos of his victims. Tess acts for personal catharsis *and* on behalf of those who could not act in any way against their violator, and just as her life was taken from her because of the pain she must live with, she merely promotes balance— the death of her former, normal, joyous life asks for the death of Big Driver. Again, as a writer, Tess could have easily imagined (and then likely enacted) a number of terrible, tortuous, and debased scenes of revenge, especially as she claims "I guess I was always violent deep down. I denied it like most of us do, but it let me dream up twelve novels where people were murdering in cold blood, so . . . that didn't come from nowhere." But she does not act upon her baseness, a bloodlust, or even a promise of pleasure; instead, she works towards *closure*, which promotes an image of balance and harmony in spite of the bloody holes in the bodies of those who have wronged her. Perhaps this is an oversimplification, but torture, imprisonment, or any other action, to Tess, would be needless and imbalanced. As such, she kills just as Big Driver killed—end of story. And the audience is hard-pressed to abandon or chastise

Tess, particularly as "This may be why King's stories, and his protagonists, resonate with us. They are mired in pain, they are awash in evil, yet they don't give in. . . . They struggle, and they do so admirably" instead of transforming into monsters themselves (Held 278). This simple exchange carries nothing superfluous, nothing excessive, and nothing irrational as Tess has carefully considered all options, has reasonably placed her well-being at the forefront of her thinking, has considered what her actions would mean for those who did not survive, and has only mirrored actions that Big Driver initiated.

Indeed, as Tess finds those who are responsible for her violation and kills them, this, at least to the enraged and even darkly imaginative reader, is fairly innocuous. Yet, it is crucial to note that as Tess enacts her plan, she has only deduced that Big Driver and his mother are responsible for her trauma; in fact, Big Driver, the man she sees as so huge that she comments upon her first encounter with him along an abandoned road "You don't ride in that truck of yours, you wear it," is actually "Little Driver," the younger, smaller son of Ramona Norville. This misstep is somewhat understandable as when Tess initially begins to investigate pathways towards seeking her justice, her source of information, Betsy Neal, asks if Tess is looking for someone who is "big, or really big." Tess does not understand the separation within Betsy's question and simply responds that the man she is looking for is "really big"; however, the "really big" man here is not the man who raped her, which results in Tess murdering the wrong person when she initially and accidentally identifies Big Driver for her violator. As Tess does not account for the possibility of misidentifying Big Driver when she tracks down the guilty party, Little Driver, the viewer initially sees a massive fault in Tess's self-created plan of Utopian justice as her common sense has failed her in that she kills a man who is reportedly innocent. She simply sees a "big" man on property with a semi-truck that has been identified as Big Driver's vehicle, and that these pieces of evidence are clear links to Ramona Norville's son; yet she fails to even think that there may be more than one offspring. It is not until shortly after Tess kills Little Driver, fulfilling her original plan, that she enters into the home shared by the brothers and discovers numerous Polaroids of the women she saw in the drainage ditch where Little Driver left her to die, and with these pictures, she remembers flashes of light during her rape and, albeit late, comes to understand that Big Driver is not as innocent as she thought as he was complicit with his brother's despicable predilections as he documented and covered-up each and every despicable act. Here, the viewer can breathe a sigh of relief as Tess is no longer an illegitimate murderer. Although after killing Little Driver afterwards Tess has *accidentally* found justice for herself by killing *all* who were responsible for her trauma, she nonetheless ends the crimes of a dysfunctional, loathsome family unit working in unison for reprehensible deeds. And even though, prior to the final scenes of the film, King exhibits caution so as to ensure that Tess is careful and, dare one entertain the thought, *reasonable* with her actions and planning, King also adeptly furnishes a sense of caution regarding Utopian justice with respect to Tess's fortuitous plan of revenge through her somewhat myopic planning that failed to recognize all parties involved in her violation and that the evidence she has gathered is somewhat wanting.

All in all, beyond creating *accidental* justice in *Big Driver*, King has ultimately and subtly suggested that there are many other concerns that the viewer would do well to contend with before outright celebrating Tess's actions. Indeed, Tess's retribution unfolds in a rather perfect and auspicious manner as her suspicions are *transformed* into facts (instead of having all facts be fully *confirmed* beforehand), which is quite troubling as the initial foundations of her plan for revenge were based upon some speculation and arguably questionable deduction. In other words, the fictional landscape of *Big Driver* creates a space of wish-fulfillment, a hope that good will indeed triumph over evil, and will do so in an arguably understandable, justifiable, and condonable manner. Such an ending actually mirrors the final lines of *Utopia* in which More states "I readily confess that in the Utopian common-wealth are very many features which in our societies I would wish rather than expect to see" as the righteous ending of the film is, to a degree, a matter of wishful thinking, or wishful thinking/writing that finds Tess stumbling into a series of killings that all turn out to be warranted from her perspective and somewhat lackadaisical sleuthing (135). To that end, perhaps *Big Driver* could, after all, be construed as another tale of terror by Stephen King in that there is a horror in believing that a perfect resolution to a despicable, tortuous act may only come about via accident, or that an eye-for-an-eye philosophy only ends up blinding both aggrieved parties. This Utopian "perfection," again, rests upon how one considers the validity and soundness of Tess's approach and execution of seeking justice, and while there is a case to be made supporting the reasonableness of Tess's actions, the neatly-tied plotlines may be too convenient, indicating that the Utopian, or perfect, road to justice can only manifest within the world of make-believe. Then again, perhaps the problematic violence in *Big Driver* is a reflection of a refreshing constant among King's works: that legitimate violence is not wholly a black-and-white matter. In short, when King prompts his audience to pause and contemplate the complexities, contexts, and variables associated with each and every act of violence within his corpus, particularly in light of Tess's imperfect execution of justice, such an attempt at promoting *thinking* alongside action certainly resonates with a real, cherished, and "utopian" common sense that is woefully absent from many acts of violence, as well as judgments rendered towards those who sincerely seek legitimate foundations for otherwise unsa-vory endeavors.

WORKS CITED

Anderson, James Arthur. *The Linguistics of Stephen King: Layered Language and Meaning in the Fiction.* Jefferson, NC: McFarland, 2017. Print.

Back in Town. Dir. Rocco Urbisci. Perf. George Carlin. HBO, 29 Mar. 1996. Television.

Big Driver. Dir. Mikael Salomon. Perf. Maria Bello, Joan Jett, and Olympia Dukakis. Lifetime, 18 Oct. 2014. Television.

Held, Jacob M. "From Desperation to Haven: Horror, Compassion, and Arthur Schopenhauer." *Stephen King and Philosophy.* Ed. Jacob M. Held. Lanham, MD: Rowman & Littlefield, 2016. 277–297. Print.

Heller-Nicholas, Alexandra. *Rape-Revenge Films: A Critical Study.* Jefferson, NC: McFarland, 2011. Print.

King, Stephen. "Big Driver." *Full Dark, No Stars.* 2010. New York: Gallery Books, 2011. 133–245. Print.

———. *Danse Macabre.* 1981. New York: Gallery Books, 2010. Print.

———. "On the Importance of Being Bachman (Introduction)." *The Running Man.* New York: Signet, 1999. v–xiv. Print.

Magistrale, Tony, and Michael J. Blouin. *Stephen King and American History.* New York: Routledge, 2021. Print.

More, Thomas. *Utopia.* Trans. Miller. New Haven, CT: Yale Nota Bene, 2001. Print.

Pâquet, Lili. "The Corporeal Female Body in Literary Rape–Revenge: Shame, Violence, and Scriptotherapy." *Australian Feminist Studies*, 33.97 (2018): 384–399. Print.

Strengell, Heidi. *Dissecting Stephen King: From the Gothic to Literary Naturalism.* Madison, WI: University of Wisconsin Popular Press, 2005. Print.

"When you Wish upon a Weinstein." *Family Guy.* Dir. Dan Povenmire. FOX, 10 Dec. 2004. Television.

Index

About the Contributors

Michael J. Blouin, one of the co-editors of this volume, is Associate Professor of English and the Humanities at Milligan University. His research interests are critical theory, popular culture, and American politics. Blouin's recent publications include *Stephen King and American History* (2020), co-authored with Tony Magistrale, as well as *Stephen King and American Politics* (2021).

Jason Clemence is Assistant Professor of Humanities at Regis College in Massachusetts. He teaches courses on British literature, film studies, writing, and humanities-based pedagogical strategies. His scholarly interests include psychoanalytic and feminist film theory, the Victorian novel, and intersections of style and grammar in undergraduate writing curricula.

Phoenix Crockett, MAT, is an educator who specializes in middle grades English Language Arts. He is from Houlton, Maine, not far from many of the settings discussed in these pages. He lives in Vermont with his wife.

Mary Findley is Professor of English, Humanities and Social Science at Vermont Technical College. Her academic interests include Stephen King, vampires, and all things related to the unquiet coffin.

Maura Grady is an Associate Professor and Director of Composition at Ashland University in Ohio. She writes on film, television, gender and fandom studies. She has published on *The Shawshank Redemption*, including, with Tony Magistrale, the book *The Shawshank Experience: Tracking the History of the World's Favorite Movie* (2016).

Stephen Indrisano is a theater technology specialist and student from Maryland. He and Phoenix Crockett attended school together at the University of Vermont, and they now co-host the "Stephen King Boo! Club," a premiere King-related podcast. He lives with his partner in Washington, D.C.

Brian Kent is a Senior Lecturer of English Emeritus at the University of Vermont. In addition to a number of articles on Stephen King, he has published essays on authors Tom Robbins and James Jones.

Tony Magistrale, one of the co-editors of this volume, is Professor and former Chair of the English Department at the University of Vermont. He is the author of twenty-three books and over eighty articles, many of them featuring the films and novels of Stephen King.

Patrick McAleer is Co-Chair of the Stephen King Area of the Popular Culture Association's Annual National Conference and has presented papers on Stephen King every year he has attended this conference since 2005. He is the author of *Inside the Dark Tower Series* (2009) and *The Writing Family of Stephen King* (2011), and he is the co-editor of *Stephen King's Modern Macabre* (2014, with Michael Perry), *Stephen King's Contemporary Classics* (2014, with Philip L. Simpson), and *The Modern Stephen King Canon: Beyond Horror* (2019, with Philip L. Simpson).

Matthew S. Muller is currently a student of Tolkien Studies and Imaginative Literature at Signum University. A veteran of the United States Marine Corps, where he deployed to South America, Africa, and Europe from 1994–1998, he earned his B.A. in English Literature from the College of William and Mary in 2002 and his MFA in fiction from City University of Hong Kong in 2016. He lives in Austin, Texas.

Sarah Nilsen is Associate Professor in Film and Television Studies at the University of Vermont. She is the author of *Projecting America: Film and Cultural Diplomacy at the Brussels World's Fair of 1958* (2011) and co-editor with Sarah E. Turner of *The Colorblind Screen: Television in Post-Racial America* (2014) and *The Myth of Colorblindness: Race and Ethnicity in American Cinema* (2019). Her current book project is an edited collection, *White Supremacy and the Media in Trump's America*.

Danel Olson is a three-time finalist for the Bram Stoker Award and winner of a Shirley Jackson Award and two World Fantasy Awards. He served as editor of the mammoth collection for Centipede Press, *Stanley Kubrick*'s '*The Shining': Studies in the Horror Film* (2015), called "a major contribution to film history and scholarship" by the *Washington Post.* Forthcoming is his Lexington book, *9/11* Gothic: *Decrypting Ghosts and Trauma in New York City's Terrorism Fiction,* based on his PhD dissertation from the University of Stirling, Scotland.

Alexandra Reuber is Senior Professor of Practice of French at Tulane University. Her most recent publications on Stephen King include: "Gothic Recall: Stephen King's Uncanny Revival of the Frankenstein Myth" in *Beyond Horror: The Modern Stephen King Canon* (2018) and "In Search of the Lost Object in a Bad Place: Stephen King's Contemporary Gothic" in *Stephen King's Contemporary Classics: Reflections on the Modern Master of Horror* (2015).

Philip L. Simpson is immediate past President of the Popular Culture Association/American Culture Association, additionally serving as Co-Chair of the Stephen King Area for the Association. The author of numerous books, journal articles, book chapters, and short stories, as well as anthology co-editor, he currently serves as Provost of the Titusville Campus and Eastern Florida Online at Eastern Florida State College on the Space Coast of Florida.

Sarah E. Turner is a Senior Lecturer in English at the University of Vermont. Her research interests include Critical Race and Ethnic Studies and Representations of Race in the Media. She has co-edited two collections on colorblind racism and media with a third forthcoming; she has also published work on King, Disney, racial reconciliation films, and popular culture.